D0622807

# Selected Economic Essays and Addresses

# Selected Economic Essays and Addresses

by

Sir Arnold Plant

ROUTLEDGE & KEGAN PAUL
London and Boston

*First published in 1974 for the Institute of Economic Affairs*
*by Routledge & Kegan Paul Ltd*
*Broadway House, 68-74 Carter Lane,*
*London EC4V 5EL and*
*9 Park Street,*
*Boston, Mass. 02108, USA*
*Set in Monotype Garamond 10 pt. 2 pt. leaded*
*and printed in Great Britain by*
*The Camelot Press Ltd, Southampton*


*ISBN 0 7100 7935 4*
*Library of Congress Catalog Card No. 74-80753*

# Contents

# Foreword

As part of its educational purpose, the Institute of Economic Affairs is collecting not easily accessible studies of market processes and/or their institutional framework. Many are by economists whose works also show an appreciation of classical economic theory, and since the essays or addresses cover several decades they will be of interest as economic history as well as economic analysis and applied economics.

This volume assembles a selection of the main essays and addresses of Professor Sir Arnold Plant. Their common link is that they were primarily designed for academic readers or audiences. They are divided into three parts according to subject and in a prefatory note to each part Sir Arnold indicates other of his readings or addresses that bear on the broad subject. The prefatory notes are thus to some extent a short list of his chief published works.

The Biographical note indicates the main features of Sir Arnold's academic career and public work. Hitherto, most of his thinking has remained unpublished, notably – and for his colleagues and students most regrettably – a study of the economics of property. Part of the value of this volume is that it reproduces pieces on three aspects of property. But much of his thinking was transmitted to colleagues and students and is reflected in their teaching and writings. Much also remains in his unpublished lectures on business administration and the structure of industry.

Many of his colleagues and former students now in high positions in industry, teaching or government round the world could speak of his work as a teacher. Two of his B.Com. undergraduate students in Cape Town received Honorary Doctorates with him in 1968 when the fiftieth anniversary of the University was celebrated: Owen McCann, then His Eminence Cardinal Archbishop of South Africa, and Clive

Corder, a prominent businessman and Chairman of the University Council.

Among his undergraduate students at the University of London, the three Ronalds of the 1930s are now Professor Ronald H. Coase of the University of Chicago, Professor Sir Ronald Edwards of the London School of Economics and Chairman of Beechams Limited, and Ronald F. Fowler, for many years Director of Statistics at the Ministry of Labour. Other former students include Sir Arthur Lewis, Professor of Economics at the University of Princeton, and Mr Arthur W. Knight, Financial Director of Courtaulds Limited. Frank MacFadzean, Visiting Professor at Strathclyde University and Chairman of Shell Limited, studied at the one-year postgraduate course in the Department of Business Administration.

I am a former student whom Sir Arnold appointed as his Research Assistant after I graduated. This Foreword gives me the opportunity to speak of his outstanding qualities as a teacher, his clarity as a lecturer and his kindnesses to me as an undergraduate. I have no doubt that many other former students will share my respect, gratitude and affection.

ARTHUR SELDON
*Editorial Director,*
*Institute of Economic Affairs*

# Biographical note

Arnold Plant was born in London in 1898, and was educated at Strand School until the First World War. He left Strand School to work in a mechanical engineering factory controlled by the Admiralty, and joined the army under the Derby Scheme in 1916. Defective eyesight prevented him from being accepted for general overseas service and the Admiralty retained him in this factory until the middle of 1918 when he was posted to the Royal West Kent Regiment. After the Armistice he returned to engineering until resigning to become a student at LSE for the years 1920 to 1923, graduating B.Com. and B.Sc.(Econ.). His first academic appointment was to a newly-created Chair of Commerce in the University of Cape Town in 1924. He was also Dean of the Faculty of Commerce from that year. In 1930 he returned to LSE as Sir Ernest Cassel Professor of Commerce in the University of London. He retired from the Chair in 1965, Professor Emeritus.

In addition to the articles referred to in the Prefatory Notes in this book, his publications include contributions to the *London Essays in Economics in Honour of Edwin Cannan* (1927) and to the South African volume of the *Cambridge History of the British Empire* (1936 – Revised Edition 1963).

During the 1930s there was much concern about the possible extinction of a viable British film industry faced by severe competition from producers, renters, and exhibitors in the USA. A series of government measures resulted in the passing in 1938 of an Act under which a Cinematograph Films Council was created. Professor Plant was appointed one of the original independent members of the Council and continued to act in that capacity until a complete change in the independent membership was announced in 1969. His work on the Cinematograph Films Council involved much contact with a number of government departments in addition to the Board of Trade, and as a temporary civil servant during the Second World War he collaborated daily with advisers to ministers over a wide range of policy matters. After the war his services as an experienced adviser were in virtually continuous demand. He received a Knighthood in the Birthday Honours of 1947.

# Acknowledgments

The editor and publishers would like to thank the following for permission to reproduce the essays in this volume: the Editorial Board of *Economica* for 'The economic theory concerning patents for inventions' (*Economica*, February 1934) and 'The economic aspects of copyright in books' (*Economica*, May 1934); the Athlone Press and the Stamp Lecture Trust for 'The new commerce in ideas and intellectual property' (Stamp Lecture, 1953); the University of Southampton and the Esso Petroleum Company Limited for 'The substance and the shadow – reflections on prosperity' (Fawley Lecture, 1956); the Institution of Mechanical Engineers for 'Engineering in an expanding economy' (Graham Clark Lecture, 1959); and UNESCO for 'The economic approach to the peaceful use of nuclear power' (Meeting on the Peaceful Uses of Atomic Energy, UNESCO, 1958).

PART ONE

# African Studies

Two articles have been selected for reprinting. The first is a contribution made in 1927 to a short-lived journal named *Voorslag*. The editorial board invited a contribution which was printed under the title 'The economics of the native question'. I had arrived at the University of Cape Town as Professor of Commerce in 1924 and was drawn at once into the problem of the economic relations between the various races living in Southern Africa. I welcomed this opportunity to set out in full article form the results of my studies in South Africa and Rhodesia. From 1924 until I left Cape Town in 1930 I was a member of the South African Committee of the *Round Table* and regularly contributed articles on these issues, following up developments subsequent to the publication of the *Voorslag* article.

The second article reprinted is one of my latest publications on this subject, the Introduction to the IEA publication *Economic Issues in Immigration*, dated 1970. In the 1930s, and since 1946, I wrote a number of articles commenting on migration problems and on economic relations in multi-racial societies. For example, *The Population Problem* presents in book form a series of broadcast talks conducted by T. H. Marshall and a number of other experts. My contribution was entitled 'Population trends and international migration'. In 1952 (revised edition 1958) Odham's issued a volume *The British Commonwealth* edited by Drummond Sheils. At his invitation I wrote a section on 'Economic problems of the Commonwealth'. Again in March 1962 *Optima* included an article which the editors had requested me to write on the Commonwealth and the Common Market.

A. P.

CHAPTER I

# The economics of the native question*

In his classic treatise on 'The American Commonwealth' the late Lord Bryce devotes a very interesting section to a discussion of the economic and social results of the former reliance of the white population of the Southern States on black slave labour for the performance of all menial work; and he was prompted by his description of the general behaviour of the class of 'poor white trash', which inevitably grew up, to make the significant comment that 'the less a man has to be proud of the more proud will he be of his colour'.

South African students of the poor white and native questions were not slow to appreciate the force of that remark. We find the able drafters of the report of the Transvaal Indigency Commission (1906–8) not only studying the American problem, but quoting Lord Bryce as a hint to the European population here. What is perhaps not so generally realised is that the refuge which some degenerate white people are prone to seek in the colour of their skin as a basis for privileged treatment is but one particular phase of the universal habit among the lazy or inefficient of seizing hold of an entirely irrelevant characteristic of their competitors and endeavouring to persuade the general public that it constitutes a sufficient ground for legislation differentiating against that particular class as a whole. It is a singular feature of people whose *economic* life is inefficient that they will go to tremendous trouble by methods of political and social propaganda to persuade the public that its interest lies in bolstering up the inefficiency of the propagandist. Whereas economic success involves continuous effort and incessant vigilance in the search for efficiency, one successful political exploit may secure for the propagandist a privileged status with a permanently

* From *Voorslag*, Durban, May–July 1927.

secure income. Those who talk most of the importance of safeguarding Western civilisation betray a complete misunderstanding of its nature.

What, after all, constitutes Western civilisation? Its basis is something more permanent and yet more intangible than the expression it finds in different circumstances. It cannot be identified with the windmill, the steam engine, the turbine, the internal combustion engine, or the substitution in general of mechanical for human energy in production; neither is it merely the employment of wage-paid labour by profit-earning capitalists; nor the supersedence of barter by a money or a credit economy; nor merely the changes which are taking place in the relationships between men and women or parents and children. All of these things are no more than the results of a more fundamental movement which differentiates what we feel to be 'Eastern' from what we claim as 'Western'.

It should not, on the other hand, be difficult to recognise behind the kaleidoscopic forms of Western institutions a steadily increasing capacity for change. Taking a long view, the march of civilisation as we know it may be regarded as the gradual breakdown of all those features of human institutions which have constituted an impediment to changes *of a certain type*, and the force which has made for those changes has been the desire of human beings for greater material welfare. In so far as increased material welfare has depended upon the increased co-operation and inter-dependence of all the inhabitants of the earth, races and peoples are destined to mix more and more as the march proceeds. The permanence of Western civilisation will depend upon our ability to adapt ourselves quickly to the changing circumstances which improved co-operation implies. Competition is the force which induces us to co-operate more economically with each other.

Whereas, therefore, Western civilisation implies the breakdown of privilege and caste in the search for greater effectiveness of co-operation, those who least comprehend its nature resent the competitive aspect of co-operation and spend their time bolstering up, or endeavouring to resurrect, caste privileges. If the competitor is a Jew, or a married woman, or an Indian, or a native, or an unapprenticed skilled worker, or a professional man who did not pay his premium as an articled pupil, then the general public is besought to clamour for legislation which will put an end to the competition. Usually it is argued not only that the successful competition is 'unfair' because of some advantage which the intruder is alleged to have (which is after all the reason why his co-operation in that particular way is advantageous), but antithetically that the competitor is untrained and incompetent as a practitioner and should be prevented from offering his wares. The old rule of *caveat emptor* is in fact attacked by the displaced seller. Where the argument that the competitor is incompetent is manifestly untrue, and the consumer declines to believe that he needs protection from what he prefers to buy, then the religion or race or colour or home life of the competitor is likely to be introduced in the hope of exciting prejudice against him.

If an infinite capacity for change constitutes the ideal condition for a flourishing civilisation on Western lines, it is clear that so long as the incompetents who imagine that their interests are vested in stagnation are powerful enough to obstruct changes which are essential to progress then the future of Western civilisation itself is endangered. While in South Africa there is a general feeling that the future is uncertain, it is not usually so clearly understood that the menace to progress comes from the very people who are loudest in their protests against 'the undercutting of Western standards of life'. Such 'undercutting', or competition, has, of course, constituted one of the most potent forces making for a higher standard among those who avail themselves of it. If by careful buying I can in future secure all that I am accustomed to have at half the price I have previously had to pay for it, I clearly have as much money left over with which to raise my 'Western standard of life' much higher; and in buying additional things I increase employment. It makes no difference whether the competition which reduces prices is the result of the introduction of machinery or of the employment of Indians or natives: in both cases 'Western standards' are raised, and employment is increased. If the introduction of the 'invention' is resisted, in order that incompetence may flourish, our 'Western standard' sinks below the level that it might have attained.

It will, of course, be objected in some quarters that this argument would hand over all the work to underpaid non-Europeans, and that Europeans would be left without income to purchase anything at all. If Western standards of life had, in fact, no better foundation than trade agreements or legislative enactments against price- and wage-cutting there would be some validity in the objection, but a moment's thought suffices to remind us that the steady improvement in the condition of the working classes in Great Britain, the USA and in other great industrial countries rests on the much surer foundation of improved education, the division of labour to suit the capacity of individual workers, and, in general, the economies of higher wages. The prospects of great economies in production through the increased employment of uneducated, unskilled brute labour at low wages are exceedingly small. Very few new 'inventions' are likely to take that form.

To resist co-operation with the native is therefore to lower our Western standards of civilisation. It is equally detrimental to our own economic interests to attempt to confine that co-operation, on the side of the native, to the performance of menial work. We may take it that those who advocate that the native should be allowed 'to develop along his own lines' have in view the prohibition of any development that may happen to be along lines which the European regards as his monopoly. The native population constitutes part of the resources on the utilisation of which depends the economic prosperity of us all, and in so far as the natives are denied the opportunity for the most effective co-operation of which they are capable, we are so much the poorer. It is gradually being realised that serious economic waste is involved in denying to the youth of a country the highest standards of education that the individual shows capacity to undergo with profit. The son of a farmer will not necessarily make a better farmer than anything else, whether European or native; and if the most effective contribution of individual natives to the welfare of society may chance to lie in industry or in the professions, there is clearly a serious economic waste involved in any policy of colour or race barriers which may be erected to avoid the necessity of re-shuffling the occupations of the less competent people who are temporarily displaced.

Fundamental as is the need for greater co-operation between the native and European sections of the community, in the economic interests of both, it must not be supposed that opposition to changes in that direction is confined to the Europeans. The most conservative parts of the East are probably not more suspicious of innovations than are the communal natives in the reserves, and commissioners reporting on the natives are continually commenting on the inevitable slowness of any radical changes, so long as many of the chiefs throw the weight of their influence against it. Their natural desire to retain the authority which they exercise in communal tribes is still a strong check to the infiltration of Western habits and ideas through the men returning from the mines and European farms. Nothing is further from the facts than the fear which seems to lurk in the minds of some urban artisans that there are legions of natives waiting for the opportunity to descend upon the towns and deprive every European of his daily bread. The native is primarily an agriculturist, and normally seeks the towns only when the pressure of circumstances forces him from the land. The native problem is still fundamentally an agrarian problem; and it is the relation of the native to the land which he cultivates which provides the key to the present discontents. A generation ago the South African Native Affairs Commission (1903–5) came to the conclusion that land tenure provided 'a common origin of many serious native problems. It dominates and pervades every other question.'

From the economic standpoint, there is little to be said in favour of communal tenure. It provides little, if any, incentive to adopt progressive methods of farming; of 'improvements' there can be no question so long as it persists. Few men will expend capital on permanent improvements in land which they are unable to transfer or bequeath, at least to a relative; and communal grazing (which is not confined in South Africa to the territories in which communal cultivation is still the rule) makes well-nigh useless any systematic campaign to raise the standard of stock. For that reason the more enlightened chiefs in the territories (where, taken as a whole, communal tenure is still by far the most general system) are anxious for the provision of suitable machinery whereby a change-over to individual ownership might be effected. That anxiety is not due merely to the inadequacy of the present area (approximately one-fifteenth of the total area of the Union) to provide on a broadly communal system of occupation for the needs of over two millions of permanent residents (compared with the four millions of Europeans and non-Europeans who secure a by no means entirely satisfactory livelihood, chiefly on an individual system, in the remaining fourteen-fifteenths). In addition, as was eloquently argued by Chief Zibi at the last Pretoria Native Conference, it is impossible to induce educated natives to remain under such conditions. The best educated members of the native community find communal life as intolerable as twentieth-century Europeans would find a return to the communal methods of their own pre-medieval forefathers. It was a pity, argued Chief Zibi, that all the educated natives left for the towns and none were left to uplift the masses. In tribal purchases the land should be surveyed and only the grazing be communal. Chiefs must grow with their people. Just as natives respected the ownership of cattle they must learn to respect the ownership of land. Over twenty years ago the Native Affairs Commissioners commented on the 'increasing number who fret under the conditions of communal life, seeking alike for the opportunity to gain independence and assert individualism. . . . Where the natives exhibit in sufficient numbers a desire to secure and a capacity to hold and enjoy individual rights to arable plots and residential sites on such lands, provision should be made accordingly under well-defined conditions.'

Lest any harassed official of the Native Affairs Department should chance to read these pages I make haste to add that the affirmation of a belief that a rapid transition from communal to individual ownership is essential implies no delusion that the granting of individual tenure immediately to every native who desired it, under the highly intricate apparatus of property law which Europeans have evolved to protect themselves, would be in any way appropriate, save for a few exceptional natives who, like some Europeans, tower probably as much in intellectual capacity as in education above their fellows. The complexity which has been introduced into real property law during centuries of evolution is the outcome of the endeavours of members of the legal profession to protect the legitimate interests of their clients in the highly involved transactions which some of us have wished to make in connection with land. Whatever views we may hold as to the desirability and possibility of simplifications, for our present purposes we must accept the view of experts that we have brought the complexities on ourselves. But, on the other hand, the law of land tenure which is involved in complex transactions is not necessary or appropriate to safeguard the rights of parties where the titles and transfers involved are not intended or likely to be other than simple in the extreme. When England, blundering as all pioneers inevitably must, led the way from communal to individual tenure of land, and illiterate agriculturists whose immemorial rights were suddenly questioned had recourse for the first time to the legal profession in their search for justice, they discovered in many cases that the decision whether they might remain as they were, or face ruin, depended on abstract questions as to whether they were customary tenants 'at will' or 'for life', or whether the lord had silently reserved the right to increase the 'fine' at transfer, or whether by some providential intervention they turned out on investigation to hold the proud title of 'copyholders of inheritance'.

In their ill-informed indignation, they blamed the lawyers when, like wild animals, they were singled out to be driven off enclosed land which their forefathers may have occupied even before the lord of the manor; and that suspicion of the legal profession has not yet been eradicated in some quarters in spite of generations of education. Students of early English economic tracts will know how fierce that indignation was, and how important was the part played by those divines who, as ever, have endeavoured to fight oppression of the ignorant. It must be added that the courts, before the end of the fifteenth century, had begun to find reasons for upholding the rights of customary tenants against summary ejection, and by 1530, although too late to amend many wrongs that had been wrought, the recognition of customary rights to property was standard legal practice, under which any occupier who had the courage, funds and knowledge to appeal to the courts might secure justice. More confidence might be reposed in the attempts of our legislators today to deal with 'squatters' (many of whose forefathers 'squatted' on the same ground actually before it was sold or granted to, or otherwise acquired, by the European owners who now clamour for their eviction) if it were known that their proposals were based not merely on a profound study of South African conditions, but in addition that experience elsewhere had been continuously in mind.

Experiments with individual tenure, and with simplified methods of transfer and modified forms of title, have of course been made in South Africa, with a success varying broadly with the degree to which the details of the scheme have been consciously aimed at suiting the capacity and aspirations of the occupiers. It should here be urged that the modifications introduced owe none of their desirability to the race or colour of the occupiers. They are necessitated entirely by the social and economic status and degree of education of the population to whom they apply; and they find their place as much in the proposals for the settlement of poor whites and for the granting of security of tenure to 'byowners' as in the case of the native peoples. The forms of tenure introduced will accordingly succeed or fail in their object in so far as they represent an intelligible reform along lines which the *occupier* understands.

For that reason it is high time that a detailed investigation were made of the present practice in communal occupation throughout the territories. Where the customary local practice in certain districts is for blood relations to succeed to holdings, the transition to a specially adapted form of individual tenure with limited rights of transfer should be facilitated. Thus, in Northern Nigeria, as the result of the report of the Lands Committee in 1910 which feared that the land would soon be heavily mortgaged, as in India, if full transfer rights were allowed, the regulations promulgated provide that 'there is no restriction on sale, transfer or bequest to a blood relation. The consent of the district head-man is necessary for the transfer to a non-related native of the same district, and the additional approval of the resident is required for transfer to a native non-resident in the district.' The occupier in Northern Nigeria is not, however, a freeholder; and the Government as trustee may expropriate in certain cases. The Economic and Wage Commission of 1925 urged the desirability of 'a complete survey of the economic position of the native people'. If an investigation could at the same time be conducted by arrangement in the Protectorates, with a view to ascertaining the present conditions of communal tribes throughout Southern Africa, the difficulties of introducing individual ownership would be greatly reduced. The same plan is not necessarily the best throughout South Africa.

South African experience of individual tenure prior to the Glen Grey Act of 1894 has shown clearly the futility of intricate systems of title and transfer. Since 1852 the experiments at Kat River (Stockenstroom), Lovedale, Paddie, Harmesfontein, Dysseldorp and Zuurbrak, Oxkraal and Kamastone all in turn proved unsatisfactory for similar reasons. Often the natives were not ready for the system; they disliked a permanent site and preferred to migrate, or the allotments were unsuitable for permanent occupation; and more often the cost of survey and title, and of conveyancing were too high, so that lots passed, on inheritance and purchase, without the title. The valuable report by Mr Vos in 1922 on Native Location Surveys attributed the chaos in the Ciskei to the fact that titles issued prior to 1894 were subject to the costly law of transfer, and recommended the cancellation of existing titles in favour of new grants, to occupiers and others who could satisfy a Commissioner as to their rights, with transfer on the lines of the 1894 Act. In the locations, however, where the Glen Grey system has since 1894 been introduced, a much more encouraging condition exists, in spite of defects which have revealed themselves as time passes. The simplified system of transfer, requiring merely the signature of the Magistrate and the payment of a stamp fee of *2s 6d*, has worked much more satisfactorily; while the provisions of field officers to see that the plot boundaries are not disregarded, and that registrations of title do not fall in arrears would eventually prove to be an economy, by obviating the necessity to re-survey the area from time to time. Mr Vos's report emphasised the importance of appointing such officers in particular in the surveyed areas of the Transkei (at Butterworth, Tsomo, Nqamakwe, Idutywa, Xalanga and Umtata) where the Glen Grey system has been applied, and urged that the plan there adopted of transferring title deeds from Capetown to the Chief Magistrate at Umtata should be imitated in the Ciskei by removing the deeds to the Chief Native Commissioner's headquarters at King-williamstown.

Under the Glen Grey Act perpetual quitrent is payable by the occupier, and holdings may not be mortgaged, sub-let or divided without the Governor's consent. The land may not be devised by will but, following native custom, passes by intestate succession to one heir; and transfers must be approved by the Administration to safe-guard the principle of 'one man one lot'. The holdings are subject to forfeiture for non-payment of dues, or failure to occupy the holding beneficially or for certain serious criminal offences. The unanimous proposals of the Southern Rhodesian Land Commissioners of 1925 that the main features of the Glen Grey system be adopted in Southern Rhodesia testifies to the success of the experiments. The Rhodesian scheme, however, provides for holdings without payment of quitrent; and it is not proposed to create separate building plots, advantage being taken of the Glen Grey experience that such plots, separated from the cultivated land, are not taken up by the occupiers, who prefer to live alongside their crops and who have almost invariably contrived to do so by 'squatting' on the adjacent commonage. An important distinction, again, is the Rhodesian decision that, while small peasant occupation is anticipated, there is no need, on account of the fortunate abundance of land, to limit the size of individual native holdings. 'Only in exceptional cases should the Native be permitted to hold more than 1000 acres in freehold' (!).

It is, indeed, the question of the supply of land available for the natives which vies in importance in the Union with that of the system of land tenure. Reference has already been made to the striking dis-proportion between the areas available per head of population in the native and non-native territories respectively. Where individual tenure has been introduced the land available is extremely limited: thus in the Glen Grey area only eight thousand plots of approximately four morgen were available, and in the surveyed areas of the Transkei the number of titles issued was (in 1922) about twenty-six thousand. In all these areas large numbers of landless natives live on the commonage, the Glen Grey district alone containing four thousand married and landless hut taxpayers in addition to the eight thousand allotment holders. The entire inadequacy of the present land provision is indeed admitted on all sides: differences of opinion arising only when methods of acquiring additional land are discussed. 'The Transkeian country', declared Colonel Muller in 1924, 'under existing conditions cannot from its own resources support all its inhabitants. At any given moment half the able-bodied are earning the money for the support of their families in areas outside their territories', as many as 90,000 being absent in 1921. Recently Professor W. M. MacMillan has estimated that the purchases of the ten thousand families in the Herschel district cannot exceed the pitiably low figure of £1 per family per month, and that of this amount about one-half has to be earned by the adult males by labour in the mines or on the farms outside the territories. Moreover, comparatively speaking, Herschel is not a bad case.

Two conclusions are unavoidable. In the first place, any policy which contemplates driving more natives from outside into the existing territories, or impeding the efforts of natives to acquire additional land outside those territories will endanger the peace and prosperity of the Union. Secondly, any policy which seeks to impose limitations on the scope or sphere of work which natives may undertake outside the territories will not only increase the distress in the native areas themselves, but react to the detriment of the European population. Not only is native labour an asset in itself, which should be given the fullest possible scope; but the purchasing power of the native communities is a consideration which the trading community can no longer afford to neglect. It is from these two aspects that the economic provisions of the present native proposals should be viewed.

As regards the acquisition of additional lands, the Native Lands Act No. 27 of 1913 prevents a native from acquiring any land outside the scheduled native areas (excepting in the Cape Province) from a person other than a native, without the approval of the Governor-General; and similarly prevents other persons from acquiring land from a native outside the native areas, or from acquiring land in a native area, without approval. The intention was to maintain the *status quo* as regards the ownership of land by natives and Europeans, until such time as the Union could be re-divided into segregate areas. The recommendation of the Beaumont Commission set up for the purpose, incorporated in the 1917 Bill, and of the five subsequent Local Committees which submitted revised schedules in 1918 all met with such strong opposition from the natives on the one hand and those European farmers, on the other, whose farms would henceforward be in a native 'reserved area', and who feared depreciation in the market value of their property, that Parliament took no further action.

The exemption of the Cape Province from the operations of the 1913 Act was the result of a decision in the Courts (in the appeal case Thompson & Stilwell *v.* Kama), and the present position is still broadly covered by the statement of the 1905 Native Affairs Commissioners that 'there has not been, nor is there at present, any bar to the acquisition of landed property by natives'. In the Orange Free State natives have been from the earliest times and still are by law debarred from acquiring land. The 1913 Act deprived the natives in the Transvaal of their right freely to buy or lease land, which had been recognised by the Supreme Court in 1905 (Tsewu *v.* Registrar of Deeds), and it operated in a similar manner in Natal. The reports of the Native Affairs Department show that, despite the 1913 Act, in urgent cases in these two provinces 55 tribal, 43 communal and 24 individual purchases of farms by natives were nevertheless sanctioned by the Governor-General up to 1921, inside the 'Local Committee areas'; and that it is not intended to establish additional European rights over Crown lands in these areas.

In the meantime, European interests have still further entrenched themselves in the Committee areas and the platinum discoveries in the Transvaal have led the Government to abandon the 'segregation' policy in so far as these districts are concerned. In the Native Lands (Amendment) Bill, the revised version of which is at present engaging the attentions of a Select Committee, the existing restrictions on the acquisition of land by natives are removed in so far as certain 'released areas' are concerned; and, where these are not available at reasonable terms, adjoining land may be added by proclamation to make up the same area, the unavailable parts of the 'released areas' being deproclaimed. Crown land in released areas and adjoining a scheduled native area is to be granted to natives only, and may not be leased for longer periods than one year to non-natives. Two-thirds of any revenue from prospecting licences or mineral law applying to released or native areas is to be applied to a Native Lands Purchase and Advances Fund; together with squatter licence fees, quitrents payable in native areas by non-natives, and funds specially voted by Parliament. This fund would seem to be a necessity if only to enable a native to provide the fencing, required under the Second Schedule of the Act if his holding in a released area adjoins the land of a non-native. Not only is he required to erect and maintain a fence at the demand of his neighbour, but the latter is to pay only half the cost, although he alone may want it.

Most important, however, is the abandonment of the segregation principle, since the natives wishing to purchase or lease part of the additional land in the 'released areas' must face non-native competition. Now that, in the fundamental matter of the acquisition of land outside the reserves, a return has been made to free competition, the equally uneconomic limitation of the *area* in which natives may purchase should also be abandoned. In so far as the native population is still in tutelage it might be justifiable, purely on grounds of administrative convenience, to stipulate that any new acquisition must adjoin land already occupied by natives; but in the case of educated natives who have attained a certain standard all such limitations are undesirable. No attempt has yet been made by those responsible for the measure to show that the proposed 'released areas' are adequate. The native spokesmen are emphatic that they are already largely occupied by natives (68,000 natives in the Transvaal already on the local Committee areas), and that the new provisions are entirely inadequate.

Chapter II of the Native Lands (Amendment) Bill is concerned with the natives residing on land outside the native territories. It is the intention by means of heavy licence fees (£3 per squatter on land actually *occupied* by non-natives, and £5 on land not so occupied) to eliminate the squatter class of native. According to the Native Affairs Department, squatting is today 'almost the universal form in which land is leased by the natives in the three northern provinces of the Union'. It is an unsatisfactory system; in particular because the mutual obligations of the occupier and the squatter are indefinite, the occupier rarely being satisfied with the services or other rent payment rendered, and the squatter having no security of tenure to encourage him to improve his cultivation. While therefore a change-over to a definite, indisputable system of labour or rent-tenancy is needed (in some instances freehold plots may reasonably be considered the squatters' due), the present proposals are tantamount to an agrarian revolution. The Chief Native Commissioner in Natal has recently hinted that 'any drastic suppression of squatting conditions would result in the unsettlement of 200,000 natives', while in the Transvaal there are on private farms 40,000 squatters and 88,000 farm labourers (liable, according to the 1913 Act, to perform at least ninety days' service per year). What is to happen to these natives, and to the farms at present dependent on their labour? The Act defines a class of 'labour tenants', who with their families are obliged to serve the proprietor of the land for at least 180 days in each year, in terms of a written contract. Applications by owners for permission to have either labour tenants or squatters must be submitted through a magistrate to the divisional council or to a special board for approval, and (although in the revised form of the Bill the fee for labour tenants has been left to be fixed by the Select Committee) the intention is to make the licensing fee a heavy one. The squatter, assuming that the owner is not prepared to submit to the licensing procedure and fee, is faced with the alternative of either binding himself under contract as a 'servant', in continuous employment, or being evicted. As a 'servant' (or even as a 'labour tenant') the native will be brought under the provisions of the Masters and Servants Acts, under which breach of contract is a *criminal* offence. No more need be said here of the general advisability of a policy of converting a class of peasant cultivators into farm labourers; but in so far as natives are compelled by pressure of taxation through licensing fees to enter into contracts as 'servants' the class of work performed will probably exhibit all the characteristics of forced labour. Until the conditions of employment on farms are such as to attract labourers voluntarily from other occupations, no devices of this type will succeed in providing efficient workers.

Assuming secondly that squatters are evicted as the result of this measure, where are they to go? The mines offer to healthy adult males long spells of contract work, away from their wives and families, and without hope of training and prospects of advancement. If the men go to the mines the families must find their way to the already overcrowded territories, where in due course they will be joined by their men. If, on the other hand, they are forced to the towns they will encounter the opposition of white and coloured workers believing in the economic fallacy of a work fund: they will find minimum wages fixed by the Wages Board which, because they must be acceptable to 'civilised' workers, will effectively limit their openings in any but the most menial of labouring work; and should they eventually demonstrate their efficiency at more skilled tasks, they will find themselves displaced once more, if the clamour of non-native workers is sufficiently strong to force the Government to add other skilled occupations to the schedule of Act 25 of 1926, which amended the Mines and Works Act of 1911. If the agrarian revolution contemplated in Chapter II of the bill is not to create an army of discontented vagrant natives, to dislocate farming operations and cause serious repercussions in the towns, its provisions must be amended so as to convert squatters by an inevitably *gradual* process into peasant proprietors or leaseholders on the one hand, and into contented labourers on the other.

There remains the problem of the European attitude towards the educated native. His place in South African life, and his capacity to contribute to the solution of the native question are both adversely affected by our general inability to think of natives as individuals or in any other way than as 'raw kaffirs'. As a result of the rapidly progressive differentiation of individuals, the communal pastoralist is today separated from the university-trained professional man by a whole range of different types and grades of natives. It is not the 'raw' native who in due course will take his place as a skilled workman in our factories, but an intelligent educated workman, Western in habits and training. So long, indeed, as colour prejudice continues, the native artisan will generally need to be considerably superior to his white colleagues before he gains admittance. It is no more reasonable to refuse full equal citizenship to natives of this type, for fear of evil social consequences, than it would be to segregate the British working man lest he should take a house in Park Lane and commence to pay his attentions to a daughter of a member of the House of Lords. In this connection a far too prevalent view was very deliberately enunciated by the present Prime Minister while addressing the Pretoria Native Conference on 3 December 1925, when he said: 'The European feels, quite rightly, that the right to vote is the fruit of centuries of civilised government and that he is the result and the heir of a civilisation in which the native does not share.' It is relevant to point out that it is the Europeans who must bear the responsibility for withholding civilisation from the native; but if the statement were intended to suggest that fitness for the franchise, and capacity to maintain and further Western civilisation are inherited characters, it will find little support among modern biologists. The social and economic forces which make up our environment operate without discrimination on all races and colours that come under their influence, and the response of our natural endowments (which seem to show no broad racial or colour distinctions) makes us what we are. While the provision for native education remains as meagre as it is today, the number of natives who will seek social intercourse and full co-operation with civilised, well educated people is doomed to remain small. The earlier sections of this paper argue that our failure to provide for the native population the opportunities for the fullest co-operation of which they individually are capable is *economically* deplorable; and the depressing outlook of many Europeans towards native questions suggests that the *non-economic* reasons for regretting our lack of intercourse with the native peoples are no less potent.

CHAPTER TWO

# Economic issues in immigration*

Historians of Britain's agricultural, industrial, commercial and financial development since medieval times have familiarised us all with the notable contribution made to this country's economic growth and strength by alien immigrants from Europe. On the whole, our governments encouraged them to come, protected their settlements from the natural hostility of local inhabitants and were content to tax rather than expropriate the financiers among them, with the regrettable and notorious exceptions of some impecunious monarchs. Such antagonism as was shown by the British people to foreign settlers was generally no different in kind from that aroused by internal migrants from other parts of the country, nor indeed from that habitually displayed against long-settled inhabitants of adjacent hamlets and towns. In this century the revolution in road and rail transport has shown up these local prejudices for the nonsense they always were, but some of us are old enough to remember how large a part they played in enlivening local gossip in country homes and inns.

As the London-born son of a mother brought up in the Peak of Derbyshire, I spent my early holidays when a small boy with working-class grandparents and uncles and aunts. Coming as I did from Shoreditch, where the bakers and barbers and tailors were mostly German immigrants, the timber merchants and cabinet-makers from Russia and Eastern Europe, and so on, I was fascinated to be told how gormless were the contemptible dwellers in near-by villages and towns. A son or daughter who married and brought home one of these 'furriners' was chided for lowering the purity and sturdiness of the local stock. My grandmother explained to me that my mother's lamentable emigration to London was the disastrous consequence of

* Introduction to *Economic Issues in Immigration*, IEA Readings 5, Institute of Economic Affairs, 1970.

her marrying a furriner drawn from an ancient North Staffordshire family living twelve miles away. Until she died full of years, my grandmother never did, nor aspired to, see the sea, and resolutely refused to visit us in London. The immigrants from Europe differed only in that their talk on first arrival was even less intelligible than the dialects of local furriners, and their manners suspiciously better, almost ingratiating. One's children were not encouraged to develop too intimate a relationship with theirs. Inter-racial marriages 'bring out the worst of both sides, tha' knows'.

After the accession of William and Mary to the throne, the arrival of a new stream of immigrants from Holland aroused the usual reactions. That well-travelled publicist, Daniel Defoe, a loyal supporter of King William, published in 1701 his satire *The True-born Englishman*, which, by the wit and outspokenness of its rhyming couplets and the rapidity with which over 20 editions were sold in two years, became the most popular piece published in King William's reign. Thereafter, no literate person in the country, indeed no one who was not too stupid to grasp the purport of what was read out to him, would wisely profess to be 'true born' or, if he did, claim that there was any virtue apart from dubious rarity attaching to his peculiarity. In a preface, Defoe remarked that

> if I were to write a reverse to the satire, I would examine all the nations of Europe, and prove that those nations which are most mixed are the best, and have least of barbarism and brutality among them; and abundance of reasons might be given for it.

I must resist the strong temptation to quote here any of the 1100 or so lines of satire by which Defoe shatters the myth of the true-born Englishman. It is clear (though not explicitly) from Professor Charles Wilson's admirable contribution 'The Immigrant in English History', printed first in this collection of six essays, that he knows his Defoe, and I am grateful in part for his essay because it has prompted me to read the satire once again.

It so happens that while I was engaged in reading these essays and writing this Introduction, there came into my hands the recently published lectures delivered in the University of Ghana in 1968 by Professor Sir W. Arthur Lewis, my old friend and former academic colleague, under the title *Some Aspects of Economic Development* (distributed in this country by Allen & Unwin). This is the sixth series of

Aggrey–Fraser–Guggisberg Memorial Lectures first instituted in 1957 with funds provided by the Government of Ghana to commemorate these three founders of Achimota College. Professor Lewis (now at Princeton) is a native of the West Indian island of St Lucia, who in the course of his varied and distinguished academic career has served as Principal and Vice-Chancellor of the University of the West Indies. In the third of his five lectures, on 'Development Planning', he discusses the problems created by the migration of foreigners, members of traditionally trading communities, into tropical Asian and African areas which had hitherto functioned only as subsistence societies. In this lecture Professor Lewis draws upon his careful study and sympathetic understanding of the history of immigration policy in Britain to formulate proposals for the improvement of immigration policy (such as it is) in the newly-independent tropical countries. I shall therefore summarise his argument here partly quoting (as I am sure he would approve and prefer) his own well-chosen words.

> The Chinese swarmed over South-east Asia; the Indian traders opened up Burma, and then East Africa; Syrians and Lebanese moved into West Africa. And at a later stage, the Ibos of Southern Nigeria, having learned the techniques of trading, moved north into the Muslim states in large numbers. There is no doubt that these traders performed a service without which rapid development would not have been possible . . . It is beyond question that they raised the economic level of the peasants as well as themselves by what they did.

Why were they so successful?

> Mainly because their culture is different from that of farmers in subsistence societies. They are willing to work 18 hours a day for six days a week. . . . In addition they have the virtues one finds in any immigrant group. Immigrants know that their success depends on their own efforts, and therefore they live by higher standards of effort and personal responsibility than people who are living in their own country. It follows also that such groups are clannish. When they have a job they hire one of their own, because they know from bitter experience that the natives among whom they live do not live by the code which success in business requires. . . . It is not race that gives Indians or Chinese or Arabs or Ibos their superior accomplishment when they live in sub-

sistence societies. The difference is wholly in the culture of immigration. Whatever the cause, the result in the second half of the twentieth century is explosive. As the indigenous populations have tried to enter business they have found themselves largely unable to compete, because they do not understand what business takes. The method of learning, which would be to apprentice their sons in other people's businesses, is closed to them. . . . So antagonisms have got fiercer until they have erupted in violent and disgusting outbursts. The story began in Burma, where shortly after independence all the Indians were driven out. . . . Then the position of the Chinese in Thailand and in Indonesia began to be threatened: a massacre of these people one of these days is not yet out of the question. Here [in Africa] the Northerners killed 20,000 Ibos in September 1966 and drove out a million from their homes. The Indians in East Africa are clearly doomed, the only question being how many will be killed before they are all driven out. Genocide is the favourite crime of our century. . . . Different races cannot live at peace within the same borders unless there is absolute economic equality between them. Racial differences bring enough trouble without their being identified also with economic conflicts.

What can be done? Professor Lewis continues:

For examples we can go quite far back in British history. In the year 1484, when large numbers of silk weavers were flooding England from France, they were welcomed by Richard III because they were bringing in a new industry. But in order to prevent them from developing into a separate clan, and in order to force them to teach their trade to English youngsters, he passed an Act forbidding a foreigner to take any other foreigner as an apprentice except his son. Henry VIII faced a similar and equally welcome influx of Protestant refugees from Holland some 40 years later. He strengthened the Act in 1523 by forbidding aliens to have any alien apprentices at all. The new skills were therefore acquired by Englishmen within a generation. This is what the Northerners should have done to the Ibos instead of murdering them. A law prohibiting non-Northerners from employing other non-Northerners, coupled with a massive educational programme for Northerners, would have solved the problem within a generation.

Professor Lewis's confident optimism concerning the efficacy of his plan to follow particular British precedents bears witness to his sense of the desperately urgent need to counter the threat of violence and mass genocide by enforcing absolute economic equality of opportunity between the indigenous and immigrant races. The parallel he draws between fifteenth- and sixteenth-century Britain and tropical countries in the twentieth century is illuminating and valuable, and commands our utmost respect, provided only that the defencelessness of the immigrants is closely similar in the two cases. In Britain 500 years ago they were the victims of persecution in their countries of origin, and Britain was their only haven offering a reasonable hope of economic and personal security for themselves and their families. Onerous conditions could therefore be imposed upon their freedom as aliens in Britain to develop their crafts and small businesses in the most efficient and productive way without depriving the country of all the immediate benefits accruing from their special skills, enterprise and industrious habits. Professor Lewis's parallel is therefore most apt in relation to the unhappy plight of Indians today facing ruin, if not worse, in the new independent states of East Africa, and of the Indians and Chinese in parts of South-East Asia. Is it, however, equally applicable to the immigrant Ibos in the Northern states of West Africa? Had they no alternative in Southern Nigeria but to emigrate to the North? Did they migrate to escape oppression or intolerable restrictions in the South on their rights to develop their trading businesses in the way they considered most effective and profitable? Apparently not; did they not go North in the belief that their profits would be higher there? If that is so, how successful would Northern attempts be to impose by legislation profit-reducing restrictions on their freedom to conduct their businesses as they thought best for themselves? Could they not transfer their trading businesses back to the South? Or does Professor Lewis envisage the imposition of restrictions on Ibo traders throughout the whole Federal region, relying on other States also to deny themselves the full economic benefits which they would gain from Ibo traders' efficiency and liking for long hours and hard work?

One device for attracting suitable and willing immigrants to speed up economic growth is the indentured labour contract for a fixed period, with or without compulsory or voluntary repatriation on the completion of the contract. On reflection it is strange that the adoption of this system in the former British Empire has aroused so much animosity in this country among self-styled 'humanitarians'. Something very akin operated on our internal labour market for some centuries, since the days of the medieval wage-fairs. A similar system has long been regarded as a sensible and humane method of recruitment of nationals into our armed Services (and indeed of aliens into the Foreign legions) – a vast improvement, say, on the former Naval press gang. As the authors of the 1948 Report by PEP on *Population Policy in Great Britain* opined, provided that the contract is freely entered into, 'there is no injustice in recruiting immigrants, under contract, for a particular industry and in making their stay in the country conditional on remaining with it for a stated period'. They thought that the admission of immigrants to work in particular industries was at that time 'temporarily desirable'.

South African mining companies have habitually recruited African workers for the diamond and gold mines on the same basis. During the last century the South African colonial governments also recruited alien immigrants from overseas under formal indentured labour contracts: first Indians and later Chinese. The Indian immigrants served their indenture terms mainly on the coastal plantations of Natal, and few of them elected to be repatriated. They took up other occupations or became traders. Some migrated to Cape Colony and the Transvaal. In 1904 there were 100,000 Indians in Natal against 97,000 Europeans. The circumstances in which Chinese indentured immigrants entered the Transvaal at the beginning of the twentieth century were special. The South African War had dislocated the arrangements of the gold mining companies for recruiting African labour, and the general economic recovery of the colony depended upon the rapid re-expansion of gold production. The Chinese immigrants were to stand in for African labour, doing only the same work. In January 1904 the Conservative Colonial Secretary in Britain gave his assent to an Ordinance of the Transvaal Legislative Council authorising the importation of indentured labour. The first Chinese arrived in July 1904, and by January 1907 the number employed was 53,856. The gap was partially filled by this 'pump-priming', and the impetus to spectacular economic expansion throughout the Transvaal was thereby restored. Humanitarian opposition in Britain to this so-called 'Chinese Slavery' played a leading part in securing the victory of the Liberal party at the British general election of January 1906. The Liberal Government prohibited the issue of further immigration licences, and insisted upon the termination of the Ordinance one year after the first meeting of the new self-governing Transvaal Legislature in 1907. It was decided that the Chinese labourers should be repatriated as their contracts expired. Australia and New Zealand, having participated in the South African war, had no compunction in making their indignant voices heard on the very idea of permitting Asiatic immigration into any British Dominion in the Southern Hemisphere.

In looking back at the early history of permanent white settlement in South Africa, it is worth recalling that at the very outset in 1652 the first Commandant of the Dutch station in Table Bay, where Cape Town now stands, would have promptly arranged the immigration of free Chinese colonists, if he had been allowed to have his way, to assist in establishing an economically viable foothold in the continent. Had his masters been the new Confederation Government of the Seven Dutch Republics, and had their desire been to establish a colony, he might have got his way. Jan van Riebeeck landed with 181 men, many of them sick. After a fortnight's quick survey of the terrain around the slopes of Table Mountain he recorded that he found everywhere

> the finest flat clay ground and other beautiful, broad, fertile soil – as fine as one could find anywhere in the world. [He had travelled extensively, and served for years in the Far East.] With the small number of men we have, however, not one-hundredth part of it could be ploughed or cultivated. It would, therefore, be suitable if some industrious Chinese were to come here for that purpose with all kinds of seeds and plants, for much better fruits could be expected here than could be hoped for at Ilha Formosa, as the soil is richer, and there are several marshy places.

Alas, Jan van Riebeeck was not the executive representative of a colonising Republic, but a Commandant responsible to the Governor-General and Council of a monopolistic Dutch East India Company with headquarters in Batavia, intent on establishing at the Cape of Good Hope no more than a refreshment station for ships passing between Holland and the Far East. The last thing the company wanted was the competition of free immigrants in or round about its station, spoiling the lucrative market of provisioning alien ships putting in for supplies. Riebeeck was firmly advised to say no more about the usefulness of free families 'raising crops and cattle and for making butter and cheese', and thenceforward he 'kept mum', making do with his original 181 men, and the services of sick members of ships' companies put ashore for convalescence at the refreshment station. This was 250 years before the introduction of Chinese indentured labourers into the Transvaal was to cause such an outcry in British politics.

Indentured labour contracts have continually run into difficulties concerning repatriation. The terms of contract normally require the approval of the government of the country from which the immigrants are drawn, as well as of the host country. As between India and Natal, the Indian government refused to sanction contracts which made the subsequent repatriation of the immigrants compulsory. The longer the sojourn abroad, the bigger the political and administrative problems of re-absorption, especially with expanding family units. Even given the utmost goodwill on both sides and a sincere determination to give sympathetic consideration to the aspirations of the immigrant and his family, agreement between the parties could prove impossible. How much bigger the problems are after the lapse of several generations!

It is not reasonable for an African government today to regard the descendants of immigrants of long ago as 'aliens' who must be deported or suffer harsh personal and economic discrimination, if not worse. This is the desperate situation to which Sir Arthur Lewis has called attention in the lecture from which I have quoted. Nor, in my view, can it be reasonable for anyone to contend that the present government of a country like India, concerned with its own population problem, is under any special moral obligation to try to create a new home for the vastly larger number of descendants of the Indian emigrants who crossed the sea to Africa perhaps a century ago.

There is another aspect of schemes for immigration under contract to which I wish to refer. I have already called attention to the views of the authors of the 1948 PEP Report on Population Policy. The factual account which that Report gave of the governmental machinery for immigration control was very enlightening to a non-specialist reader such as myself. I cannot recall seeing since then any detailed comprehensive study of the evolution of this control machinery, the criteria to which governments have appealed in operating it, and the economic implications of the decisions taken.

As I understand the position, immigration control in Britain stems from the Aliens Act of 1905, as amended by the Aliens Restriction

Acts of 1914 and 1919. Under this legislation, the Aliens Order of 1920 was issued, and this Order still provides the basis of control. To quote some passages from the PEP Report of 1948:

> The Home Secretary can prohibit the entry of any non-British national and also has power to order the deportation of aliens on certain grounds, though as to the admission of immigrants wishing to take up employment he is guided by the Minister of Labour.

Then follows what is to me a tendentious passage:

> In so far as immigrants are permanently satisfied with lower standards . . . they constitute a threat to the interests of the British working class. . . . The sweated industries which developed in Britain half a century ago depended largely on the exploitation of immigrants. . . .

The Report then went on to explain that

> As a rule it is the Government's policy to place foreign labour only in jobs where suitable British labour is not available. The Government schemes are supported by the Minister of Labour's Joint Consultative Committee, on which the Trades Union Congress is represented. . . .

The Report does, however, record that

> The Economic Survey for 1947 declared that 'The old arguments against foreign labour are no longer valid'. The price of safeguarding the interests of British labour in this way has been a much slower rate of absorption of foreign workers than might have been hoped, particularly in the case of mining.

I find this account of the situation in 1948 very disturbing. To me it is altogether too reminiscent of South African controls, as I knew them years ago, of immigration and migration in the supposed interests of civilised white labour. How have the British machinery and governmental attitudes and policy concerning immigration control changed over the last 22 years? As regards the factual position, I know that the British Nationality Act of 1948 introduced a new term 'citizenship', so that British subjects of the United Kingdom and Colonies became also citizens; and that the Act also specified the conditions under which application could be made for a Certificate of Naturalisation. I am aware also that it sets out the circumstances in which naturalised persons can be deprived of 'citizenship'. It has not entirely escaped my notice that since 1958, with the attainment of independence by former Colonies and dependencies, a series of Acts each relating to a specific former dependency contain special provisions with regard to loss of UK citizenship concerning that State.

What effect has all this had on immigration into the United Kingdom? The six learned contributors whose essays are presented in this collection have provided a formidable and rich meal for our enjoyment. Readers with digestions as weak as mine may find some of the ingredients difficult to assimilate. In such circumstances one hesitates to ask, like Oliver Twist, for more: but I for one would welcome another study. I think that many of us need to have, as soon as may be, an account both factual and analytical, both comprehensive and in detail, of the evolution of government legislation, procedures, attitudes and policies concerning the immigration of foreign workers into the United Kingdom from 1945 to the present day. Is there a volunteer?

I have been much enlightened by my study of these essays, and I warmly commend them to others.

PART TWO

# Property and Ownership

In the early 1930s my mind was very much occupied with the problems of property and the economic functions of ownership. The two papers on patents and copyright reprinted here from *Economica* embodied material which had been assembled, as so often happens, over a considerable period. The patents article incorporated the substance of an address delivered to Section F of the British Association meeting at Leicester in September 1933; that on copyright was the Presidential Address to the London Economic Club in 1934.

Reference to the opening paragraphs of my British Association Paper shows that in September 1933 I was already convinced of the significance of David Hume's philosophical sentiments and principles.

The course of Hume's intellectual activity in the middle of the eighteenth century is familiar to all students of philosophy and I have no intention of dwelling upon it here. The *Treatise of Human Nature* not having proved a success, he resolved to re-cast it in a more satisfying form. A first section published in 1748 covered the field of 'Human Understanding', and this was followed in 1751 by a second section covering the 'Principles of Morals'. In the concluding sentence of the 'Advertisement' (or Foreword) to the re-cast material from the *Treatise of Human Nature*, Hume declared that he wished the new version to be received as his definitive statement. 'Henceforth', he wrote, 'the author desires that the following pieces may alone be regarded as containing his philosophical sentiments and principles.'

I wish to dwell briefly on some aspects of the second section of this re-cast version, viz. that which covered the 'Principles of Morals'. I do not now recollect how long before 1933 I first perceived the significance of David Hume's analysis. I do know quite definitely that my interest arose out of my acquiring a second-hand copy of Hume's *Essays Literary Moral and Political*, published by Routledge on 30 May

1894 as Number 75 in their edition of Sir John Lubbock's 'Hundred Books'. (The evidence for this is not without interest. Apart from all the other essays in the No. 75 volume, the 1748 and 1751 re-casts of the *Treatise of Human Nature* material are called 'An Inquiry Concerning . . .', whereas I think all other editions I have acquired since then used the spelling 'Enquiry'. In all my own references to these works of Hume I have used 'Inquiry'. The Routledge edition has always served as my working copy. Hume's 'Inquiries' became the starting-point for my own thinking and writing and teaching, and remain an essential part of them. I believe a preference for 'inquiry' over 'enquiry' could well be sustained on grounds of best English usage; that apart, I have retained it in a sense of loyalty to the Routledge edition to which I owe so much.)

In November 1958 I delivered some lectures at Trinity College, Dublin, under a Foundation dating back to the late eighteenth century known as the 'MacDonnell Lectures', Political Economy being considered a not inappropriate field of discourse to satisfy the terms of the rubric. It was an invitation I welcomed. As an enthusiastic student of the history of economic thought I greatly esteemed the contributions which political economists in Ireland had made to the progress of the subject.

The part played in this development by Richard Whateley is well known. In 1831 he was appointed Archbishop of Dublin. He had for two years previously held the Chair of Political Economy at Oxford. One of his first acts as Archbishop was to endow out of his private purse a Professorship of Political Economy at Trinity College, Dublin, modelled on the Oxford Chair. Political economists in Ireland, particularly after the creation of this Chair, have made noteworthy contributions to the advancement of knowledge and particularly to its application to the land problems of their country. Especially remarkable is the number of them who made it their business to become established authorities on the law of real property.

These were eminent men who rendered valuable service to Ireland, and I wished to pay my tribute to them. Accordingly, I gave the relevant MacDonnell Lecture the title 'Political economy and the functions of ownership'. Included among them were some famous political economists who accepted invitations to occupy Chairs of Political Economy outside Ireland, as for instance at University College, London, in circumstances which enabled them to broaden their range of discussion and research, without, however, requiring them to abandon or neglect their major interest in Irish land controversy which might be kept fresh by their continuing to hold an Irish Chair contemporaneously. What was much more rare was for an eminent Irish political economist to take a post abroad where continued participation in Irish land politics was quite impracticable even if he had a mind to it.

The outstanding case is that of William Edward Hearn (1822–88). His breadth of erudition was in itself quite exceptional. He was educated at Trinity College, Dublin, leaving in 1849, eighteen years after the endowment of the Whateley Chair (at that time occupied by W. N. Hancock) to become Professor of Greek at Queen's College, Galway. Five years later, in 1854, he emigrated to accept appointment as Professor of Political Economy and other subjects at the University of Melbourne. Until his death thirty-four years later Irish land problems ceased for him to be more than illustrative material. Hearn's rare analytical powers and breadth of erudition were displayed in his path-breaking book *Plutology* (first edition 1864), the first of three substantial volumes produced in Melbourne before his death in 1888. Each of them testifies to his detachment as a scholar and complete freedom from any desire to take part in political propaganda. The second treatise followed in 1879, fifteen years after the first edition of *Plutology*, and may perhaps be described as a scientific study in social anthropology, entitled *The Aryan Household, its Structure and its Development; an Introduction to Comparative Jurisprudence*. The year before his death, Hearn produced in 1887 *The Government of England, its Structure and its Development*. In terms of contemporary writers I myself find some affinity of approach between Hearn's *Aryan Household* and Leslie Stephen's *The Science of Ethics*, and between Hearn's *Government of England* and the kind of study of the State of Victoria that Walter Bagehot might have made from London.

Inspired by David Hume's approach I resolved to apply myself to the somewhat arduous task of research into patent and copyright law, treating them as arising under 'Section III: of Justice'. To what extent, for instance, does patent law promote invention or hamper it, and effectively combat the pressure of special interests in maintaining or even increasing scarcity? (Jeremy Bentham hoped that he and his brother Samuel might grow rich by a well-devised patent system. He actually expressed the view that it 'produces an infinite effect and it costs nothing'.) This research was greatly assisted after I had been appointed to the Chair of Commerce at the London School of Economics in 1930 by the generous award of a grant to finance the appointment of a research assistant. My studies were stimulated by occasional invitations to contribute articles on special problems.

In March 1949 I addressed a Sessional meeting of the Chartered Auctioneers' and Estate Agents' Institute on 'Land planning and the economic functions of ownership'. The substance of this address was published in the Journal of the Institute in May 1949, and reprinted as a separate paper which was given an extensive circulation.

I contributed to a *Bank Review* an analysis of revised British patent and copyright regulations of 1949. In spring 1951 I wrote on 'Property in programmes' for the *BBC Quarterly*. Much of the argument developed in these publications was subsequently incorporated in the Stamp Memorial Lecture, 1953, 'The new commerce in ideas and intellectual property', which is reprinted here.

A. P.

CHAPTER 3

# The economic theory concerning patents for inventions*

1 Patents for inventions comprise a special form of property, created by statute law. In the United Kingdom, for instance, patents 'sealed with the seal of the Patent Office [which] shall have the same effect as if it were sealed with the Great Seal of the United Kingdom, and shall have effect throughout the United Kingdom and the Isle of Man' are granted under the Patents and Designs Acts, 1907 to 1932, every patent relating to one invention only and having a duration of sixteen years in the first instance; subject to fulfilment of the conditions laid down in the Acts.

2 The statutes creating patents in the various countries impose limitations on the exercise of the property rights which they comprise, but these are not the only peculiarities of this form of property. Despite the limitations, property rights in patents are more potent than is generally true of private property. The significance of private property in the economic system was enunciated long ago with great clarity by David Hume in his *Inquiry Concerning the Principles of Morals*. Property, he argued, has no purpose where there is abundance; it arises, and derives its significance, out of the scarcity of the objects which become appropriated, in a world in which people desire to benefit from their own work and sacrifice. Systems of Justice, he went on, protect property rights solely on account of their utility. Where the security of property is adequately assured, property owners generally see to it that scarce 'means' are directed to those uses which, within their knowledge and judgment, are most productive of what they want. Such is the diffusion of private property and of the desire to use it,

* Substantially a paper read before Section F of the British Association at Leicester, September 1933. From *Economica*, February 1934.

that it is at any rate generally true that there is not a sufficient concentration of ownership of the supplies of a particular good, and of all the easily substitutable alternatives for it, to enable the owners to control the prices of the property they own. Neither the withholding, nor the disposal of the property of any one owner will in general affect appreciably the price of the commodity in question. Hitherto, this inability of property owners to control prices has been generally approved. If we except recent tendencies towards 'planned monopolies', most proposals to interfere with property rights have been aimed in the past at prohibiting the concentration of supplies of particular commodities under a single ownership, in order to prevent the property owners from raising the price by withholding part of the supply.

3 It is a peculiarity of property rights in patents (and copyrights) that they do not arise out of the scarcity of the objects which become appropriated. They are not a *consequence* of scarcity. They are the deliberate creation of statute law; and, whereas in general the institution of private property makes for the preservation of scarce goods, tending (as we might somewhat loosely say) to lead us 'to make the most of them', property rights in patents and copyright make possible the *creation* of a scarcity of the products appropriated which could not otherwise be maintained. Whereas we might expect that public action concerning private property would normally be directed at the prevention of the raising of prices, in these cases the object of the legislation is to confer the power of raising prices by enabling the creation of scarcity. The beneficiary is made the owner of the entire supply of a product for which there may be no easily obtainable substitute. It is the intention of the legislators that he shall be placed in a position to secure an income from the monopoly conferred upon him by restricting the supply in order to raise the price.

4 It may be assumed that the statutes creating these patent and copyright monopolies would not have been placed, or allowed to remain, upon the statute books in the absence of a widespread expectation of public advantage from their operation. Economists have of recent years found new difficulties in stating the effects of monopoly upon the magnitude of the national income, but it is nevertheless still broadly accepted that monopoly conditions tend to promote the diversion of the scarce means of production from a more to a less generally preferred utilisation. It is of interest, therefore, to review the expectations of those who approve of the patent system, to consider

the implications of those expectations, and the extent to which they have been realised. Are those expectations reasonable in themselves? Are the devices which have been adopted for their realisation appropriate? Has their operation resulted in objectionable consequences which may not have been foreseen?

5 As we have seen, the purpose of patents for inventions is, by giving an inventor the control for a definite period over the disposal of his invention, to make it easier for him to derive an income from it. With what objects? As soon as we enter into an examination of motive, we are, of course, venturing upon uncertain and debatable ground. It will, nevertheless, I think, be generally agreed that the ultimate aim is to encourage inventing. This is undoubtedly the expectation and hope of the vast majority of disinterested advocates of patents. The aim of all advocates, whether inventors themselves or not, is to make inventing pay better, and those at any rate who are not inventors hope for more inventions as a consequence. Even those supporters of the patent system who would describe their argument as purely ethical in character would probably agree that their ultimate concern is that inventors, *qua* inventors, should be enabled to survive. They may argue that their concern is to see that producers of inventions are not robbed of that which ought to be, even if it may not be in common law, their property; and yet their interest in inventors is very likely derived from a more fundamental belief that inventions are especially good in themselves, that the production and utilisation of inventions ought, therefore, to be encouraged, and that the way to attain that end is to extend the sphere of private property so as to increase the profitability of 'inventing', and of the exploitation of inventions, as compared with other occupations. We are surely entitled, therefore, to attribute the existence of the patent law to a desire to stimulate invention.

6 In order to examine the effects of the patent system on invention it is, therefore, necessary first of all to ask what determines the amount of invention that takes place, and we must start with a working definition of 'invention'. To give it a wide enough meaning – much more comprehensive, by the way, than that to which patent law has come to be applied – invention is the devising of new ways of attaining given ends. We might widen the definition still further, by including the devising or suggesting of new ends themselves as inventions, but this would probably involve too great a departure from ordinary usage. We may all agree that a new machine for making cigarettes is

an invention but that a suggestion for the abandonment of cigarette-smoking in favour of something else is not. If we define invention as the devising of new ways of attaining given ends it will be best to make the 'given ends' as concrete as possible by excluding from the category of 'invention' any change in consumers' taste.

7 This somewhat comprehensive definition of invention enables us to include, as we surely must, all new ways of attaining given ends, although many may not be immediately, if ever, adopted. A new device, employing a recently discovered and revolutionary scientific principle, may be mechanically excellent, and yet not capable of commercial exploitation. The time and extent of its adoption will depend upon price conditions. Changes in relative prices may lead to the abandonment of one much utilised process and the substitution of another, devised long since but never before adopted.

8 A useful distinction has been drawn by Professor Pigou between different types of change in economic conditions (and has been applied to inventions by Dr J. R. Hicks), distinguishing those which are 'autonomous', occurring spontaneously rather than in response to any environmental impulse, from those which are 'induced' by environmental changes and owe their origin therefore to circumstance. Different writers have assessed very differently the relative importance, as regards their number, of inventions which fall into these two categories, and when we carry the analysis a step farther, and attempt a classification, within the second category, of the various circumstances which may induce invention, still more difference of emphasis is revealed in the views of the various authorities.

9 Spontaneous or 'autonomous' inventions include those which arise from the existence of what Professor Taussig calls the 'instinct of contrivance'. So far as these are concerned, necessity is not the mother of invention; the act of inventing rather is a necessity in itself. The inventor cannot help it. Just as some people, who may never be recognised as poets, continue to pour out volumes of verse, so others may spend their time or part of it in devising contrivances or inventions. Sir Josiah Stamp in his stimulating essay on 'Invention' (Watt Anniversary Lecture, Greenock, 1928, reprinted in *Some Economic Factors in Modern Life*) inclines to the view that the flow of invention is largely explained in this way. 'The inventor', he says, 'is still *sui generis*, and emerges from the ranks of engineers, physicists, and chemists, not indeed as a "sport", but as a special product, which is touched by no

"economic spring". The sense of curiosity and the idea of fame play a greater part than the economic reward.' Not all of the inventors, however, whose output is involuntary, are impervious to prospects of gain. Like artists, some may turn their talent to profitable use. The amount and rate of flow may be invariable, but its direction may be influenced by inducements of one sort or another. Inventing may be spontaneous, but the nature or form that it takes may be controlled by circumstance. It will probably be generally agreed that the number of 'involuntary inventors' whose output is completely unaffected by economic conditions is at least as small as that of artists who work without regard to the saleability of their output.

More definitely in the category of 'spontaneous' inventions are those which are made by accident, for the most part no doubt as the chance by-product of activity directed to some other purpose. Every scientific worker knows how frequently an inquiry leads to discoveries which answer questions very different from those which prompted the investigation. Undoubtedly, in the field of invention, contrivances are accidentally hit upon in the same way; but in all probability, the majority of these 'chance' inventions are also indirectly 'induced' – one stage removed, as it were – for the greater part of the activity out of which they arise is influenced by circumstance. Of a somewhat similar character, again, are the inventions of 'amateurs' who, when inspecting the specialised technique of a particular field of production, being prompted by curiosity rather than hope of gain, are enabled by their unusual possession of experience of some other technique to suggest improvements and new devices which fail to occur to the minds of practitioners themselves. The timing, at least, of such inventions is undoubtedly largely fortuitous.

10 Induced inventions owe at any rate their nature, if not their volume, to the circumstances of time and place. One very potent cause affecting the amount of inventions is clearly the rate of growth of scientific knowledge. The greater the volume of new scientific discoveries, the more rapid will become the rate of application of these discoveries by inventors to purposes of production. Invention does not, of course, wait upon the completion of scientific discovery. As William Edward Hearn wrote seventy years ago, in what is surely still the best theoretical discussion 'Of the Circumstances which Determine the Extent of Invention' (in his *Plutology*, ch. xi): 'The knowledge that is imperfect for the purposes of speculation is often a sufficient guide

for the daily business of life.' 'Even at the present day', he adds, 'many processes of our most successful arts have not yet received a scientific explanation. . . . But in all empirical arts, the limit of improvement is soon reached.'

11 A second influence on the nature, if not on the volume, of new invention is specialisation and the division of labour.

The specialisation which has been made possible by the great increase in the number of scientific workers has in itself tended to increase the rate of scientific discovery. Similarly, the division of labour in production has exerted an influence on invention. Adam Smith made the point perhaps too forcibly (*Wealth of Nations*, Book I, ch. i) when he observed that 'the invention of all machines by which labour is so much facilitated and abridged, seems to have been originally owing to the division of labour'. W. E. Hearn and, following him, W. S. Jevons (*Principles of Economics*) both criticised the extravagance of Smith's language, calling attention to the number of important inventions which have emanated from unexpected quarters. Yet they did not deny the obvious truth that specialisation in product and the division of labour make possible the detailed consideration of technological processes, and that inventions of new processes do arise out of such continuous and intimate consideration of detail. Whether there is in consequence a net addition to the *volume* of invention, as distinct from a change in its nature, is another matter.

12 It is true that the growing mechanisation of industry withdraws ever more of the active and trained minds from actual machine operation and may in that way reduce the number of inventions that would otherwise be made in that field, but it would be a very incomplete account of the effects of the division of labour on invention that stopped there. Specialisation has, of course, released the more able and ingenious and mentally alert workers from routine tasks for the performance of just such special tasks as inventing. It has made possible the career of professional 'inventor'. It has moreover resulted in the increased wealth of communities, which has made possible the increase of knowledge by the endowment of research, and the spread of knowledge and the training of ability by the endowment of education. These in turn have increased on the one hand the field for invention, and on the other hand, the number of active inventors.

13 Increasing wealth, the division of labour, the progress of science, then, are clearly circumstances which induce in these various

ways the invention of new processes and devices. It remains to add another circumstance, which provides the incentive for the making of particular inventions, and that is the existence of favourable price conditions. Dispute there may well be as to the effect of price changes, and of the consequent emergence of new opportunities for profit and new probabilities of loss, on the *volume* of invention that takes place as a whole in a given period, but as to the important *directive* influence of price conditions upon by far the greater part of inventive effort there can be no doubt at all. Hearn wrote: 'The principal circumstance which affects the progress of inventions is the strength of the motive for their use. When the demand is sufficiently strong, the supply generally overtakes it. . . .' The price conditions which induce invention in particular fields are those which offer a special return to inventors in those fields. The inventions may be induced either by the possibility of quite exceptional profits to those who can cut costs still further during times of flourishing trade, when an industry is already profitable, or by the imminence of certain loss to entrepreneurs who have fixed investments in industries which are depressed, and whose only hope is an innovation which will reduce expenses below receipts. During the postwar years, for instance, inventions have been induced by price conditions in both the coal industry and the rubber industry on the one hand, and in the motor-car and radio industries on the other.

14 Hitherto, the interest of economists in the relation between inventions and industrial fluctuations has been concentrated mainly on the part played by inventions in the causation of fluctuations. (Cf., e.g., Mr D. H. Robertson's *Study of Industrial Fluctuations*, and Professor Pigou's *Industrial Fluctuations*.) The problem of the reverse effects of business fluctuations on the flow of inventions is a no less fascinating subject of study, about which a number of unargued and contradictory statements have been made. It is important to distinguish between the making of an invention and its adoption. Sir Josiah Stamp, in the paper already referred to, says: 'On the whole I incline to the view that the periods of rapid and important invention tend to be periods of larger differential profits.' The view is not supported in the paper by evidence or argument. Professor Pigou in his *Industrial Fluctuations* (ch. iv, p. 43) is concerned mainly to refute the proposition that fluctuations in general business activity may be initiated by variations in the rate at which ordinary minor inventions and improvements are made. He

argues that even in the case of major inventions it is the decision to exploit inventions rather than the making of the invention itself that is the major cause of disturbance, the time and intensity of exploitation being largely determined by the state of business confidence. 'There is', he says, '... a strong probability that invention as a whole will fluctuate very much less than invention in any given representative occupation' – i.e. he implies that there is a transfer of inventive activity from one industry to another, expansions in one field being compensated more or less by declines in invention elsewhere; and he states definitely that 'there is evidence that in slack periods technical devices and improvements accumulate in the sphere of knowledge, but are not exploited till times improve'. The nature of the evidence is not stated. It presumably relates to the statistics concerning the rate of exploitation rather than of invention itself. Such an accumulation of inventions during depressions is compatible with increasing, stationary or declining absolute rates of invention, being purely relative to the rate of exploitation, which one might reasonably expect to decline when business confidence is at a low ebb. It is of interest to notice, however, that elsewhere in the same study (p. 12) Professor Pigou asserts that 'in periods of depression the amount of *intelligence* put into production is, in general, larger, partly because relatively inefficient business men are compelled to sell out to others, but mainly because those who remain in business "are put on their mettle, and exert themselves to the utmost to invent improved methods, and to avail themselves of the improvements made by others".' This would imply an increased rate of both invention *and* exploitation during depressions, at least on the part of those who remain in business.[1]

15 In the meantime certain conclusions may be hazarded concerning induced inventions; first, that every price change, by creating cost difficulties in certain fields and opportunities for profit-making in others, provides a double stimulus to invention, and second that the larger the price change the greater will be the stimulus to invent. Third, during periods of disturbance of the general level of prices, a more general stimulus to inventions and to the exploitation of existing inventions may be expected, for we know that individual price relationships are disturbed whenever, for monetary reasons, the general price level shifts. Fourth, any government measures designed especially to reward inventors, whether by subsidisation or by the patent system, i.e. the grant of monopoly rights over the utilisation of their inventions,

may be expected, because of their influence upon price conditions, to affect the flow of inventions. It is with the patent system that we are here primarily concerned. Despite the publication of a large body of specialist literature, in the nineteenth century in particular, on the merits of patent systems, they have received scant attention by economists in the standard treatises.

16 The patent system may, on the one hand, be expected to affect the making of inventions in two ways. The first is to divert inventive activity into those fields in which the monopoly grant will be expected to prove most remunerative. It may, secondly, affect the total amount of inventive activity. The patent system may, on the other hand, exercise another effect of perhaps equal importance. It may influence the ability or willingness of entrepreneurs to make use of new inventions after they have been made.

17 It will be convenient to consider first the effect of the patent system on the amount of inventive activity. Considerable difference of opinion on this aspect of the question is revealed by the scant references made by economists who go out of their way to praise the patent system. On the one hand there is the view, perhaps best represented in our own time by Professor J. B. Clark in his *Essentials of Economic Theory* (ch. xxi), that without the patent system there would be very little inventing, and very little adoption of inventions by producers, at all. 'If an invention became public property the moment that it was made,' he says, 'there would be small profit accruing to any one from the use of it and smaller ones from making it. . . . The system which gave a man no control over the use of his inventions would result in a rivalry in waiting for others rather than an effort to distance others in originating improvements. This fact affords a justification for one variety of monopoly. . . . Patents stimulate improvement, and the general practice of the nations indicates their recognition of this fact.' For the expression of a very different view we may turn to Professor F. W. Taussig (*Inventors and Money-Makers*), who throws doubt upon what he designates as the view of the older utilitarians, that 'men contrived simply because this was conducive to gain, and would not contrive unless prompted by the experience and prospect of gain', and suggests instead that invention may arise mainly as a spontaneous manifestation of a human 'instinct of contrivance'. If this is so, 'we may be led to conclude', he adds, although it is not his conclusion, 'that the patent system, for example, is a huge mistake.' Later, he

observes that 'the defenders of patent legislation often descant on the public benefit from inventions as if there were a special moral desert on the part of the projectors and patentees. They put their case badly. What deserves emphasis is the influence of calculated profit in directing the inventor's activity, spontaneous though it be, into channels of general usefulness.' The patent system is commended because it directs rather than increases inventing activity. Professor Pigou puts the same view still more definitely (*Economics of Welfare*, 2nd edition, Part II, ch. viii): 'The patent laws aim, in effect, at bringing marginal private net product and marginal social net product more closely together. By offering the prospect of reward for certain types of invention they do not, indeed, appreciably stimulate inventive activity, which is, for the most part, spontaneous, but they do direct it into channels of general usefulness.' The only supporting evidence is a reference back to Professor Taussig.

18 The economists of the early nineteenth century who considered the question were as definite as Professor J. B. Clark that inventions would practically cease if the patent system were abandoned. Jeremy Bentham was in no doubt at all (*Rationale of Reward*): 'With respect to a great number of inventions in the arts, an exclusive privilege is absolutely necessary in order that what is sown may be reaped. . . . He who has no hope that he shall reap will not take the trouble to sow.' John Stuart Mill's argument was similar (*Principles of Political Economy*, Book V, ch. x, s. 4). As Professor Taussig said, the utilitarians assumed that the patent system was responsible for the greater part of inventing activity. The question which they one and all failed to ask themselves, however, is what these people would otherwise be doing if the patent system were not diverting their attention by the offer of monopolistic profits to the task of inventing. By what system of economic calculus were they enabled to conclude so definitely that the gain of any inventions that they might make would not be offset by the loss of other output? By no stretch of the imagination can the inventing class be assumed to be otherwise unemployable. Other product which is foregone when scarce factors are diverted in this way completely escaped their attention.

In the view of Bentham, the patent system 'produces an infinite effect, and it costs nothing'. Jean Baptiste Say, although subsequently more critical, made a similar mistake in his *Traité* (Prinsep translation, Book I, ch. xvii): 'Privileges of this kind no one can reasonably object to; for they neither interfere with, nor cramp any branch of industry, previously in operation.' The withdrawal from them of scarce resources is ignored. To John Stuart Mill, again, the only public loss was merely the postponing of a part of the increased cheapness which the public owe to the inventor.

Manufacturers, although some of them were inventors themselves, who gave evidence advocating the abolition of the patent system before a Select Committee of the House of Lords in 1851, were no doubt enabled by self-interest to perceive the loss more clearly. I. K. Brunel, for instance, believed that because of the patent laws people spent their time trying to invent, who would do better for themselves at other things. In particular, he maintained that workers wasted their time and ruined themselves, trying to think out patentable inventions, when development would be much quicker if they were not thus distracted from making improvements and refinements of a non-patentable kind. In the 'sixties James Stirling, famous in another connection for his rebuke of John Stuart Mill at his capitulation to a sentimentally 'soft school of political economy', emphasised the dangers of an over-stimulation of inventions by the patent system. Yet at the beginning of this century Professor J. B. Clark was still writing: 'If the patented article is something which society without a patent system would not have secured at all – the inventor's monopoly hurts nobody. . . . His gains consist in something which no one loses, even while he enjoys them.' No inkling here that the patent inducement to invent diverts scarce human effort from other production, and that the subsequent exploitation of patents again interferes with the disposition of scarce factors which would obtain under competitive conditions.

19 If the views of Professors Taussig and Pigou, that the *amount* of inventive activity is in the main unaffected by the inducement offered by patent monopolies, come to be substantiated, the traditional case for the system will have been destroyed without further need for criticism; but it would surely be unreasonable to accept their view without strong supporting evidence. It seems unquestionable not only that a very considerable volume of inventive activity must definitely be induced by price conditions, but also that that activity is diverted by price movements from other types of endeavour as well as from other fields of invention. Entrepreneurs faced with new difficulties or with new opportunities will divert not only their own attention, but that of every technician who can be spared, from the business of

routine production to that of urgent innovation. They will not rely exclusively upon those types of professional inventors whose autonomous output pours out in a stream of unvarying size, and some of whom may be prepared, in return for the inducements which the entrepreneurs can offer, to transfer their spontaneous activity to their service. It cannot be assumed that all who are capable of innovation spend their whole lives in inventing. Many of them are also able administrators and production controllers; some in the past have been clergymen and barbers, and in our own time there is a steady flow of technicians from the research laboratories of pure science into those of industrial invention and out again. Price changes, particularly if prices appear likely to take a new 'set', may therefore be expected to lead to an increase of invention and a decline in other activity.

The patent system makes possible this type of price movement. It enables those who have the monopoly of the right to use a patented invention to raise the price of using it for the whole term of the patent, within the limits fixed by the elasticity of demand, and in that way to derive a larger profit from the invention than they could otherwise obtain. The effect must surely be to induce a considerable volume of activity to be diverted from other spheres to the attempt to make inventions of a patentable type.

20 It will be convenient at this stage to consider both kinds of diversion together, i.e. from other kinds of activity into invention, and from one kind of inventive activity to attempts to make such patentable inventions as will, in the expectation of the inventor or of those directing his efforts, produce the greatest possible remuneration under a régime of monopoly. It will be recollected that Professors Taussig and Pigou declare the merit of the patent system to be the inducement it offers for the production of inventions of greater 'general usefulness' than would otherwise be made.

It will be clear first of all that there is one class of inventions, on the making of which the patent system can exert no effect at all, namely those arising spontaneously, whether by accident or as manifestations of an 'instinct of contrivance', in persons whose inventing is uninfluenced by all economic stimulus. It is hardly likely that this class is very important in volume or in kind.

The making of all other categories of patentable inventions may, however, be induced by the patent system. It does not follow, of course, that they will necessarily all be made in response to this inducement, for in the absence of patents a sufficient price incentive might be present, in open market conditions, to direct inventive activity to the same field; but in so far as the inducement is furnished only by the expectation of a patent monopoly, a diversion of resources takes place and other production is foregone. What grounds are there for concluding that the output induced by this type of monopoly has any greater claim to be regarded as 'generally useful' than that which would have been induced in its absence by the price conditions of the open market? I suggest that such a conclusion runs counter to all general presumptions concerning the disposition of scarce productive resources in a régime of monopolistic control as contrasted with open competition. The nearer that market conditions approximate to pure competition, the less likely does it become that any entrepreneur or property owner will find it possible to influence prices by withholding supplies, and the more likely in consequence does it become that all resources, being put to the uses which maximise the incomes of their owners, will yield their greatest aggregate product. In perfect competition all production will take place at lowest cost per unit produced. How can it be argued that any departure from such a condition, induced by the grant of monopoly power to raise prices and increase a sectional income by restricting output, will achieve greater 'general usefulness'?

The only conceivable line for such an argument to take would seem to be that *ultimately* the inventions of a patentable type which will be made in response to the grant of a temporary monopoly will possess a sufficiently greater general usefulness than would result from the other inventions or other output immediately foregone, to outweigh the immediate loss. There surely exists no scientific reason for making any such claim for *patentable* inventions in general, as compared with alternative output. It is conceivable that exceptional cases may arise in which a new mechanism becomes socially desirable for a specific and very special purpose, and that prolonged research and experiment seem inevitable for its perfection, while no remuneration is likely to be forthcoming in the interim from models which are not wholly successful. In such cases, special inducements might be necessary to secure the end in view. Thus, for example, if a flying machine were needed capable of non-stop flights round the Equator, and machines with smaller ranges were of no utility, entrepreneurs might not be forthcoming and there might be a case for a special fund to finance the making of the invention. A patent system applicable to inventions in general clearly cannot be justified, however, by exceptional circumstances of this kind. Economics, in short, has not yet evolved any apparatus of analysis which would enable us to pronounce upon the relative productivity of this particular infant industry – the production of inventions; nor does it provide any criteria for the approval of this method of special encouragement.

21 The contention still remains for consideration that the patent system is necessary in order to secure the exploitation, if not the production of inventions. The main argument is that entrepreneurs will be reluctant to invest in plant which others may also acquire for purposes of competition. It need not detain us for long. It cannot be assumed that patentable inventions in general necessitate new investment in such large units that fears of duplication will provide a frequent deterrent to entrepreneurs. It is still exceptional for a single specialised productive unit to be sufficient to meet the bulk of the demand for a product. Neither can it be assumed that inventors would cease to be employed if entrepreneurs lost the monopoly over the use of their inventions. Businesses employ them today for the production of non-patentable inventions, and they do not do so merely for the profit which priority secures. In active competition, the condition in which new devices are most promptly imitated, no business can afford to lag behind its competitors. The reputation of a firm depends upon its ability to keep ahead, to be first in the market with new improvements in its products and new reductions in their prices.

A hundred years ago it was also argued as a merit of the patent system that it provided an inducement to inventors to make public the nature of their inventions so that they would eventually be generally available for wider exploitation. When businesses were small, and processes might remain one-man or family affairs, secrecy and monopoly might indeed persist longer in open competition than under the patent system, just as it is reputed to do still within the Maskelyne family of conjurers. But the conditions of industrial production have changed in this respect. With large-scale manufacture, few valuable processes can now be conducted on so small a scale that prolonged secrecy is feasible. Possibly – it is a question requiring intimate technical experience – there may exist chemical processes in which the nature of the product defies analysis and reconstruction of the method of manufacture, and in which the nature and proportions of the ingredients can effectively be maintained as the secret of a few people; but such cases, if they indeed exist outside the pages of detective fiction and sensational literature, must surely be exceptional, and unlikely to be eradicated by the inducements of temporary patent protection.

22 If the theoretical basis of the patent system is indeed as uncertain as this analysis suggests, the actual provisions of patent legislation cannot but be arbitrary. It is impossible to share Jeremy Bentham's enthusiasm. To him 'an exclusive privilege is of all rewards the best proportioned, the most natural, and the least burthensome'. . . . '[A patent] unites every property which can be wished for in a reward. It is variable, equable, commensurable, characteristic, exemplary, frugal, promotive of perseverance, subservient to compensation, popular, and revocable.' I propose to refer to a number of features of the patent system as it exists which are of particular relevance to the preceding discussion.

23 There is first the question of the types of innovation which are covered by the patent law. A very great deal of invention goes on outside its range, without any inducement beyond that provided by the operations of the open market. One need only point to the so-called fashion trades, in which the rate of invention reaches probably its highest point, and to the non-patentable refinements and improvements every day being added to all kinds of industrial product. In the last three hundred years there has been an enormous amount of litigation in this country concerning the nature of 'a new manufacture'. To the student of economics it makes instructive reading. 'Biological inventions' – innovations in plant-breeding for the production of special types, for instance, which are of undoubted economic significance in the agricultural and pastoral industries – are excluded. They may be freely adopted by competitors. Yet they continue to be made. Medical practitioners, partly no doubt on account of traditional altruism and partly as the result of the lead, if not the drive, of their professional associations, make very little use of the patent laws; and yet the work of medical invention goes on. The whole field of scientific discovery lies outside the scope of the system, although inventors and manufacturers may owe the fortunes they have made from patented products in the main to the workers in pure science whose discoveries they have applied. The task of distinguishing a scientific discovery from its practical application, which may be patentable – as for example in the

field of wireless – is often baffling to the most subtle lawyer. Associations of interested and discontented scientists do not fail to press their claims for inclusion. There are the notorious Ruffini proposals, for instance, for the grant of monopolies to scientists covering their published discoveries. Similarly, in the field of minor industrial inventions, there is strong pressure for an extension of the patent system, to supplement the registration of designs by a short-period patent protection of particular arrangements of mechanism, on the lines of the German *Gebrauchsmuster*. How can it be shown that the 'patentable' class of innovations possesses so much greater usefulness than all these others that it should be specially encouraged by monopoly?

24 Second, there is the system of reward itself. It operates in favour of only one or one group of the many participants in the progress of an invention from the birth of the scientific discovery to the emergence of the patent monopoly. The scientific discovery itself may be the culmination of the research and of the tentative hypotheses of many scientific workers: the possibility of applying it in a particular device may occur almost simultaneously to large numbers of industrial technicians; priority in the formulation of the provisional patent application may be a matter of days or of minutes. But one application alone can satisfy the requirement of this man-made law that the patent shall be granted to 'the first inventor', who receives a monopoly of the use of it for sixteen years, in this country, with the possibility of an extension for another ten. The grant of a monopoly renders almost nugatory the labours of all the rest, for any refinements they may subsequently invent in this type of device will, if patented, be much reduced in value by the requirement that acknowledgment shall be made, in the patent specification, of the prior 'invention'. Lotteries in open competition there may well be; but the lottery of the patent system awards but one prize, and that a monopoly, while those who subscribe most of its value may be precluded from qualifying for the prize.

The existence of a monopoly in fact operates to divert the attention of inventors from what may well be the most fruitful field for further innovation. In the case of inventions which cannot be patented, a particularly useful device at once attracts the attention of other specialists who seek, maybe competitively, to refine and improve it and to adapt it to the widest possible use. The blocking effects of patent monopolies check these surely beneficial tendencies; competitors, instead of helping to improve the best, are compelled in self-preservation to apply themselves to the devising of alternatives which, though possibly inferior, will circumvent the patent. It is a particular case, but one which is very widespread, of the maldistribution of resources which is consequent upon the existence of monopoly.

The term of the patent grant must inevitably be arbitrarily determined, even if each invention were separately considered. A fixed period of years for all and sundry expediently avoids countless difficulties, the range of which may be gauged from the efforts of the courts to determine, in the case of applications for extensions, the 'nature and merits' of an invention; in order to decide whether the patentee has been 'inadequately remunerated' and the period, if any, for which an extension shall be granted. Economists will well appreciate why the Royal Commission of 1862, which included Lord Overstone, was strongly opposed to any extensions whatever. Yet if there were a parallel provision, that any person interested might apply at any time during the life of a patent for its revocation on the grounds that the patentee was already more than adequately remunerated, some interesting legislation would certainly ensue, and the decisions of the Courts, however lacking in principle, might well be preferable to the existing fixed minimum term.

25 Special interest attaches to the provisions which have been gradually inserted in the patent laws during the past hundred years with the object of mitigating 'abuses' of the system, meaning thereby such use of the monopoly power as appeared obviously in conflict with the general interest. From the 1840s, side by side with the movement for the simplification of the patent law, there continued for a generation a strong agitation for the abolition of the whole system. It had the support of *The Times* and of *The Economist*. The strong Royal Commission of 1862–4, though precluded by its terms of reference from doing more than recommend amendments, was clearly opposed to the whole system. Professor Thorold Rogers read two papers against both patents and copyrights before the British Association in 1864 and 1865; while Members of Parliament and manufacturers carried on a continuous propaganda. The movement was not confined to England; in the late 'sixties a number of economists in France, including M. T. N. Benard and Michel Chevalier, wrote against patents; in Germany, Bismarck attacked the system in 1868 in the North German Federal Parliament; in Holland, the patent law was repealed in 1869. In

England, however, the Act of 1852 gave such an impetus to the patenting of inventions that in the 'seventies the attempt at abolition was gradually abandoned in favour of the more easily practicable policy of mitigating its most obvious evils. The official examiner system of search for anticipations of new claims was introduced and gradually extended; the cost of securing patents was reduced, for the benefit of poor inventors, and payments reduced in the early years so that inventors should not be compelled to allow their protection to lapse before they had had a reasonable time in which to arrange for the exploitation of their invention. International conventions were arranged to secure more reciprocity in the treatment of foreign inventions, and to reduce in that way the competition to which manufacturers under licence were otherwise liable from foreign producers outside the jurisdiction of the laws of this country. I propose in the remainder of this paper to confine myself to two only of the modifications which have been introduced into the patent legislation of this country, viz. the sections governing the grant of 'compulsory licences' and the more recently introduced 'licences of right'.

26 Provision has been made for fifty years now for the grant of compulsory licences in the event of certain allegations, which could be made by any person interested, being found by the competent tribunal to be true. From the first, one of the grounds has been that the patent is not being worked in the United Kingdom, and that satisfactory explanations of the failure to do so are not forthcoming. This manifestation of protection is of interest, particularly in relation to the question of the effect of such provisions on the amount of output which the patentee will find it profitable to produce, but it need not detain us here. Another ground has from the first been that the demand for the patented article in the United Kingdom is not being met to an adequate extent and on reasonable terms. The Board of Trade originally, then subsequently the Judicial Committee of the Privy Council, and now the Comptroller of the Patent Office (subject to appeal to the Courts) have in consequence had thrown upon them the duty of deciding, in cases in which the law confers a monopoly upon an inventor in order that by restricting the use of his invention he may derive an income, whether the output is 'adequate' and the terms 'reasonable'. The competitive output being ruled out, what monopoly output and price can be more 'reasonable' than that which pays the monopolist best? The handling of this problem by the appointed

tribunals once more makes instructive reading for the student of economics: but the responsibility of the tribunal does not rest there. It is called upon, in addition, to settle the terms upon which compulsory licences are granted. The Royal Commission of 1862 had recommended against compulsory licences precisely because it regarded the practical difficulties of fixing the proper terms as insuperable. 'On this question of price', they urged, 'individual opinions must be expected to vary widely.' Arbitration would not be satisfactory 'where neither precedent nor custom, nor fixed rule of any kind could be appealed to on either side'. The Patents and Designs Acts today make an amusing endeavour to help out the unfortunate assessor by directing his attention to certain guiding considerations. The first two are worthy of notice here:

[Patents and Designs Act, 1907 (as amended)
Section 24 – (1) (*b*)]

(i) he shall, on the one hand, endeavour to secure the widest possible user of the invention in the United Kingdom consistent with the patentee deriving a reasonable advantage from his patent rights;

(ii) he shall, on the other hand, endeavour to secure to the patentee the maximum advantage consistent with the invention being worked by the licensee at a reasonable profit in the United Kingdom.

Possibly those responsible for this formula might be satisfied if the assessor contrived to induce both the full competitive output and the maximum monopoly profit at the same time.

It is enlightening to examine the extent to which since 1919 the Comptroller has attempted to interpret these instructions. By the end of 1931, out of less than fifty applications, many of which were subsequently withdrawn, nine grants were actually made. Three were however discharged on appeal, and in the case of the remaining six it appears that it was not necessary for the Comptroller to fix terms.

The same duty of fixing terms, failing agreement between the parties, falls upon the Comptroller in the case of Licences of Right. In the same period, 7533 patents were endorsed, but in only seventeen cases was an application made for the settlement of terms. At the end of 1931, three of these applications had been withdrawn, one was suspended by request of the parties, and thirteen were still pending.

In no case, therefore, had the Comptroller been persuaded to attempt the feat of following the instructions of the Act.

27 Licences of Right furnish us with an economic curiosity. The 1919 Act, presumably with the object of inducing monopolist patentees not to restrict so narrowly the supply of the invention during the life of the patent, offers the remission of half the fees subsequently payable to all patentees who request that their patent be endorsed 'Licences of Right', the effect being that any person may thereafter be entitled as of right to a licence to use the invention upon terms to be agreed or settled by the Comptroller. The large number of endorsements – 7533 to the end of 1931 – is striking, although of course a small percentage of the total number of patents in force during the period (about 20,000 new complete specifications being added each year). The fact that in all cases the licence fee has been fixed by agreement without recourse to arbitration by the Comptroller would suggest that the patentee secures a royalty not far different from that which he believes will adjust the total output to the amount which maximises his monopoly profit.

If we were to make the assumption that the adjustment of volume of output to given price conditions takes place promptly, and that different firms have broadly the same production costs, the position would then be that the volume of output would remain more or less the same as that which would emerge under the ordinary patent system, while the patent office would have forfeited half its revenue to little good purpose, so far as the general public is concerned. We cannot, however, assume either that production costs of different firms are identical, or that a sole licensee will rapidly expand his output and sales to the point of maximum net revenue. It therefore appears very probable that the Licence of Right system, by enabling any producer to try his hand at producing the patented article, facilitates the operation of competitive forces in concentrating output in the firms which have lowest costs, and encourages the rapid spreading of production over a number of producers, so that the aggregate output is in fact increased more rapidly to the point of maximum monopoly profit (if the patentee fixes his terms to his best advantage) than would otherwise be likely (if it does not in fact exceed that amount for a time, to the loss of certain licensees). This device almost certainly serves to increase output, for without it the monopolist would probably not as rapidly decide to grant as many licences to the producers whose costs are lowest.

Without, therefore, injuring the monopolist's interest, so long as licence terms continue to remain at the point he himself selects, the Licence of Right system tends to correct one of the *practical* objections to the patent system, i.e. the slowness of the expansion of the output of patented articles. If, therefore, it could be reasonably assumed that the Comptroller would continue successfully to evade the alarming task of fixing terms, there would be much to be said in favour of modifying the patent system so that Licences of Right became the normal practice. In the case of copyright, in which the device was first applied, the problem of terms could be settled – if crudely – by fixing a royalty of so much per cent of the price of the book or gramophone record or piano-roll as the case might be. So simple a solution is hardly applicable to inventions, and if disputes between patentees and licensees became frequent some other rough-and-ready rule would need to be devised.

28 Expedients such as Licences of Right, nevertheless, cannot repair the lack of theoretical principle behind the whole patent system. They can only serve to confine the evils of monopoly within the limits contemplated by the legislators; and, as I have endeavoured to show, the science of economics as it stands today furnishes no basis of justification for this enormous experiment in the encouragement of a particular activity by enabling monopolistic price control.

There is today widespread alarm at that increasingly rapid rate of obsolescence of industrial equipment, which is the reverse aspect of the quickening of technical progress. Everywhere we encounter the protests of owners of specialised plant and of specialised workers at the changes which convert property and specialised skill into 'surplus capacity'. In so far as the new enterprises compete for their resources, capital and labour, in open competition with existing businesses, economists have strong grounds for the presumption that the gains from their success will outweigh the losses. If, however, innovation is especially encouraged, to the loss of other production, by monopoly price conditions, is it not conceivable that there may be relatively 'too much invention of the wrong kind', and, in consequence, 'too much obsolescence and displacement of specialised ability? Can it be that the patent system is in part responsible for our present economic troubles?

## Note

1 I cannot trace any attempt hitherto at statistical investigation of the relationship between disturbances in industrial activity and variations in the rate of invention. Professor Pigou, having in mind, of course, the reverse connection, considers that 'it is not in fact possible to demonstrate a close statistical correlation between the making of industrial inventions and *neighbouring* disturbances in general industrial activity'. That may well prove to be true. I am myself much disposed after somewhat close and prolonged study to hope that the detailed records of patent applications available over a long period in this and other countries can be made to throw light on this and the other related questions. The returns are available separately for different categories of industry (in this country, for instance, over a long period, there are 146 categories), those concerning provisional applications provide excellent evidence of the date at which inventions are made, and the subsequent history of the patents can be used for a study of the timing of the actual exploitation. In particular instances, the influence of adversity as well as of prosperity within an industry upon the display of inventiveness can easily be traced beyond reasonable doubt. With due care it may be possible also to draw conclusions with regard to the relation between the display of inventiveness and industrial fluctuations in general. The work is progressing, but further discussion must be reserved for another occasion.

CHAPTER 4

# The economic aspects of copyright in books*

If an economist needed encouragement or justification for devoting time to the consideration of the effects of copyright legislation on the output of literature, he might find it in the stimulating introduction which Professor Frank H. Knight has contributed to the reissue of his *Risk, Uncertainty and Profit*. 'Having started out by insisting on the necessity, for economics, of some kind of relevance to social policy – unless economists are to make their living by providing pure entertainment or teaching individuals to take advantage of each other,' he discusses the conditions of relevance of economics to social policy, and his 'first and main suggestion' is that an 'inquiry into motives might well, like charity, begin at home, with a glance at the reasons why economists write books and articles'.[1] Direct monetary profit from the sale of what they write does not figure in Professor Knight's suggestive discussion of the motivation of economist-authors; although for three, if not four, centuries the advocates of property in the right to copy have argued as though book production were the conditioned response of authors, publishers and printers to the impulse of copyright legislation. An inquiry into the rationale of copyright seems therefore both worth while in itself and likely to prove of general interest among students of economics.

There is, of course, a special difficulty in discussing the subject of copyright, in that a writer has an unavoidable bias. How many of us approach the topic in the spirit evinced by H. C. Carey in his *Letters on International Copyright*? 'The writer of these Letters had no personal interest in the question therein discussed. Himself an author, he has

* Presidential Address to the London Economic Club, 13 March 1934. From *Economica*, May 1934.

since gladly witnessed the translation and republication of his works in various countries of Europe, his sole reason for writing them having been found in a desire for strengthening the many against the few by whom the former have so long, to a greater or less extent, been enslaved. To that end it is that he now writes, fully believing that the *right* is on the side of the consumer of books, and not with their producers, whether authors or publishers.'[2] T. H. Farrer, at that time Permanent Secretary to the Board of Trade, found it necessary to observe, when reviewing the proceedings of the Royal Commission on Copyright in the *Fortnightly Review* (December 1878), that authors, who were the principal witnesses, are interested witnesses: 'printed controversy is therefore, on the whole, one-sided.' It is rather like relying on articles in the daily newspapers for views on the waste involved in Press advertising. Bias, and fear of bias, make an author's judgment on copyright a little unreliable. His readers must exercise particular vigilance.

## 1 Book production without copyright

A convenient approach to the whole subject is to try to visualise the organisation of production of books, which we select as a typical commodity for the purpose of this inquiry, in the absence of any sort of copyright provisions. We may define 'the absence of copyright provisions' as the circumstances in which the buyer of a literary product is free, if he so desires, to multiply copies of it for sale, just as he may in the case of ordinary commodities. Would books be written in such circumstances, and would they be published? Would firstly authors, and secondly publishers, find it possible to make arrangements of a sufficiently remunerative kind to induce them to continue in the business of book production?

## 2 The unpaid author

It should be observed at the outset that part of the output of literature is written without thought of direct remuneration at all. There are authors – scholars as well as poets – who are prepared to pay good money to have their books published. It is conceivable that their output is in some cases quite unaffected by demand conditions: so long as they go on paying they will go on writing and distributing their books. There is secondly an important group of authors who desire simply free publication; they may welcome, but they certainly do not live in expectation of, direct monetary reward. Some of the most valuable literature that we possess has seen the light in this way. The writings of scientific and other academic authors have always bulked large in this class. Economists are relatively fortunate in serving a market which so frequently provides a margin above costs of publication for the remuneration of the author; their colleagues in other faculties are usually only too pleased to secure publicity for their contributions to our literary heritage without financial subsidy from themselves. Publications are, of course, in varying degree essential for their careers, in professions other than that of authorship. They seek recognition of their claims as scholars; and published work they must have, even at the cost of paying for it. Speak to them on the subject of direct immediate return, and they reply in terms of numbers of offprints or 'separates'. In just that way were authors quite generally paid in this country in the sixteenth century: they sold their manuscript outright to the publisher for perhaps at most one or two hundred copies: on occasion a little money might also pass.

For such writers copyright has few charms. Like public speakers who hope for a good Press, they welcome the spread of their ideas. Erasmus went to Basle in 1522, not apparently to expostulate with Frobenius for daring to print his manuscript writings, but to assist the printer in the good work. The wider the circulation, the more universal the recognition the author would receive.

## 3 The payment of authors without copyright

What, however, of a third group of authors – the professional scribes, who write for their living? Whether they sell their writings to publishers, who buy them because they hope to sell copies, or whether they publish them direct, their living depends on the direct proceeds from their writing, and in both cases their receipts depend on the number of copies sold. Clearly, they – both author and publisher – would gain directly from the restraint of all reprinting that resulted in a diminished sale of their own copies. If the purchase of a copy ceased to carry with it the right to make further copies from it for sale, the author and original publisher might contrive to do much better for themselves, by the simple monopoly device of restricting the number of copies offered on the market. They would do still better if they were given the power to control also the supply of directly competing books, as early publishers had in this country. It goes without saying, of course, that that undoubted fact is not an adequate reason why the general public should give them either degree of monopoly power.

The belief has been widely held that professional authorship depends for its continued existence upon this copyright monopoly; or upon an alternative which is considered worse, viz. patronage. Even if that were true, it would still be necessary to show beyond reasonable doubt that professional authors were worth retaining at such a price as copyright. The output which monopoly alone can evoke is not normally regarded as preferable to the alternative products which free competition would allow to emerge. Patronage itself may not be wholly an evil. There seems to be no reason why a person who wants certain things written and published should not be at liberty to offer payment to suitable people to do the necessary work. If the task is uncongenial, some authors will need high remuneration, and others will no doubt decline any terms; but many a builder has been willing in the past to erect even monstrous dwellings for rich men who had their own ideas about architecture. Patronage has in the past provided us with some magnificent literature, music, pictures, buildings, and furniture. There have been patrons who have given artists a very free hand in their work. Civil servants, secretaries of commissions, lawyers and others have conceived it their normal duty to express in imperishable language the views of their employers, with whom they may personally have been in disagreement. To Macaulay, nevertheless, speaking in the House of Commons at the second reading of Serjeant Talfourd's Copyright Bill in 1841 (5 February, *Hansard*, Vol. LVI), patronage was the only alternative to copyright; and it was so objectionable that it justified copyright. 'I can conceive no system more fatal to the integrity and independence of literary men, than one under which they should be taught to look for their daily bread to the favour of ministers and nobles.' . . . 'It is desirable that we should have a supply of good books; we cannot have such a supply unless men of letters are liberally remunerated, and the least objectionable way of remunerating them is by means of copyright.' . . . 'The system of copyright has great advantages, and great disadvantages.' . . . 'Copyright is monopoly, and produces all the effects which the general voice of mankind attributes to monopoly.' . . . 'Monopoly is an evil.' . . . 'For the sake of the good we must submit to the evil; but the evil ought not to last a day longer than is necessary for the purpose of securing the good.' ... 'The principle of copyright is this. It is a tax on readers for the purpose of giving a bounty to writers. The tax is an exceedingly bad one; it is a tax on one of the most innocent and most salutary of human pleasures; and never let us forget that a tax on innocent pleasures is a premium on vicious pleasures.' But Macaulay nevertheless preferred copyright to patronage.

Is there no other alternative, in the absence of copyright? For the moment it will be sufficient to remark that professional writers *have* contrived in the past to secure a price for their product, in such circumstances, provided always that a market exists for it at all. And it must be borne in mind that copyright in a particular work cannot itself *create* a demand for the kind of satisfaction which that work and similar works may give, it can only make it possible to *monopolise* such demand as already exists. Ultimately there must be patrons among the public, whom the author must serve if he is to sell his product. In the early days, authors were sometimes curiously employed. Italian paper-makers in the fifteenth century integrated forward, and organised staffs of writers to work on their paper, in the hope of thereby making the market for their product more secure.[3] We are reminded of the present-day integrations of paper manufacturers and newspapers employing journalists. In the days of manuscripts there was never, so far as we know, any thought of author's copyright. Manuscripts were sold outright, the author knowing that the buyer might have copies made for sale; and the first buyer knew that every copy he sold was a potential source of additional competing copies. In selling copies, he would therefore exploit with all his skill the advantage he possessed in the initial time-lag in making competing copies. Moreover, copies of copies naturally fetched lower prices, for errors in transcription are cumulative; and the owners of original manuscripts could sell first-hand copies at special prices. They therefore received a more permanent margin from which authors could be paid. It was all very like the present-day trade in new fashion creations – the leading twenty firms in the *haute couture* of Paris take elaborate precautions twice each year to prevent piracy; but most respectable 'houses' throughout the world are quick in the market with their copies (not all made from a purchased original), and 'Berwick Street' follows hot on their heels with copies a stage farther removed. And yet the Paris creators can and do secure special prices for their authentic reproductions of the original – for their 'signed artist's copies', as it were. Augustin-Charles Renouard, the writer a century ago of two important books on patents and copyright, quotes in his treatise *Des Droits d'Auteurs* (1838) an estimate that there were 10,000 manuscript copyists in Paris and Orleans alone at the time of the invention of printing. Booksellers were then middlemen between the buyers of copies and the copyists: it was in part a 'bespoke' trade. Copying was not by any means confined to the existing stock of classical works by dead authors, for despite the copyists the age has left a legacy of literature of its own. Unprotected by copyright, publishers were able to pay their authors then, just as dress creators can pay their designers today.

Was this all altered by the invention of printing? In fact, the making of copies was regulated almost at once; but we know beyond any doubt that the reason was not to ensure that authors were better remunerated. The early history of book production in this country is most illuminating on this whole question, and it will be touched upon in a moment. For the present, it will suffice to observe that four centuries after the days of Caxton, many English authors were regularly receiving payment from publishers in a country which had no copyright law for foreign books. During the nineteenth century anyone was free in the United States to reprint a foreign publication, and yet American publishers found it profitable to make arrangements with English authors. Evidence before the 1876–8 Commission shows that English authors sometimes received more from the sale of their books by American publishers, where they had no copyright, than from their royalties in this country. From the economic standpoint it is highly significant that, although there was no legislative restraint on the copying of books published abroad, competition remained sufficiently removed from that abstract condition of 'perfection', in which there could exist no margin between receipts and costs for the remuneration of authors, for 'handsome sums' in fact to be paid. In the first place, there was the advantage, well worth paying for, which a publisher secured by being first in the field with a new book. To secure priority American publishers regularly paid lump sums to English authors for 'advance sheets'.[4] Secondly, there was a 'tacit understanding among the larger publishers in America that the books published by one should not be pirated by another'.[5] Each notified the other of arrangements he had made.[6] What of other publishers who might be tempted? It was explained, thirdly, to the Royal Commission of 1876–8 'that the practice of all the great houses in America (there are some three or four large publishing houses with very great capital), if anybody publishes one of their books, is to publish a largely cheaper edition at any cost, and they would make any pecuniary sacrifice rather than not cut out a rival'.[7] 'Fighting editions' in the book-publishing trade served the same purpose as 'fighting brands' in the cigarette business, 'fighting ships' on the shipping conference routes, and 'fighting buses' in postwar London passenger transport. Yet, fourthly, perhaps the most important check on the rival publisher, whose competing edition would in any case be late in the field, was the low-price policy which the American publishers adopted. American editions might cost one-half as much as the English issue; one-quarter or even one-eighth of the English price was very frequent. In such circumstances, the American public enjoyed cheap books, the American publishers found their business profitable, and the English authors received lump sums for their advance sheets and royalties on American sales.[8]

The significance of priority in the market, coupled with a suitable size of edition and a corresponding price policy, as a deterrent to competition is emphasised by an illustration. In an appendix to his book on *The Marketing of Literary Property*, published in 1933, Mr G. H. Thring gives a number of accounts of the costs of book production. Taking his figures for a crown octavo volume of 288 pages, eleven point, twenty-nine lines per page, an edition of 1500 copies would involve approximately £300 to cover all publishing costs, pay 10 per cent to the author and leave a profit of 16⅔ per cent to the publisher on all the costs, including royalty. That would mean an average wholesale price of 4*s* per copy, and a retail price of, say, 6*s*. If the book were a success, and there were no copyright law, a rival publisher might very probably come into the market with a larger and therefore cheaper edition which would deprive the author and first publisher of at least part of their anticipated receipts. They might, of course, lower the price as soon as success showed itself to them, and reprint at once on a larger scale, before competitors could formulate plans. A publisher who was more skilful in judging public taste might, however, have embarked in the first instance on an edition of, say, 3000 copies, and if he calculated on receiving the same total amount of profit himself from the venture and on paying twice the previous total royalty to the author, the total sum involved might be about £382, or 2*s* 9*d* per copy wholesale, corresponding to, say, 4*s* retail.[9] A price as low as that would surely make competitors hesitate before issuing, late in the day, the still much larger rival edition which would be necessary to make possible an appreciable *further* cut in price. If a competing edition were issued much more cheaply on poorer-quality paper and possibly unbound, it would more probably tap a new market than divert the old. The abolition of copyright need not therefore result in the complete abandonment of the business of book production either by publishers or by professional authors.

## 4 The early days of copyright

Our speculations will be made more fruitful if we pause to inquire for a few moments into the nature and effects of copyright regulations in this country.

The earliest records are hardly less enlightening than those of our own generation. Regulation began in Tudor times with the usual system of royal patents, conferring upon certain persons the monopoly of the right to print particular books or classes of books. The patent system was of course applied by a series of impecunious monarchs to all sorts of enterprise, but printing was a special case, in due time expressly exempted (together with the manufacture of armaments) from the Statute of Monopolies (21 James I, ch. 3) of 1623. The printers did not fail to turn to their own advantage the determination of the Crown to control the output of the printing press. Many of the early patent grants were, in their prime, profitable monopolies; one, for example, comprehending all grammars in the Latin tongue, another the Bible, a third covering all dictionaries, a fourth all books on law, and so on. A specialist writer, confronted by a buyer's monopoly for his class of work, had little hope of early publication, still less of a profitable sale of his manuscript, if the monopolist had on his hands a large stock of a competing book already printed. After 1557, when the general control of the industry was entrusted to the Stationers' Company,[10] a comprehensive attempt was made at rationalisation in the interest of its members. Each printer's rights to print were registered by the Company, and rights were assignable by one member to another. Whenever exceptional profits attracted interlopers, the case against unregulated competition was argued by the Company with a skill which our present-day trade associations hardly excel. Already in 1583 the report of Christopher Barker went to show that the patent monopolies were not what they had been. For instance, the 'most profitable copy' in the country, a Latin grammar for children, carried fixed charges which left the printers little more than prime costs; 'the printer with some greater charge at the first for furniture of letters, hath the most part of it always ready set: otherwise it would not yield the annuity which is paid therefor'. Monopolies cut into each other: Barker himself had the patent for the Book of Common Prayer, but Master Seres had one for a psalter comprising the most-used parts – 'where I sell one book of common prayer, which few or none do buy except the minister, he furnisheth ye whole parishes throughout the realm, which are commonly a hundred for one.' Master Seres skimmed the cream. The industry already suffered from serious surplus capacity: 'there are 22 printing houses in London, where 8 or 10 at the most would suffice for all England, yea and Scotland too.' There were too many printers with narrowly specialised skill: 'who do both know and confess that if privileges were dissolved they were utterly undone, having no other quality to get their living.' And there were the interlopers, challenging the patent monopolies and making public collections for legal expenses: 'of which company being five in number, one John Wolfe, now prisoner in the Clink, is the chief.'

The era of the Star Chamber's decrees and censorship was a happy time for the members of the Stationers' Company. Compared therewith, confusion reigned as soon as the backing of the Star Chamber was removed by the Long Parliament in 1641, and the Company's petition of 1643 to Parliament for greater powers of regulation[11] was cunningly designed to make the flesh of an uncertain authority creep. 'Too great multitudes of presses' set up by 'Drapers, Carmen and others', were alleged to be in work, indiscriminately printing 'odious opprobrious pamphlets of incendiaries'. The ear of government thus attuned, the petition proceeds to business. Even members of the Company were ignoring property in copies, and if one complain he 'shall be sure to have his copy reprinted out of spite'. The copyright monopoly is 'a necessary right to stationers; without which they cannot at all subsist.' . . . 'Property in copies is a thing many ways beneficial to the State, and different in nature from the engrossing, or monopolising some other commodities into the hands [of] a few, to the producing of scarcity and dearth, amongst the generality.' The stationers then pass to a statement of the case for copyright which would not discredit an 'economic adviser' to a modern publishers' association. The first consideration is that books are luxuries, the demand for which is elastic, and therefore monopoly cannot harm the public:

> Books (except the sacred Bible) are not of such general use and necessity, as some staple commodities are, which feed and clothe us, nor are they so perishable, or require change in keeping, some of them being once bought, remain to children's children, and many of them are rarities only and useful only to a very few, and of no necessity to any, few men bestow more in Books than what they can spare out of their superfluities. . . . And therefore property in Books maintained among stationers cannot have the same effect, in order to the public, as it has in other Commodities of more public use and necessity.

The second consideration is that copyright monopoly would result in more and cheaper books:

> A well-regulated property of copies amongst stationers, makes printing flourish, and books more plentiful and cheap; whereas Community (though it seems not so, at first, to such as look less seriously, and intentively upon it) brings in confusion, and many other disorders both to the damage of the State and the Company of Stationers also; and this will many ways be evidenced.

Their reasons recall the oscillation theory of modern specialists in the mysteries of perfect competition. Over-production would result from an absence of copyright:

> For first, if it be lawful for all men to print all copies, at the same time several men will either enviously or ignorantly print the same thing, and so perhaps undo one another, and bring in a great waste of the commodities . . .

and under-production also:

> Secondly, the fear of this confusion will hinder many men from printing at all, to the great obstruction of learning, and suppression of many excellent and worthy pieces.

Booksellers' risks and costs would increase:

> Thirdly, Confusion or Community of Copies destroys that

> Commerce amongst stationers, whereby by way of Barter and Exchange they furnish books without money one to another, and are enabled thereby to print with less hazard, and to sell to other men for less profit.

Even professional authors come in for consideration:

> Fourthly, Community as it discourages stationers, so it is a great discouragement to the authors of books also; many men's studies carry no other profit or recompense with them, but the benefit of their copies; and if this be taken away, many pieces of great worth and excellence will be strangled in the womb, or never conceived at all for the future.

Copyright should pass to heirs and assigns without term:

> Fifthly . . . many families have now their livelihoods by assignment of copies . . . and there is no reason apparent why the production of the brain should not be as assignable . . . as the right of any goods or chattels whatsoever.

And finally, in view of the foregoing:

> 'Tis obvious to all, that (if we will establish a just regulation) foreign books must be subjected to examination, as well as our own, and that all such importation of foreign books ought to be restrained as tends to the disadvantage of our native stationers.

The case for copyright has rarely been stated as comprehensively as in this early petition. Parliament responded promptly with the requisite Ordinance of 1643 (virtually a re-enactment of an old Star Chamber decree), to which we owe at least the inspiration of John Milton's *Areopagitica* of the following year. Under the Commonwealth, political censorship was continued, and after the Restoration the office of Licenser was revived by an Act of 1662 (13 and 14 Car. II, ch. 33) which was little more than a new version of the former ordinances. The Act expired in 1679, was renewed in 1685, continued again till 1692, and then re-enacted for two more years. It lapsed finally in 1694. Until then, the control of the Stationers' Company continued over all copyright, which had to be registered in its books; but thereafter its authority to restrain reprinting ceased.

## 5 Competition, and the first Copyright Statute

As we have seen, authors could expect little benefit to themselves from the patent system. The printer who enjoyed the patent right for a particular class of book had a buying monopoly for all manuscript books in that class, and authors were in his hands. Under the control of the Stationers' Company, as members began to compete among themselves for the right to issue new books, authors were gradually enabled to bargain with more success. In the seventeenth century some of them were in a position to sell the rights to publish only one edition of a stated number of copies; and cash payments, in addition to the delivery of the authors' copies, became more general. The bulk of the publishing business came into the hands of the London booksellers, who were, of course, members of the Stationers' Company. Their contact with the market made them good judges of books which would sell, and they could therefore offer better terms. On occasion they shared the risks in expensive publications by taking over stock from each other by exchange or purchase. It was at the end of the seventeenth century that competition from publishers and printers outside the Stationers' Company became really severe. The era of political and religious censorship was passing, and the Company could no longer interest the Government in the control of the new printing presses springing up throughout the country. The doctrine of perpetual copyright which the Company had endeavoured to establish, on the evidence of assignments registered in its books, began to be flouted on all sides by the country booksellers, particularly after the Licensing Act lapsed in 1694. The London booksellers made a series of unsuccessful attempts to secure new legislation, and it was not until the eighth year of Queen Anne that they secured the passage of the first Copyright Statute.

## 6 The 'perpetual copyright' question

In view of the claims which the Stationers' Company had hitherto made, the terms of the Copyright Act of 1709–10 are significant. In the case of existing books, the Act gave the authors, or if they had transferred their rights (which, of course, they almost invariably had) the then proprietors, the sole right of printing them for twenty-one years and no longer. In the case of new books, the author was given the sole right of printing them for fourteen years from the date of publication, and, if then still living, for one further term of fourteen years. The penalty for pirating was forfeiture and a fine of one penny per sheet, the protection extending only to books registered at the Stationers' Company. It will be noticed how closely the Act followed the patent system for inventions, as preserved in the Statute of Monopolies of 1623. The London booksellers, who must by then have despaired of ever securing the perpetual copyright which at one time they had claimed, had no reason to oppose the grant, enforceable in the Courts, of fourteen years of monopoly power for every new book they bought outright, although some of them subsequently protested when they realised that the second period of fourteen years granted to authors who were still living was the author's property to sell again.[12]

Authors themselves were placed in a much better bargaining position. Their success depended upon individual popularity and reputation. As regards 'bargaining power', they needed only to avoid committing themselves far ahead in any one contract, for if their books sold well they could rely on booksellers to bid up each other. The career of David Hume as an author well illustrates the position.[13] In 1739 at the age of twenty-eight he sold the rights to the first edition in two volumes of his first book, *A Treatise of Human Nature*, 1000 copies to be printed, to John Noon, bookseller, for fifty guineas and twelve bound copies. A year later, the third volume, *A Discourse Concerning Morals*, was ready, and although Noon was very willing to take it Hume found it more profitable to contract with Thomas Longman, to whom Francis Hutcheson had referred him.[14] In subsequent years he issued several editions of his *Essays* through Kincaid, Donaldson, and ultimately the very astute London publisher, Andrew Millar. In 1754 we find him engaging with Edinburgh booksellers to publish 2000 copies of the first volume of his *History of Great Britain* for £400; but Andrew Millar paid him £700 for the rights to one edition of the second volume, and the same for the subsequent section (in two volumes) on the Tudors. In 1759, twenty years after selling his first book, Hume contracted with Millar to write the early section of the *History*, 'from the beginning to the accession of Henry VII', for £1400, 'the first previous agreement ever I made with a bookseller'. Millar apparently also bought the 'full property' in the first two volumes of the *History* for another eight hundred guineas. Nevertheless, David Hume had reason to protest frequently against the sharp practices of Andrew Millar, who deceived him continually concerning the size of editions and their rate of sale, and reprinted an edition without giving the author the agreed opportunity to correct the text.

Andrew Millar took a leading part in the renewed attempt which the London booksellers made in the middle of the eighteenth century, despite the Copyright Act of 1709, to establish their claim to perpetual copyright.[15] The traffic in 'copyrights' of existing books was continued, as though that Act had not been passed; the London booksellers probably depending on each other to respect assignments recorded in the registers of the Stationers' Company. Millar had in 1729 bought *The Seasons* from James Thomson, and duly registered his property in it. In 1763, fifteen years after Thomson's death, another bookseller, Robert Taylor, republished *The Seasons*, and Millar brought an action three years later in the Court of King's Bench. By a curious majority decision, the Court found in 1769, after Millar's death, that the 1709 Act did not take away the author's perpetual copyright which, the Court declared, had existed at common law, and which in this case the author had assigned to Andrew Millar. On the basis of that decision, perpetual copyright was for five years thereafter the law of England. The country booksellers were not prepared to let the matter rest there; Donaldson, the Edinburgh bookseller, republished *The Seasons* once again. Becket, who had purchased the Thomson copyrights at the sale of Millar's effects, secured an injunction against him in the Court of Chancery, and Donaldson in 1774 appealed to the House of Lords. The House invited eleven judges to answer a number of questions on the effect of the Act of Queen Anne, and by six to five they declared that it took away the perpetual rights of authors. The House of Lords, with the lay peers taking an active part (Lord Camden wiped the floor with the London booksellers), voted twenty-two for Donaldson and eleven for Becket.[16] 'Thus for ever', says Birrell, 'perished perpetual copyright in this realm.' The London booksellers, as David Hume advised them to do, made earnest attempts to secure another law, but their prosperity was against them, and opinion was too strong. They did better when they emphasised in those days the interests of authors, just as a century and a half before they found it most profitable to profess anxiety for the safety of the realm. Statutes of 1801 and 1814 extended the period of copyright to the life of the author or for twenty-eight years, whichever period was the longer. Putting on one side the ethics of the question, it seems unlikely that the extension of the term enabled authors to *sell* their copyrights outright to publishers for much greater prices, or had any considerable effect on the output of new literature.

## 7 The Copyright Act of 1842

This rapid survey of the early history of copyright in this country will have served its purpose if it makes more clear the interests concerned in the important changes introduced into the law by the Act of 1842 (5 and 6 Vic., ch. 45), which remained in force right through the remainder of the nineteenth century and was only superseded by the present Copyright Act of 1911. The Copyright Act of 1842 had the effect in general of adding another fourteen years to the monopoly period. Copyright was made to extend for the life of the author plus seven years, or forty-two years from the date of publication, whichever period was the greater. There may be doubt whether the volume of authorship was thereby increased, but it certainly increased the profits to be made from the sale of successful books. The immediate occasion for the passing of this important measure is of interest; if the evidence of a publisher of the time is to be accepted,[17] the Bill found favour in the House of Commons 'because it was understood to be for the special benefit of the family of Sir Walter Scott, whose copyright was about to expire under the old law'. More specific and less far-reaching means of achieving that particular end might well have been devised.

For seventy years the Copyright Act of 1842 exercised a far-reaching influence on the output and prices of English books in the United Kingdom. Even before it was passed, critics of the copyright system were calling attention to the high prices which resulted. In 1837, for instance, the Keeper of Printed Books at the British Museum, Thomas Watts by name, advocated in the *Mechanics' Magazine* the adoption of the 'compulsory licence' or 'royalty' system, by which, since any person who paid to the author a fixed percentage of the selling price would be free to print any book, competition between publishers could be allowed while securing remuneration for authors.[18] During the nineteenth century, the differences between the prices of books in England and the United States were enormous. T. H. Farrer (afterwards Lord Farrer), Secretary to the Board of Trade, presented long sch edules of comparative prices as evidence to the Copyright Commission of 1876–8.

## 8 The defence of high prices

The defence of high prices in England which the publishers then advanced was the same as was employed in 1643. 'Four books out of five which are published do not pay their expenses. . . . The most experienced person can do no more than guess whether a book by an unknown author will succeed or fail.'[19] It was argued that copyright is essential in order that the monopoly profits from successful books might cover the losses. The question is worth a little consideration. Without copyright, publishers no doubt would not issue all the books which copyright elicits, for competition would reduce the receipts from those which succeed. The higher the profits from the copyright monopoly, the greater the willingness to publish the doubtful successes. The odds in the gamble are made more attractive. Given copyright, therefore, a larger proportion of available manuscripts will be accepted by one publisher or another, and more people will continue to write who in competition would abandon hope of seeing their manuscripts in print and would turn to other occupations. Monopoly is, of course, a common enough device for securing in this way the diversion of scarce resources to particular uses. It is involved in the patent system for inventions, in the chartered-company method of opening up 'new' territories, in the 'public utility corporation' for the provision of services, and so on. What is generally overlooked by the more enthusiastic advocates of these schemes is the alternative output which the resources would have yielded in other employment. T. H. Farrer, giving evidence before the 1876–8 Commission, no doubt had these considerations more or less clearly in his mind when discussing the weaknesses of copyright. 'What we want, I believe, is more good books and cheaper good books; but we do not want more books; we have too many books at present. Some persons, whose opinions are deserving of much consideration, wish to do away with copyright in order to diminish the number of books, and to reduce the number of those who make authorship a trade. They think that to do so would be a gain to the public in providing better books, and that it would not discourage those who write for the sake of reputation or for the sake of truth, and less for the sake of money. I do not say that I agree with these persons, but I think they are right in thinking that we have, under the present system, too many books.'[20]

The fact is, of course, that the eminent publishers who have called attention to the inevitable element of risk in the conduct of their affairs have been prone to exaggerate the unreliability of their judgment in selecting manuscripts for publication at their own risk. Suppose it to be true that four books out of five fail to pay: are they *all* – were they *ever* all – issued at the risk of the publisher? Faced with really risky propositions, do they not suggest to the luckless author that he should share the risk with them, or bear the whole costs, or secure a subsidy from elsewhere? Would it indeed be sound business for a publisher to subsidise definitely hazardous enterprises out of the monopoly profits gained through copyright? Insurance companies select the risks they bear, and publishers do likewise, notwithstanding the fact that the funds *they* risk arise in part from monopoly profits. Where guess-work is a fair description of the publishing business, copyright no doubt increases the amount of risk-bearing by lengthening the odds receivable on the winners. It fails, however, to describe a great part of the book-publishing trade. The fortunes of publishers vary enormously, but the differences are not by any means attributable to luck alone. The authors who (it is of interest to observe) were included on the 1876–8 Royal Commission had had experience with publishers of widely varying success. To Dr Wm Smith, for instance, 'only one book in four is a very moderate calculation of the books which are successful, of the books which pay their expenses'. Anthony Trollope on the other hand had 'learned from two publishers within a short period that not one book in nine has paid its expenses, and that still they have been able to carry on the trade'. The comment of the Secretary to the Board of Trade was that 'the public and the successful author must have to pay handsomely for the publishers' unsuccessful speculations'.[21] To the extent that publishers are successful in selecting books which sell, for issue at their own risk, and in requiring the authors to finance the publication of the remainder, copyright legislation does not have the effect of inducing them to undertake more risk-bearing. If the intention be to secure the publication of books for which in a free market authors would have to pay, more certain methods of achieving that end could certainly be devised. And if it could be assumed that there are public reasons for subsidising the production of such books, students of public finance will probably agree that more equitable means could be found of distributing the cost. It is not, however, to be expected that many people would support the principle of indiscriminate encouragement of all books which publishers regard as unlikely to sell in sufficient volume to cover their cost. And this is precisely the result which copyright may secure.

## 9 The fixing of prices: author *v.* publisher

It may be useful at this stage to set out the interests of authors and publishers respectively in the prices to be charged for books under copyright monopoly. It is not to be supposed that both parties are necessarily best served by a price which restricts the supply of a book to the point of maximum net profit to the publisher. The author's interest will depend rather on the terms of his contract with the publisher, and generally he will be better served by a larger edition and lower selling price than will pay the publisher best. Where the publisher is the entrepreneur, he is concerned to maximise the surplus of aggregate receipts over aggregate costs. The author on the other hand, if paid a fixed sum per copy or a percentage of the published price, has no concern with costs. If paid a fixed sum per copy, the author's receipts will be greater, the lower the final price and the greater the number of copies sold; if he receives a percentage of the published price, his receipts will be greatest when the *gross* receipts from sales are maximised, not (like the publisher) when *net* receipts after deduction

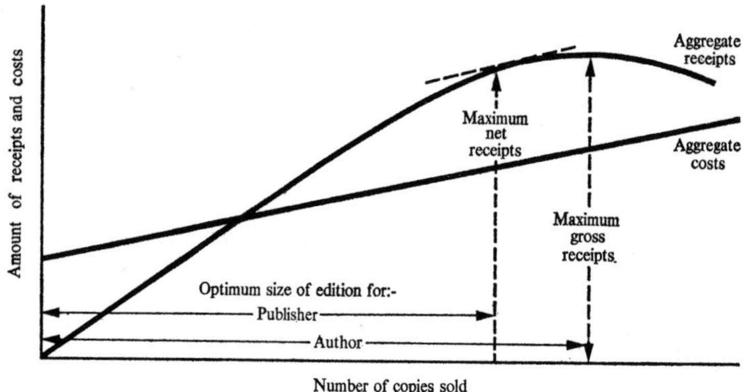


*Figure 1 Aggregate receipt and cost curves*

of costs are greatest. Since every additional copy printed adds something to the *aggregate* costs of an edition, *net* receipts and the publisher's profit are maximised at a smaller output and higher price than would result in the greatest *gross* receipts and author's income. The divergence of interest is shown clearly in Figure 1 exhibiting aggregate receipt and cost curves.

The author is therefore usually interested in securing a price and output nearer to the competitive figures than those which pay the publisher best. Only when the author becomes a joint entrepreneur, and shares the net profits with the publisher after the deduction of costs, do their interests in monopoly restriction coincide; and only in the case in which the author takes the whole risk and pays the publisher a commission based on costs or gross receipts is the author concerned to issue a smaller edition at a higher price than the publisher would wish for.

## 10 Price discrimination at home and abroad

In the nineteenth century the extremely high prices which English publishers exacted for books, behind the copyright law, led to the emergence of the circulating libraries, which became in due course a powerful vested interest standing in the way of a low-price policy. As the most important buyers of new books, particularly novels and biography, and dependent upon high book prices for public support, the circulating libraries attained to a position in which they could insist upon the publishers maintaining high prices to the public for a term of years while supplying the libraries at less than wholesale rates.[22] By issuing first an expensive and later a cheaper edition, the publishers practised a very profitable form of price discrimination in the home market; but the libraries enforced a longer delay than some of them desired.

A discriminating price policy for the overseas markets has long been a regular feature of the publishing trade. Circulating libraries may pay less than booksellers for their supplies, but 'colonial editions' usually sell at still lower prices. In the nineteenth century the reasons were diverse: the colonial communities were poorer, less interested in books and more cheaply supplied from other countries, particularly the United States and even the Continent, despite the difference of language. Notwithstanding dumping, the prices charged by English publishers for export were too high to meet the requirements of British colonial policy. In 1835, apparently, the India Council decided to admit the cheap American reprints of English books into India: the taste for the English language and literature could not be cultivated widely enough at the prices ruling for English editions.

## 11 The 'compulsory licence' or 'royalty' proposal

In such circumstances it is not surprising that increasing attention came to be paid to proposals for encouraging competition between English publishers by the introduction of the compulsory licence or 'royalty' system. As has been said, the Keeper of Printed Books at the British Museum advocated the system as early as 1837. R. A. Macfie, who had for years pressed the same proposal in the case of patents for inventions (the 'licence of right' system was eventually introduced on a voluntary basis in 1919), gave evidence before the Copyright Commission of 1876–8 in which he outlined a scheme under which any publisher might issue an edition of any book on payment, during the term of the copyright period, of a percentage of the published price to the author or his assigns. Thereby the supply of successful books, and quite possibly the remuneration of authors, would be increased. In Italy the law already provided for this system, at the end of a long term of ordinary copyright. The Canadian Government had just passed a law, as a measure of protection against pirated editions from the United States, permitting Canadian publishers to reprint English books on payment of royalty to English authors. Sir Charles Trevelyan and many others favoured the adoption of the system in England; but the Secretary of the Board of Trade, though personally sympathetic and strongly in favour to the free importation of cheap Canadian reprints into England, advised the Commissioners that the proposal was scarcely a practical question at the moment.[23] Only one of the fifteen Commissioners ultimately viewed it with favour; the rest, including the authors, feared that if publishers' profits were reduced, unproven books would not be so willingly published. Herbert Spencer gave evidence against the proposal, citing his own experience as an author of philosophical works. According to his figures, it was twenty-four years after the publication of his first book before the losses on his works had been recouped. It should, however, be said that he included in the costs of publication his own 'cost of economical living' during the period, that despite the copyright law he apparently had to issue the books at his own expense and risk, and that his receipts from sales in America (where he had no copyright to keep up prices) were apparently greater than from those in England. He estimated his net profits on sales in 1876, twenty-six years after publishing his first book, at 41¾ per cent, and he naturally feared that a law which allowed any publisher to reissue his books on paying him a royalty of 10 per cent might not yield him the same income. He regarded himself as entitled to a monopoly because in his view the demand for his works was inelastic for a fall in price: the royalty system, he thought, 'would be especially injurious to the particular class which of all others needs encouragement', the books described by the chairman of the Commission as 'of the graver class which do not appeal to the popular tastes'. Students of philosophy were fair game for monopolistic authors.

## 12 The Copyright Act of 1911: the introduction of the 'royalty' system

These considerations, therefore, were responsible in 1878 for the decision of the Commission that 'it is not expedient to substitute a right to a royalty defined by statute, or any other right of a similar kind' for copyright as it then existed. It is consequently of particular interest to observe that thirty years later it was largely due to the pressure of a group of publishers, in another field, for the *adoption* of the royalty or compulsory licence system that the present amending and codifying Copyright Act of 1911 (1 and 2 Geo. V, ch. 46) was framed and passed. The publications in question were mechanical reproductions of musical compositions. In 1908 a revised International Copyright Convention was signed in Berlin, and by its thirteenth article ratifying countries were invited to confer on authors and composers the exclusive right of authorising such reproductions. A departmental committee of the Board of Trade was appointed in 1909 to consider the consequential changes that were desirable in the copyright law of this country. Hitherto a large business in mechanical reproduction had been built up by gramophone companies and manufacturers of perforated music rolls and the like, on the assumption that authors and composers had no right to restrain the reproduction of their works by these means. Those who prefer such language might say that the trade coolly pirated musical works. The companies feared a serious disturbance and restriction of their business if the thirteenth article became law in this country: one large concern might secure rights so extensive as practically to exclude the others. They therefore presented important evidence before the departmental committee, unanimously demanding a compulsory licence system for musical compositions, on the lines of an Act of 1909 which had just been passed in the United States, in order that they might retain their existing freedom to reproduce published music, subject only to a new liability to pay remuneration to the composer. Not every musical composition, however, is capable of perfect performance on a barrel-organ; and composers who gave evidence objected strongly to the compulsory licence proposal, insisting on their right 'to control the mode in which their pieces are produced and the character of the instrument which produces them'. The Committee with one dissentient reported in favour of the thirteenth article and the composers, and against the compulsory licence system. Nevertheless, the 1911 Copyright Act (Section 19) made provision for compulsory licences for 'records, perforated rolls, or other contrivances by means of which . . . [musical works] may be mechanically performed'.

The method adopted in this country for remunerating the composer differs from that in the United States, where a fixed specific royalty of two cents was made payable on each gramophone record. The gramophone companies favoured the American system, and in their evidence before the departmental committee they opposed a royalty system based on a percentage of the selling price of the record, on the ground that a composer would then be 'paid for the value put into it by the interpretation of the great artiste'. There was further the problem of deciding one rate of remuneration for all composers. Both difficulties had been anticipated in 1838 by A.-C. Renouard.[24] The basis adopted in the Act was, after the first two years of its operation, 5 per cent royalty on the retail selling price of the contrivance, with a minimum of one half-penny for each separate musical work in which copyright subsists. The Board of Trade is empowered, after public inquiry, to vary the rate by provisional order, at minimum intervals of fourteen years; and the administration of the system is controlled by the Board by regulation, apparently without insuperable difficulty.

The Act of 1911 again increased the duration of copyright in general, but in the same clause a most important innovation was inserted, at last introducing the royalty system into book publishing for the last twenty-five years of the copyright period. During that time, any person may reproduce a published work, after giving written notice and on paying royalties of 10 per cent of the published price to the owner of the copyright on all copies sold. No great difficulty seems to have arisen in administering this clause. The increase in the term of copyright, in accordance with the Berlin convention, to the life of the author and a further period of fifty years is hardly likely to have affected the terms of original publishing contracts and the output of authors' manuscripts; but the new royalty system now makes it possible for at any rate the second generation of readers after the death of an author to enjoy a wider circulation of his books at lower prices, in spite of the increase in the copyright period.

## 13 Some conclusions concerning the necessity for copyright

The conclusions concerning the necessity for copyright which emerge from this survey may now be summarised. The parallelism with the case of patents for inventions is of course very marked. In the first place, expectation of direct reward explains only a part of the total output of literature, just as it fails to account for more than part of the inventions which are made. Second, just as professional inventors continue to be paid for their services in fields in which the patent system does not apply, so also have professional authors in modern times been remunerated for their writings, whether by payment of a lump sum or by way of royalty on the sale of copies, in a country in which they were unprotected by copyright law. The publishers of new books are simply a special case of the manufacturers who exploit new but non-patentable inventions for which they pay the inventor. (Where no payments have to be made to authors, and the demand for the book is not in serious doubt, publishers are not of course deterred by fear of competition from issuing an edition. Of that fact the abundance of contemporary editions of standard works selling successfully against each other at different prices and in a variety of formats, affords a continual demonstration.) Third, copyright monopoly, like patent monopoly, enables the privileged producers to increase their receipts from successful products by restricting the supply, and in so far as experience and special skill are unavailing when a publisher tries to gauge the relative chances of success of certain kinds of manuscript books, copyright will, as we have seen, lead to an increased volume of risk-bearing. This consideration applies, however, over a definitely limited range of books; and it is extremely doubtful on reflection whether there exist any public reasons for the *indiscriminate* encouragement of the literature that falls into this category. Nor is there any reason why the increased volume of risk-bearing which copyright may elicit from certain publishers should materialise in the form of books alone: a prudent business man might well spread the risk more widely to include some racing or a gamble at Lloyd's with his book publishing. The odds might be still more attractive. It is at least doubtful whether book buyers and successful authors should be specially selected, by the effects of copyright on the price of the books which sell, to provide the fund which increases the element of gambling inherent in the book-publishing business.

More authors write books because copyright exists, and a greater variety of books is published; but there are fewer copies of the books which people want to read. Whether successful authors write more books than they otherwise would is a question of 'the elasticity of their demand for income in terms of effort' – they may prefer now to take more holidays or retire earlier. Some of them are in any case well advised to write different books – instead of writing what they would otherwise want to say or have to say, they find it more remunerative to write the sort of thing for which the demand conditions are most appropriate for ensuring the maximum monopoly profit.

The expectation of higher profits from book publishing as the result of copyright tends to increase the number of publishers in the business. Keen competition between publishers will enable the authors, whose copyright monopoly they are anxious to share, to make better bargains; with the result that the remuneration of publishers will tend to fall to the market rate of return on their capital and skill in other fields. Apart, however, from the increased volume of unpleasant 'remainders', the prices of books will remain above the competitive level so long as copyright subsists.

There is, of course, no system of economic calculus which supports the contention that output of the type which monopoly induces is 'preferable' to that which emerges from the different disposition of the same scarce productive resources resulting from the competitive bidding of the open market. One special weakness of copyright monopoly as an administrative device is the *non-discriminatory* nature of the encouragement it affords to ventures which are too risky to be embarked upon in a free market. It is not difficult to imagine particular cases in which literary effort might well be specially encouraged on public grounds. Large undertakings involving many expert contributors and expensive illustrations might not invariably find sufficient backers and 'advance subscribers', in view of the large capital outlay to be made by the first publishers, to make them commercial propositions. Yet if there were public reasons for financing particular ventures of this sort, subsidies provided from general taxation have more to commend them than a copyright monopoly; and if that system were politically impossible, it would surely be better that copyright monopoly be limited to such enterprises, by some such system as that in which the Comptroller of Patents is at present authorised to grant *exclusive* licences to manufacturers to exploit inventions which 'cannot be . . . worked without the expenditure of capital for the raising of which it will be necessary to rely on the patent monopoly' (Patents and Designs Act, 1907, as amended, Section 27 (3), (c)). It is, however, a far cry from hard cases of this sort to a comprehensive system of copyright for *all* new books. To the economist who studies the statements of the case for and against the copyright system as we know it, there is no document more satisfying in its logic than the minority report in which Sir Louis Mallet, a member of the Royal Commission on Copyright of 1876–8, stated the arguments against the continuance of the monopoly. His conclusion was that in the absence of copyright 'it will always be in the power of the first publisher of a work so to control the value, by a skilful adaptation of the supply to the demand, as to avoid the risk of ruinous competition, and secure ample remuneration both to the author and himself'.[25]

## 14 A practical proposal

In 1878, however, the abolition of copyright was to Sir Louis Mallet 'a question of the future'. That is still true. As he observed, 'in a matter which affects so large and valuable a property, and so many vested interests as have been created under copyright laws, it would be both unjust and inexpedient to proceed towards such a change as has been foreshadowed, except in the most gradual and tentative manner'. By a very simple change in our copyright legislation, the next important step forward might now be taken. It is practicable, in that it merely changes the date at which part of the already existing and tested administrative machinery set up under the Copyright Act of 1911 comes into operation in the case of every copyrighted book; and, further, in that the price policy already adopted by many publishing houses for their most successful books already conforms very closely to that which the simple change would ensure for all books which are reprinted after the first edition. As long ago as 1771, David Hume wrote to his publisher William Strahan: 'I have heard you frequently say, that no bookseller would find profit in making an edition which would take more than three years in selling.' In 1876, John Blackwood told the Copyright Commission: 'Every publisher now is aware from actual experience that in order to reap the full benefit of a book, he must work it in a very cheap form as well as an expensive one.' In our own day, it is surely the common practice of publishers to issue a cheap edition of successful books very promptly after the first expensive issue has served its purpose with the circulating libraries. If the now existing compulsory licence or royalty system (Copyright Act, 1911, Section 3) were made to operate a few years – say, five years – after first publication, instead of being delayed as at present until twenty-five years after the death of the author, security for publishers against competition would be preserved until their first editions were either disposed of or 'remaindered', remuneration for authors would continue on all sales throughout the full copyright period, and the public would no longer have to wait more than five years for cheap copies of the books they wish to buy. The first edition might still be issued by the publisher at the price which best suited his pocket under conditions of monopoly, but if he wished to retain the whole of the business the compulsory licence system would then compel him to follow the present practice of many publishers and reissue his successes before the end of the five-year period at a price low enough to deter competitors. There is, of course, nothing to prevent the successful sale, side by side, of a number of editions by various publishers at different prices and in different formats; and in many cases the author's remuneration from his 10 per cent royalty under the compulsory licence system would be greater than it is at present. There remains the theoretical objection, which we have already noticed in connection with the existing royalty provision, to fixing one percentage of royalty for all books and to giving authors a share in the value added by paper-makers and printers and binders to the more expensive editions; but their practical significance can hardly be deemed to outweigh the obvious public advantage to be derived from the change. The most widely read authors would still secure the greatest royalties from books selling at the same price, and something can even be said for allowing authors additional remuneration if their books are capable of sale in expensive as well as cheap editions. The change would, of course, tend to reduce the volume of risk-taking on purely speculative publications – a consequence which, it has already been argued, is hardly likely to involve any considerable impoverishment of our literary heritage. Particular cases might still form the subject of special provision. The objection might be raised that academic texts and scientific treatises, which undergo constant revision for each edition, might then be re-issued in obsolete condition; but with the adoption of the system, authors would surely see the wisdom of permitting the necessary alterations to be made to keep reprinted editions up to date. Drastic modifications would no doubt be made to an increased extent in the form of entirely new works – a development which indeed from other points of view has much to commend it. There cannot be any question that it would be in the public interest to ensure low prices for books as early as possible after the fate of the first edition has revealed that a demand exists for them; and it is an important feature of the proposed amendment that it involves no new administrative principle, that it enables the continuance of, if not indeed an increase in, the remuneration of authors whose books the public want, and lastly that it simply confirms and extends throughout the book-publishing business the price policy which successful publishers already pursue in their own interests.

## Notes

1 London School of Economics Series of Reprints, No. 16, pp. xxv–xxvi.

2 H. C. Carey: *Letters on International Copyright* (Preface to 2nd edition. New York, 1868) and *The International Copyright Question Considered* (Philadelphia, 1872). Carey was at one time a publisher himself.

3 See Putnam: *Books and Their Makers.*

4 E.g. Evidence of G. H. Putnam.

5 Evidence, Professor John Tyndall, Question 5795.

6 E.g. Evidence of G. H. Putnam.

7 Evidence, Professor T. H. Huxley, Question 5610.

8 E.g. Evidence of T. H. Huxley, Question 5610. 'I myself am paid upon books which are published there: my American publisher remits me a certain percentage upon the selling price of the books there, and that without any copyright which can protect him.' Also John Tyndall, Question 5775: '. . . I make an arrangement with my publishers . . . in New York, and they every year send me an account of their sales and allow me a certain percentage on the retail price of my books.' Asked (Question 5791) if the percentage were as large as it would have been if he had had copyright in America, his answer was: 'I cannot say, but I should be inclined to think so, because I am in the hands of a most high-minded publisher. I believe that I should gain no advantage by the copyright in America that I do not possess at present. But though I should be unaffected, on public grounds I hold that a copyright ought to exist.'

Cf. also Herbert Spencer in a letter to *The Times*, 21 September 1895, reprinted in *Various Fragments* (1900): 'For a period of thirty years, during which English works had no copyright in America, arrangements initiated about 1860 gave to English authors who published with Messrs ——— profits comparable to, if not identical with, those of American authors.'

9 The relevant detail of the costs, based on figures of Mr Thring, is:

| | *Edition of 1500 copies* | | | *Edition of 3000 copies* | | |
|---|---|---|---|---|---|---|
| | *£* | *s* | *d* | *£* | *s* | *d* |
| Composition | 46 | 2 | 6 | 46 | 2 | 6 |
| Machining | 15 | 10 | 6 | 22 | 19 | 0 |
| Paper | 18 | 18 | 0 | 37 | 16 | 0 |
| Binding | 36 | 0 | 0 | 54 | 0 | 0 |
| Brasses for cases | 1 | 12 | 0 | 1 | 12 | 0 |
| Jacket | 12 | 11 | 0 | 13 | 3 | 0 |
| Author's Corrections | 6 | 0 | 0 | 6 | 0 | 0 |
| Advertising | 60 | 0 | 0 | 60 | 0 | 0 |
| Postage, etc. | 10 | 0 | 0 | 10 | 0 | 0 |
| Royalties | 40 | 0 | 0 | 80 | 0 | 0 |
| Profit | 50 | 0 | 0 | 50 | 0 | 0 |
| | £296 | 14 | 0 | £381 | 12 | 6 |

10 On the Stationers' Company see *A Transcript of the registers of the Company of Stationers of London, 1554–1640 A.D.*, edited by Edward Arber, 1875. I am indebted for many of the references concerning this period to the researches of Miss M. Plant. I have modernised the spelling in quotations.

11 See Edward Arber, *op. cit.*, Vol. I.

12 For an entertaining and informative account of this period see Augustine Birrell: *Seven Lectures on the Law and History of Copyright in Books* (Cassell, 1899).

13 See *The Letters of David Hume*, edited by J. Y. T. Greig.

14 Letter, 4 March 1740, to Francis Hutcheson: The same bookseller 'is very willing to engage for this, and he tells me that the sale of the first volumes, though not very quick, yet it improves. I have no acquaintance among these folks, and very little skill in making bargains. . . . There are two favours, therefore, I must ask of you, viz. to tell me what copy money I may reasonably expect for one edition of a thousand of this volume, which will make a four shillings book: and, if you know any honest man in this trade, to send me a letter of recommendation to him that I may have the choice of more than one man to bargain with.'

And again, letter, 16 March 1740, to the same: 'I must trouble you to write that letter you was so kind as to offer to Longman, the bookseller. I concluded somewhat of a hasty bargain with my bookseller from indolence and an aversion to bargaining, as also because I was told that few or no bookseller would engage for one edition with a new author. . . . I . . . also engaged myself heedlessly in a clause, which may prove troublesome, viz. that upon printing a second edition I shall take all the copies remaining upon hand at the bookseller's price at the time.'

15 The three famous cases of Tonson *v.* Collins, 1760; Millar *v.* Taylor, 1766; and Donaldson *v.* Becket, 1774. For a convenient account, see Birrell, *op. cit.*

16 It is of interest to note that David Hume at once wrote to Wm Strahan, the successor to Millar's business, suggesting the transference afresh to him of Hume's property in his most recent alterations to his works. 'If nobody can reprint these passages during fourteen years after the first publication, it would effectually secure you so long from any pirated edition.' (Letter, 1 March, 1774, in *The Letters of David Hume.*)

17 Cf. Evidence of John Henry Parker, a retired publisher, before the Royal Commission on Copyright of 1876–8.

18 Cf. Evidence of R. A. Macfie, before the same Commission, and see also A.-C. Renouard: *Traité des Droits d'Auteurs*, Paris, 1838.

19 *Edinburgh Review*, October 1878; article on the Report and Evidence of the Royal Commission on Copyright. Cf. also The Humble Remonstrance of the Company of Stationers, London, to the High Court of Parliament, April 1643: 'Scarce one book in three sells well, or proves gainfull to the publisher.'

20 Evidence of T. H. Farrer, the Secretary to the Board of Trade, 13 March 1877, Question 5080.

21 Evidence, 16 March 1877, Questions 5191–2–3.

22 See evidence to the 1876–8 Commission, e.g. George Routledge: '. . . In the case of novels published for the circulating libraries, you must give the trade a certain time [before lowering the price], or else they will not take them.' Sir Charles E. Trevelyan: '. . . No doubt if the monopoly were abolished the circulating libraries would collapse.'

23 Evidence of T. H. Farrer on 31 January 1877: 'It is, however, at the present moment in this country, scarcely a practical question. . . . Whatever advantages a system of royalty might have, it would require new machinery of an elaborate kind, and it would disturb existing arrangements, and be opposed by existing interests. It is, therefore, not worth while now to discuss it, nor am I prepared to meet the various difficulties of detail which would no doubt arise in considering it. To do so would require a far greater knowledge of the practice of the trade than an outsider can pretend to. But judging from the little I have been able to gather I should not think them insuperable.'

24 See his *Traité des Droits d'Auteurs*, Vol. I, § IX, p. 463. Of the royalty system, he wrote: 'What makes it inadmissible is the impossibility of arriving at a fixed general rate of remuneration, and the extreme difficulty of collecting it. [To focus the problems involved in drafting legislation, he took as an example the payment to be made by a publisher to the possessor of a first edition of Fénelon's *Télémaque* issued in 1699. If this had never been reprinted, he thought that a rate of payment might be determined, but if it had been reprinted in various editions it is completely impossible to fix a rate which would be equitable.] One might perhaps overcome the obstacle to collection, with sustained effort, but as to fixing the royalty, regulating this becomes impossible. . . . Will the law be required to determine a fixed royalty? What could be more unjust than a fixed rate, applied generally to things essentially unequal? . . . If your royalty is fixed on a proportional basis, each *Télémaque* at, say, two hundred francs, will produce, just for the right to reproduce it, more than each completely manufactured copy in the other edition will be worth (at twenty sous) and yet it will still be the same text which will have no more intrinsic value in the one case than in the other.'

25 The uniformly high quality of reasoning in Sir Louis Mallet's minority report can be appreciated only if it is read as a whole, but a small extract may perhaps be quoted with advantage:

> Property exists in order to provide against the evils of natural scarcity. A limitation of supply by artificial causes, creates scarcity in order to create property. . . . It is within this latter class that copyright in published works must be included. Copies of such works may be multiplied indefinitely, subject

to the cost of paper and of printing which alone, but for copyright, would limit the supply, and any demand, however great, would be attended not only by no conceivable injury to society, but on the contrary, in the case of useful works, by the greatest possible advantage. . . . The case of a book is precisely analogous to that of a house, of a carriage, or of a piece of cloth, for the design of which a claim to perpetual copyright has never, I believe, been seriously entertained.

CHAPTER 5

# The new commerce in ideas and intellectual property*

'I do not choose a subject [for a public lecture] necessarily because I think I know a great deal about it, but rather because I have, at various times, put myself questions to which I do not know the answers, and the choice of a title to cover them forces me in the meantime to find the answers if I can.' These words were written by Josiah Stamp over twenty-five years ago. In his addresses and published works, Lord Stamp sought invariably to break new ground. He believed that comprehensive works on the Principles of Economics are best written by the professorial economist, while the development of the subject lies, to an important extent, in specialist works, 'proceeding from the centre of economic theory outward'. But as his sphere of activity widened, he found that 'the realistic economic life meets all the streams of practice, custom and idea impinging upon it, infiltrating it at a score of distinct points. . . . Why not [he asked] sometimes change the direction of study, and drift *from* outside on some of such streams *into* the heart of economic territory?'

My choice of a topic for this Stamp Memorial Lecture follows his precept. I feel that he might have approved it.

## I

My topic is the new commerce in ideas and intellectual property. At the outset I had better say what I have in mind. If ideas are to be put on record at all, and certainly if anyone is to be given some sort of

* Stamp Lecture, 1953. Published by The Athlone Press, University of London, 1953.

property right in them, they must be expressed in, or reduced to, a material form. I shall be concerned only with ideas which have attained to that degree of concreteness. It may then be decided that certain property rights shall be attached to them by statute law, over and above the ordinary property right accorded to the owner of the original exemplars under common law. It has become the custom in informed circles to divide these special property rights into two categories, Intellectual Property embracing those types that are accorded copyright or analogous protection, and Industrial Property covered by patents, registered designs and trade marks. I shall confine myself to the types of ideas, as for example literary, dramatic, musical and artistic works, for which special rights of Intellectual Property are granted or claimed. When I refer to the commerce in these ideas I have in mind the economic processes by which, first, ideas are given the material form in which it becomes practicable, and may also be thought expedient, to attach special property rights to them, and by which, second, the ideas are communicated to other people either in the perishable form of performances or in the more durable form of copies. By the *new* commerce I mean to imply that the market conditions of demand and supply in which these economic processes are conducted have become so greatly transformed by the march of civilisation and by technological advances as to call urgently for a reconsideration of many of the assumptions underlying copyright legislation.

Consider for a moment the change in conditions of demand, in the extent of the market for these products, since copyright privileges, first introduced into this country four hundred years ago, assumed their present general pattern. It will suffice merely to enumerate some of them:

(*a*) the vast increase in total population, and, with improved means of transport, in the numbers accessible as a potential market to any one producer;

(*b*) the spread of education and the change in human habits and tastes;

(*c*) the great growth and wider distribution of purchasing power;

(*d*) the increase in leisure, and the new requirements for vocational training;

(*e*) the improvements in artificial lighting and in the heating of buildings;

(*f*) the prolongation in the average length of life;

(*g*) the new aids to declining sight and hearing with advancing years.

Changes such as these have transformed the economic conditions of supply, because of their effect on the size of the potential market for a performance, or for a single edition of copies, and on the period over which an edition must be held in stock before a sufficient number of copies can be disposed of to recoup the investment incurred.

The technological advances which have revolutionised production are far too numerous to be catalogued and assessed here individually, but it is necessary at least to indicate their general character and significance.

In printing, new inventions and improved methods of production since the first introduction of movable type have greatly reduced unit costs of production, particularly when the initial edition can be large and when further editions are called for. I should remind you, for example, of the effects of:

(*a*) replacing hand casting and setting of type by mechanical type-setting;

(*b*) the making of stereotype copies of master-type so that gangs of printing machines can produce identical copies in parallel;

(*c*) the use of power-operated and rotary presses, feeding the paper continuously into the press from rolls;

(*d*) remote type-setting by one central compositor, so that simultaneous editions of identical copies can be produced on printing presses each located in a convenient regional centre of population;

(*e*) the elimination of the cost of keeping type standing, and the reduction of the overall costs of issuing reprint editions, by use of photographic methods of reproducing printed works;

(*f*) the replacement of the slow and costly methods of hand engraving in printing copies of illustrations and artistic works, by the industrial applications of photography to block-making.

These and similar advances in technique have transformed the structure of printing costs, and in particular the relation between the initial investment in preparing for an edition and the subsequent recurring unit costs of multiplying copies.

I am bound also to make reference to the many-sided contribution which we owe to the development of photography. Permanent records of transient data can be made with infinitely greater speed and accuracy, and at lower cost, than by any previous method, and an indefinite number of copies, each of the same high degree of fidelity, can be produced very cheaply. Micro-photography may solve the problem of storing and transporting bulky records. Cinematography has profoundly affected the economics of theatrical entertainment, by bringing a uniform quality of performance to all classes of the community, wherever situated, and today instructional films make a growing contribution to education and training.

Two other main streams of recent technological advance have undermined the traditional concepts of intellectual property and copyright privilege. The first is the recording and reproduction of sound, the second the broadcasting of sound and television.

The combination of the vibrating diaphragm, the microphone and electric power have now given to fleeting sound the permanence of the printed word. No human voice, no musical performance by human agency, intended to be recorded and overheard, no sound, even those which are outside the range of the unassisted ear, need now be missed by anybody, anywhere and at any time that he might wish to pay his share of the cost of recording it and reproducing it. The sound film has virtually superseded the silent picture in our cinemas. We stand only at the threshold of even more revolutionary improvements, consequent upon the development of wireless transmission. At its outset it effected an enormous saving of specific capital investment by superseding long-distance cables in telegraphic and telephonic communication. The development of broadcasting systems throughout the world since 1919 has brought all classes of society, in the role of listeners to sound broadcasts and more latterly as viewers of television programmes, into closer communication, at least at the reception end, with other social classes in the same community and with other communities. Transmission is instantaneous, its range is rapidly becoming universal, and it is equipped to record and store its programmes for reproduction down the ages to come. Broadcast-receiving apparatus is already far more generally installed in domestic households, and certainly in the kitchens, than the telephone. For the great majority it remains, for the present, a one-way communication; but for all that, in potentiality if not in achievement, broadcasting represents the most significant advance yet made in the communication of ideas. Taken in conjunction with cinematography, it is already challenging, in priority, the movement towards universal literacy among the underdeveloped communities throughout the world. For many purposes, the necessity for learning first to read has already been by-passed. Why bother, it has been said, to read about things that can be seen and heard?

Much of this progress was not even contemplated when the latest Copyright Act of 1911 became the law in this country. These new advances have changed the nature and the incidence of the risks involved in the commerce in ideas. The pattern of receipts and expenditure, and in particular the cost-structure at the various stages in the business of communication have been disturbed and re-cast. Copyright privileges now have a changed significance and effect. Some are obsolete and impede progress, others may need strengthening if desirable developments are to be speeded up. Outworn privileges have a tendency to become hard-set. Their melting-point is high, and high temperatures may have to be generated before they can be resolved. Sectional interests are strongly mobilised, and the legislation has become highly technical. Moreover, many of the privileges which are most highly valued by important groups of interests are now entrenched in international conventions, the existence of which may tend to discourage efforts at reform of national legislation by those who believe that radical changes are necessary in the public interest.

It is because I am convinced that important new opportunities are within our grasp, if the formidable impediments to their realisation can be overcome, that I invite you to join me in an examination of the rationale of Intellectual Property as now defined, and in the consideration of the desirability of introducing amendments.

I have derived much assistance from the study of the Report published in October 1952 of a Copyright Committee appointed in April 1951 by the President of the Board of Trade to consider the whole matter 'with particular reference to technical developments and to the revised International Convention for the Protection of Literary and Artistic Property signed at Brussels in June 1948', a convention which, I am glad to say, has not yet been ratified by this country. The Committee received a great deal of evidence and elicited important new information, which is conveniently assembled and, if I may venture to say so, very competently analysed in their Report. While I find myself in disagreement with much of their argument and conclusions, I do gratefully acknowledge my indebtedness to the Committee for the help which I have derived from their Report in bringing the important issues more clearly into focus.

## II

Let us ask ourselves, first of all, how and to what extent the publication of literary works is or is not likely to be affected by the grant of copyright privileges to the author.

Many people find it convenient to commit ideas to paper without any intention or desire to allow their manuscripts to circulate generally, much less to be published. In the free world these manuscripts are beyond question theirs to preserve, sell, bequeath or destroy. Eminent authors have felt unable to die in peace until their friends have been able to assure them that their unpublished manuscripts have been safely burned.

Once published with his consent, an author's work is destined irretrievably for the public domain. If the Courts decide that a publication is offensive, they may order all copies to be destroyed; but if the author regrets publication, the most he can do is to try to buy up the copies which have been sold, and, if he has retained the copyright, decline to authorise new editions so long as the law permits him to do so. In this country, copyright continues after the author's death, but for over a hundred years it has been the law that, once he is dead, the Judicial Committee of the Privy Council may over-ride the wishes of his literary executors and authorise re-publication, or performance of a musical work, on such terms as it may determine. It is, in my view, in the interests of scholarship and historical research that this safeguard should be preserved, and I am disturbed to find that it is seriously proposed that it should be abandoned. David Hume came to regret the publication of his *Treatise of Human Nature* and would have suppressed it if he could. His biographer, John Hill Burton, provided the conclusive answer when he wrote:

> The bold and original speculations of the *Treatise* have been and to all appearance ever will be part of the intellectual property of man; great theories have been built upon them, which must be thrown down before we can raze the foundation. That he repented of having published the work, and desired to retract its extreme doctrines, is part of the mental biography of Hume; but it is impossible, at his command, to detach this book from general literature, or to read it without remembering who was the author.

A great deal of publication which goes on, in the field of scholarship and in ordinary business, is in no way affected by copyright, and would continue if copyright were completely abolished. Publication is paid for by those who wish for it, to propagate their ideas, to enhance their reputation, or more generally (as with advertisements) to promote some other interest. The author believes that the cost of publication is an investment which, if necessary, he is prepared to make for reasons other than any direct return which publication may bring him. The same is not true of literary works written expressly or partly with an eye to direct profit from the sale of copies. Without an initial period of copyright, a great deal of publication would not take place at all. What can we say about the possible effects of the duration of the copyright period upon the quantity and quality of authorship which takes place?

In this country over two and a half centuries, the period of copyright has been gradually increased from fourteen years from the date of publication, with a further period of fourteen years if the author were still alive at the end of the first term, to the present period (since 1911) of the author's life and fifty years after his death. These prolongations of the period of copyright privileges, and of the special payments which flow from them, are very pleasant for their recipients, whether authors and their heirs or publishers who have acquired the rights. The important economic questions are whether the increases in price which they involve are necessary to secure the flow of output to which they apply, and whether any additional literary output induced by prolongation of the period of copyright is generally to be preferred, from the standpoint of the public, to the alternative occupations which the authors might otherwise have had to turn to. It seems to me very doubtful whether the extensions have induced many *new* writers to apply themselves to authorship for profit. Would anyone ever have been deterred by a privilege restricted to twenty-eight years who would have responded to the offer of a longer period? What of the effect on authors who have settled down to their career? As regards the *quality* of their literary output, it is questionable whether the progressive extensions beyond twenty-eight years have influenced them when planning more- or less-serious works. So far as the *quantity* of their output is concerned, the only likely general effect of prolonging their income from work already published would seem to be to *reduce* the aggregate output of authors over their lifetime as a whole. As I see it, therefore, the prolongation of copyright payments and of the consequent higher prices of the products are not economically necessary. If it could be shown that the writing of works of enduring and exceptional literary value had depended upon long periods of copyright, and extended terms had been confined to them (on the lines of the permissive extensions of patent rights now so rarely granted to exceptional inventions), a reasonable justification for the extensions might be advanced; but that does not seem to me to have been the case.

It may be objected that in confining my attention to the economic aspects of the question, I evade the main case for conferring special privileges on authors, composers and artists. A majority of the public may wish to confer special awards on successful practitioners in these fields of creative work, even though the effect may be to encourage them to sit back a little, and a liberal copyright policy may be a convenient way of showing generosity towards them. It may be thought that the author's continuing royalties are not a large part of the price of books, and providing that they accrue to him and his family one should not be niggardly. As an occasional writer myself I had better say no more about that. But if we are concerned to encourage authors to concentrate more of their energy on the production of serious literary works, I suggest that this might be more certainly achieved by an amendment of Government policy in a quite different direction. For many of the outstanding contributions to scholarship and technological improvement, the relative periods of investment of effort in production, and of reaping the reward, are quite the reverse of those which might justify longer periods of copyright. The work of producing a major work of scholarship may absorb the productive energy of the author over many years, during which his current income is seriously reduced, compared with what he could have earned from less absorbing effort. On the other hand, the reward is frequently concentrated into a very short period after publication. A seminal contribution may have great vogue for a very few years and give rise to an abundant progeny from a host of followers, stimulated to make important new advances of their own. These new contributions by other authors may quickly supersede the original work. The receipts of the pioneer author, to whose prolonged effort the community owes so much of the whole advance, are however still subject today to income tax and surtax in the short period of recoupment with the most niggardly allowance for spreadover. Long periods of copyright, after the bulk of his sale has taken place, are of little avail. In such circumstances the few exceptional authors who are capable of important contributions may be sorely and unnecessarily tempted to turn aside from long-term projects.

When we turn from authorship to the economics of the publishing business, very different considerations apply. The risks of publishing new literary works are different in nature and in extent from those of authorship. The investment of time in arranging a publication is usually much less than in writing the manuscript, and the quality of effort involved is quite different. Publishing is a manufacturing, or more accurately, a merchant-converter business, so organised that it need involve little specific investment in equipment. While the plant involved in book production, that is, in paper-making, type-setting, printing and binding is often expensive and highly specialised, it is, for the most part, owned and operated by separate firms. It certainly need not be integrated with the business of publishing. It is not usually capable only of making the books which happen to be launched by a particular publisher, and certainly not only of the manufacture of a particular book which happens to be a new work. The publisher invests cash in the issue of an edition which he plans, the actual making of which however he usually contracts out to a number of industrial firms. That is the maximum extent of his risk. It is clearly generally greater for most new books than for most reprints, for which the market has already been tested, and it is greatest of all for new works on particular subjects by hitherto unknown authors. A publisher frequently does not bear all the risk himself. He can offer terms which require the author to take, at any rate, part of it. A new author may be required to advance the whole or part of the cost of the edition, the amount to be repayable out of sales; royalty payments may not commence until sales have recouped costs, and rates of royalty may be generous or the reverse. Nevertheless, the publication of new works by unknown authors involves special risks, and the business offers opportunities for the development and exercise of specialised skill in assessing the market for a manuscript. Publishers are not common carriers, required within the limit of their capacity to undertake all the business offered to them. They are free to pick and choose, and some find it advantageous to specialise. Many of them are highly expert in assessing the market, and there is sufficient competition in most fields of general publishing to ensure that the terms they generally secure for the risks they take are not extortionate. Yet throughout the history of publishing in this country, the most successful publishers have insisted, when occasion suited, on their fallibility. They regard the making of some mistakes as inevitable. A new title by a new author is usually something of a gamble.

When an author transfers his copyright privileges in their entirety to his publisher, the publisher secures a term of monopoly for the works he contracts to issue. He cannot be undercut by rival editions of the same works, and his receipts from those which continue to sell are increased. The gambling element remains, but the odds are increased, and winners may prove very remunerative. The longer the monopoly period, the greater the revenue accruing to the publisher from works with a lasting popularity. Prolongation of the period thus encourages the entry of more starters. More publishers enter the trade, and individual publishers will back more outside chances. A dark horse, cheaply acquired, may do well, but there will be more losses. There will be a greater waste of resources diverted to speculative publishing from other fields in which the willingness of buyers to take the product is more certain. I can see no reason for hope that the more speculative ventures which come off will possess, in general, sufficient exceptional merit to compensate for the additional waste involved. The economic problem therefore amounts to this: If we accept the view that special encouragement should be given to the publication of new works, and that the most convenient means is to allow publishers an initial term of monopoly, how long should that term be?

It would, I think, be most generally agreed that publishers should be protected for the period over which they normally plan to hold a first edition in stock, in the hope of selling sufficient copies to recoup the costs involved. Many people would probably go further, and favour a longer period, to encourage publishers to launch several speculative works in the expectation that the total costs would be covered by the sale of further editions, under copyright protection, of those which went well. Book buyers may well feel that such a policy will increase the chance of some books being published which they will wish to acquire. But if we are to be realistic, our theory must be related to the way publishers normally plan their operations. A special case for a monopoly for publishers cannot rest on the general proposition that if business men are enabled to make monopoly profits, some of them will be devoted to good works. The relevant question seems to be this: when publishers plan their investments in the issue of editions of new works, do they in fact bring into their budgetary calculations any problematical receipts from sales more than five, or shall we say, ten years ahead? In the case of very expensive ventures, such as encyclopaedias, do they include in their budgets any expectations of revenue accruing from sales as far ahead as twenty years? I venture to assert that such long-term planning is unusual in any branch of industry other than durable constructional work, building operations and land use. In publishing, it must be rare indeed.

The point which I am inviting you to accept is that there is no logical case for making the period over which we might wish to assure a continuing income to successful authors coincide with that for which a monopoly might reasonably be accorded to the first publisher of a new work. Quite different considerations are involved. The economic function of publishers is closely analogous to that of merchant-converters and manufacturers in those parts of the textile trades which are subject to fashion change. If a textile-maker wishes to protect his innovations in the field of design, privileges are accorded him by the Registered Designs Act of 1949. He must register a design before publication, and it is then protected for five years only in the first instance, with possible extension, on payment of a fee, for two further periods of five years each and no more. The Board of Trade has the invidious responsibility for making rules under the Act which determine which 'designs' are excluded from the Registered Designs Act, 'being articles which are primarily literary or artistic in character', and thereby entitled to full copyright protection. In their wisdom they have accordingly laid down, for instance, that designs of printed paper, intended to be reproduced more than fifty times, for use as wallpaper, may be accorded under the Designs Act the very limited period of protection, whereas artistic or literary work, intended similarly for reproduction as, for example, calendars, to be hung (not stuck) on a wall, may be protected under the Copyright Act, without formalities or registration, for the full period of the author's or artist's life and fifty years thereafter. In drawing the borderline between the two, the Board has had the assistance of various Departmental Committees on Patents and on Copyright, but the more I study the grounds for the important distinctions which have been made, the less justification can I find for them in terms of differing economic circumstances of supply and production.

At various times, and in various countries, this important distinction between copyright for the authors and protection for the first industrial reproducer of copies of their work has been recognised in legislation. In this country, the first Copyright Act of Queen Anne gave protection in two terms of fourteen years each, the second being a fresh grant to the author, so that he could re-contract afresh with other publishers. Similarly today, in the United States, after a first period of twenty-eight years, a second and final term of twenty-eight years is accorded, on application, to the author, or if he is no longer living, to a member of his family, or his executor or next of kin; but to no other owner of the first right. The original publisher is not eligible to apply for an extension, nor can the rights for a second term be assigned in advance to him or to anyone else. The important innovation of combining an initial term of monopoly for the original publisher with a further period of open licence, under which the author continued to receive royalties, while the competition of publishers encouraged the issue of cheap as well as more sumptuous editions, was first adopted, I believe, by Italy, under the Copyright Law of 1865. The first term was forty years, or the author's life: then a further term of forty years was allowed, during which anyone might republish on payment to the owner of the copyright of a five per cent royalty on the selling price, which had to be marked on the work. This provision in the Italian law was continued for sixty years.

Forty-two years ago, the royalty open-licence system was at last introduced in this country under the terms of the Copyright Act of 1911. Section 3 of the Act extended the duration of copyright to the author's life and fifty years thereafter, with the important proviso that, at any time after the expiration of twenty-five years from the death of the author, any person may reproduce a published work on giving notice of his intention in a form to be prescribed, and on payment, to the owner of the copyright, of royalty at the rate of ten per cent of the published price in respect of all copies sold by him. Thereafter, for at least the latter part of the copyright period, the issue of cheap reprints has no longer been a matter to be decided, with an eye solely to his own interest, by a publisher enjoying a monopoly privilege. It may of course be, and it frequently is, to his interest to issue a cheaper reprint at any time. We are assured that most publishers almost invariably do so, during the monopoly period; but how soon they do so, and at what price they sell the reprints is for them as monopolists to determine. Since the proviso to Section 3 was introduced, however, their interest requires them, as the copyright term approaches the twenty-fifth year following the death of the author, to take account of the imminent competition of other publishers, and particularly of those who specialise in reprints of popular works, and to see to it that supplies are adequate to meet the demand at selling prices as low as their competitors would be prepared to make them. As we have seen, recent advances in printing technique, the use, for example, of photographic processes and improvements in the rapid production of large editions have greatly facilitated the business of reprinting. As never before, we have the means, if we will allow them to be applied, to bring books in popular demand to the people quickly at competitive prices. When one compares the periods of protection accorded to manufacturers under the Patents Act and the Registered Designs Act with those enjoyed by publishers under the Copyright Act, the conclusion seems to me irresistible that the open-licence royalty system should be made to operate much earlier in the copyright period.

I was gratified to discover from the recent Report of the Departmental Committee on Copyright that the Committee follow the same line of argument in the parallel cases of the manufacture of gramophone records and the production of cinematograph films. They recognise that these industries 'undoubtedly call into play a variety of skills, in part technical, in part artistic, and the companies spend large sums both in manufacturing equipment and in the payment of those artistes whose performances are reproduced', but they 'do not regard either, when treated as a work distinct from the original musical or dramatic material which they record, purely as "an original literary, dramatic, musical or artistic work" within the generality of the terms of the Copyright Act'. They 'cannot escape from the conclusion that gramophone records and cinematograph films approximate more closely to industrial products than to original literary or musical works'. They call attention to the great disparity between the terms of protection given to other industrial products, under the Registered Designs Act and the Patents Act, and those given under the Copyright Act, and recommend that the period of protection in these two cases be reduced from fifty to twenty-five years. The scope and term of copyright subsisting in the authors' and composers' works incorporated in the records or films would not be affected.

I should remind you that the production of an ordinary feature film normally involves an investment at least a hundred times larger than that incurred by a publisher when he issues an edition of a new work, and the risk of loss is very great indeed. In the case of gramophone records, the manufacturer is not protected under the Copyright Act, as publishers are, from the competition of rival manufacturers, who are free to issue their own recordings of the same musical composition. There is no case therefore for leaving publishers alone in a privileged position. But instead of recommending a parallel reduction in their term of protection, the Committee proposed a change in the reverse direction. They recommended that the publishers' monopoly period be prolonged by twenty-five years to coincide with the full duration of the author's copyright.

The consideration which weighed with the Committee was their judgment on a question of immediate expediency. The United Kingdom has not yet ratified the latest revision of the International Convention for the Protection of Literary and Artistic Works. The terms of the new Convention, signed at Brussels in 1948, have been interpreted as requiring this country, if it acceded to it, to abandon its open-licence royalty system for literary publications. I would remind you that the original Convention was signed in Berne in 1886, and ratifying countries became members of what is known as the Berne Union. Revised Conventions were adopted at Berlin in 1908 and at Rome in 1928. The United Kingdom has acceded by ratification on each occasion, and membership of the Union has not hitherto stood in the way of development of the important distinction introduced in the Copyright Act of 1911 between the term of author's copyright and the period of protection accorded to the original publisher. Publishers who are concerned largely with new works have a different interest in this matter from those who specialise more in reprints. In 1935, the Belgian Government circulated a number of 'Propositions avec exposés des motifs', one of which proposed in effect that since this country allowed competing British publishers to reprint copyright works during the latter part of the copyright term, in competition with the original publishers, foreign publishers should equally be entitled to engage in this reprint business. A Departmental Committee on International Copyright was appointed at the time to examine these proposals, and I am bound to say that the interests of the reading public do not appear, from their report, to have weighed heavily on their minds. They recommended against supporting this movement towards freer trade in reprints, and considered it would be preferable for the British Government to abandon the open-licence royalty period altogether. Nor were they content to rest there. They called attention to a further safeguard of the interests of the reading public which this country might remove at the same time. Ever since the Copyright Act of 1842 our legislation has contained a provision designed to prevent the owner of a copyright, after an author or composer has died, from having the last word if he should refuse to allow the republication or the public performance of a work. Thus, under Section 4 of the Copyright Act of 1911, a complaint can be made in the last resort to the Judicial Committee of the Privy Council, which may order the copyright owner to grant a licence and may decide the terms and conditions. I have already stressed the value of this safeguard to historians and other students of literature and music who desire ready access to the social heritage of works left by the past generation. It has served as a reminder to copyright owners that there is a public interest in the exercise of their privilege which will, if necessary, be protected, and its importance is in no way diminished by the fact that enactment of the safeguard has in itself sufficed and that it has never, in consequence, been found necessary to apply it. The Committee of 1935, however, chose to regard that fact as evidence that the safeguard was unnecessary, and considered that, if the Government decided to repeal the proviso to Section 3, then Section 4 should go with it.

Thirteen years elapsed, however, before the next International Conference was held. On occasions of this sort the pressure to extend and strengthen monopoly privileges is usually strong, and it appears that at Brussels, in 1948, the representatives of some other countries contended that these sections of the British law were not consonant with the Convention. This was certainly not true of the existing Convention and those which preceded it, for these expressly gave member countries the right to legislate on these matters as they chose, and as indeed this country chose to do in 1911, and Italy had done as long ago as 1865. If it were no longer to be so under a new draft of the relevant Article 7 of the Convention, the British representatives could have opposed the new draft. If defeated, the United Kingdom was entitled under the rules to reserve its existing right to apply the new draft only in so far as it was consistent with its domestic law. At Brussels, for example, it acted precisely in this way when Article 11 was adopted at the Final Plenary Session. The Declaration then made by the United Kingdom Delegation is worth quoting here:

> The United Kingdom Delegation accepts the provisions of Article 11 of the Convention on the understanding that His Majesty's Government remains free to enact such legislation as they may consider necessary in the public interest to prevent or deal with any abuse of the monopoly rights conferred upon owners of copyright by the law of the United Kingdom.

That reservation was equally applicable to Article 7, but a similar declaration was not made in that case. In consequence, the United Kingdom was left in a somewhat embarrassing position. Ratification is apparently interpreted as requiring the Government to repeal the proviso to Section 3 and Section 4. If it accepted this interpretation, it had three courses open. It could ratify and put amending legislation in train: a reluctant Government might then still find it impossible to make parliamentary time to get the legislation through! Second, it could do nothing, and wait for the Berne Union members to decide, in practice, that the United Kingdom had ceased to be one of them. Third, it could endeavour to re-open negotiations, if necessary by asking that a further Conference be summoned.

For what it is worth, my own view is, I trust, by now abundantly clear to you. I believe that the public interest requires that the Government should reject this recommendation, and formally announce its intention to abide by the principle explicitly set out in the Act of 1911, while reserving the right to vary the length of the term, within the full copyright period, during which the open-licence royalty system may operate. It would then be left, for the time being, to the good sense and judgment of each member country in the Berne Union to decide whether or not to continue on that understanding the mutually beneficial reciprocal arrangements with this country which have persisted hitherto.

At worst, this course would not necessarily involve our 'going it alone'. The USA, among other countries, has never been a member of the Berne Union. There is also a separate Pan-American Union. Since 1947, under the auspices of the United Nations Organisation, the General Conference of UNESCO, as the lineal descendant of the International Office for Intellectual Co-operation, has set itself the task of putting copyright protection on a world basis. In 1951 it authorised the communication of proposals for a Universal Copyright Convention to the governments of all countries, and invited comments. Because of the diversity of views, the experts thought it wise to circulate three alternative drafts of Article IV relating to the duration of copyright. The first was: *either* twenty-five years from first publication *or* the author's life and twenty-five years after his death; the second, this same minimum period in any country, and as much longer as was provided by the law of each contracting State; the third was similar to the second, but with a minimum period of the life of the author and thirty years after his death. All three proposals contemplated minimum periods shorter than that laid down by the Brussels Convention of the Berne Union. Thirty-four countries communicated their comments, and in 1952 fifty countries were represented at an Inter-governmental Conference on Copyright at Geneva. A Universal Copyright Convention was there adopted, and signed on behalf of thirty-six countries, for submission to all countries with an invitation to accede by ratification. The minimum duration of protection fixed under the Convention is twenty-five years, or author's life and twenty-five years after his death for countries which calculate their period on the basis of the author's lifetime; and if under 'national treatment' the duration is longer, the same period will operate in those countries in the case of works of foreign origin. It is of interest to note that this coincides with the views communicated before the Conference by the United Kingdom, and bears a reasonably close resemblance to the law of the USA.

Present practice in the United Kingdom and in the United States is not as dissimilar as appears at first sight. Both countries divide the copyright period into two parts in order to break the monopoly of the first publisher. It is true that America has retained the more logical system of starting the period from the date of first publication, while the United Kingdom has introduced the uncertainty of the duration of the author's life. It is also unfortunately true that America still retains the notoriously protectionist 'manufacturing clause' which, in the case of works in the English language, restricts the grant of full copyright to those printed from type set in the United States, but this requirement has already been tempered in a way which promotes importation of serious works. *Ad interim* copyright for five years is now granted in the case of works in the English language printed outside the United States, and a maximum of 1500 copies may be imported. One thousand five hundred copies is a reasonable proportion of a normal first edition of a scholarly work, and the opening of the American market to that extent greatly improves the prospects of successful publication of a large range of books produced, for example, in the British Commonwealth. If further editions are called for, the requirement that continued copyright protection shall be conditional upon the publication of an American-made edition before the end of the five-year period is in these circumstances a less formidable, though still highly regrettable obstacle. In these matters of copyright the reading public throughout the English-speaking world have everything to gain from a closer co-ordination of policy throughout the British Commonwealth and the USA.

## III

I turn now to consider the complicated situation which has arisen as the result of new technological developments relating to public performances. I refer particularly to the remarkable advances which have been made during the present century in the recording of performances and the multiplication of copies of these records for subsequent reproduction of the performances, and to the still more recent development of broadcasting and television whereby performances may be enjoyed simultaneously by an indefinitely large number of listeners and viewers. It will suffice for my purpose if I concentrate on performances of music and plays.

The law gives the owner of the copyright, in literary and musical works, the sole right to authorise performances in public. Plays and musical compositions are intended to be performed rather than merely read, and dramatists and composers usually hope to earn more from public performances than from the sale of copies. As to what constitutes a public performance, the trend of legal decisions has been to interpret it so widely that almost any performance outside the purely domestic circle is included, and each public performance of a work must be authorised or licensed by the owner of the copyright. In the case of plays, it is relatively simple for the dramatist, or at any rate for his professional agent, to keep track of intending performances and to negotiate terms. A play usually makes up the whole or is one of the main constituents of the programme. Copyright owners in these cases normally negotiate individually, and in making terms they may be as generous or as exacting as they choose. Music presents more difficulty. Concerts are more numerous and widespread than dramatic performances, and in most cases they are not confined to the works of one composer. Many may be involved in a single concert. It is therefore very convenient, if not indeed necessary, for musical composers to organise themselves into groups or societies for the purpose of licensing concert performances, and this arrangement has advantages also for the organisers of concerts, in that it reduces the number of separate negotiations for licences which they have to undertake. The convenience of collective bargaining, at any rate to the owners of musical copyrights, is so great that a single organisation, the Performing Right Society, acts, except in the case of musical plays, on behalf of almost all musical publishers and popular composers, who assign their rights to the Society. As long ago as 1929, a Select Committee reported that 'apart from classical and educational music, the Society controls 90 per cent, or even more, of the performing rights in copyright music'. It has in fact a substantial monopoly of such copyright music.

This simplification of general procedure has gone so far as to prevent the negotiation of the terms best suited to individual cases. As members of the Society, composers and music publishers assign to it all their rights. Licence fees are pooled, and each copyright owner whose music is performed receives the share of the pool which the Society allocates to him. It is not necessary for a collecting organisation to operate on that basis. Copyright owners might fix their own tariffs and instruct the collector what terms to charge and to collect. Concert promoters would then choose from a detailed tariff list and no doubt some copyright owners would do better and some worse than they do under the Society's arrangements. I am indebted to the Report of the Copyright Committee 1952 for an admirable summary of the actual *modus operandi*. The Society does not furnish a list of all the compositions in which its members have an interest, nor does it license every performance individually. Wherever possible it charges an inclusive fee for a hall, and the entire repertoire of the Society's members is then available for performance. This simplification means that the division of the pooled receipts between composers of different types of music, and between composers and publishers, must inevitably be arbitrary. For instance, a composer may have assigned all his rights to a publisher, but the rules of the Society prohibit the payment to the publisher of more than one-half of the amount due on any composition, and the ordinary division is two-thirds to the composer and one-third to the publisher. In allocating the entire pool, the fees from different classes of entertainment are segregated and the payments to individual composers take into account the frequency of performance of each work and also discriminate in favour of 'more-serious but less-popular music'. If this is unfair to the composers of 'less-serious but more-popular' music, and they are aware that it goes on, they nevertheless have not seceded. Perhaps they feel they do sufficiently well as things are, and take pleasure in the thought that they support culture. It is also the fact that they have no alternative easily open to them.

As regards the general public interest, the Performing Right Society classifies its customers. So, of course, do individual dramatists. They expect more from a large West End theatre than from a small village dramatic society, and almost everyone would agree that they are entitled to get more. The Society operates a number of tariffs applicable to entertainments given under different conditions, ranging from those organised in concert halls, music halls and dance halls to hotels, cafés, flower-shows, and even gatherings for which no separate admission charge is made, such as meetings at Women's Institutes, music-while-you-work in a factory or music-while-you-eat in a works canteen. It has never refused a licence to any organiser of an entertainment who is prepared to pay what the Society decides is the appropriate fee. In fact, it operates a discriminating monopoly as completely as do most public utility corporations, and differs from them only in that its tariffs are not subject to the approval and control of a public authority. I will say no more about the matter here, beyond remarking that the recommendation of the recent Copyright Committee that the tariffs of such collecting organisations should be subject to independent review will surprise no one.

It is when we come to the new development of arranging public performances of recorded music that we encounter a host of new problems, which were not envisaged, or clearly foreseen, when the Copyright Act of 1911 was passed. Until that Act became law, composers were powerless to prevent manufacturers of records and similar appliances from reproducing versions of their compositions without making any payment. The Act gave the composer, for the first time, the sole right to authorise a recording. He need not do so, if he dislikes records, or decides that the sale of records might weaken the interest in live performances of his compositions to an extent that would reduce his aggregate receipts from both sources. The relevant terms of the Act are of peculiar interest. Various manufacturers then in business feared that protection of the composer might give particular manufacturers a monopoly advantage, and they were successful in getting a clause written into the Act, Section 19 (2), which provides that once a composer has authorised one recording other makers may, as of right, produce versions of their own, subject to certain formalities and to the payment of a prescribed royalty on each record sold. The manufacturers each have copyright protection for their own records, but from the outset of recording the composition enters, so far as record-making is concerned, the open-licence royalty arena. In this case, the terms of the Brussels Convention do not prevent member countries from allowing a term of protection for a record different from, that is of shorter duration than, the minimum term of authors' and composers' copyright.

The major difficulty which has since emerged arises out of public performances. When the legislation of 1911 was under consideration the manufacturers made it clear that they had no desire to control the performing right in their records. They considered that public performances would be a great advertisement, both for the record and for the composer, and they asked for legislation which would secure two results: first, provide that when a composer consented to a recording being made, he parted also with the full performing right in the recording, and second, entitle any person who bought a gramophone and a supply of records to give public as well as private performances without incurring any further obligation. There seems no reason to doubt that when Section 19 of the Copyright Act became law, it was generally supposed that its provisions secured both results. No one, of course, is in a position to assert categorically that that was the intention of Parliament, but it was at least generally assumed that record manufacturers had obtained what they wanted, namely, protection against pirating their own recordings, freedom to the buyer of a record to give public performances without further obligation even to the composer, and, most important, no power themselves to control the use of the records once they were sold. The industry operated, and developed rapidly, on that basis for more than twenty years; but as time went on, a number of interested groups came to regard the absence of control over public performances as an objectionable restraint on their opportunities to secure additional profits. In a court action in 1933, the Carwardine Case, it was decided that the effect of Section 19 of the Act was contrary to that which had for so long been generally assumed. It was held that the Act had, in fact, given the record manufacturers the control over performing rights. The manufacturers promptly formed a private company, Phonographic Performances Ltd, which has since acted as a collecting agency handling the licensing of all public performances of recorded music. It has a strong monopoly position. It operates a system of tariffs. But it is itself subject to collective pressure from groups of performers whose services are required for the making of records, and who are determined to see that records do not replace them wherever they might be employed in person. The licensing policy of the collecting agency is greatly affected by this pressure. For example, at the request of the Musicians' Union, licences are refused for any entertainment where musicians could be employed, and the BBC has been compelled to restrict severely the number of hours each week during which gramophone records may be broadcast. The Union has announced its ultimate aim to be the complete suppression of all use of gramophone records by the BBC. The collecting agency 'voluntarily' allocates a share of its licence revenue to various groups: 20 per cent to performing artists, 12½ per cent to the Musicians' Union and 10 per cent to publishers. There has been widespread criticism of the restrictive licensing policy adopted by the agency, and the recent Copyright Committee came to the conclusion that the rights given by the Carwardine decision 'have been enforced in an arbitrary and autocratic manner, with the minimum of consideration'. Yet the Committee was informed by the agency that the fees from performances were of little or no importance in relation to the total receipts of the gramophone companies, and the manufacturers stated that no account was taken of them when deciding whether or not to make a record, or when computing their costings.

The performers are not, however, content with indirect control, but demand some sort of copyright which would enable them directly to control the use of records. They already have protection against unauthorised commercial recordings of their performances, under the terms of the Dramatic and Musical Performers' Protection Act of 1925. Performers need not record if they think they will be better off without, and if they do make records they would no doubt all like to be able to fix their own tariff of licence fees for public performances and augment their incomes in that way. But their interests are significantly divided. The solo performers, in general, have no fear that record playing will reduce the demand for their appearances in person, and their interest might be best served by a scale of tariffs adjusted to maximise their income from public performances of records. On the other hand, the players in orchestras and bands, and the chorus singers, are more generally concerned to insist upon punitive rates and positive refusals of licences, since public performances from records will, in their view, reduce the other demands for their services. Thus the Incorporated Society of Musicians, which represents the solo performers and singers, told the Copyright Committee that 'an increase in recording and broadcasting is accompanied by an increase in the number of musicians'. These new developments have stimulated public attendances at concerts. The soloists find that the greater the sale and the wider the use of their records, the greater the interest in their appearances in person. The one market helps the other, and they can be more selective in the engagements they accept. In the case of the members of orchestras and choruses, who are in much more plentiful supply, the appeal made by their personal appearances is not always so markedly superior to that made by their records, to say nothing of records made by their competitors. The organisers of a small dance or a church garden party, or similar social gatherings in which some incidental music would be appreciated, often have to consider cost very carefully, and a selection of good recordings by well-known orchestras is likely to be widely preferred to a public appearance by the best orchestra which the funds available would permit the organisers to engage for the occasion. The grant to the record manufacturers of the power to license, or to refuse to license, the use of records has provided not only the manufacturers, but the performers and other suppliers of the services needed by the record makers, with a direct incentive to form combinations with the object of imposing restrictions. The manufacturers would no doubt have liked to augment their incomes from public performances of their records, but the 'rank and file' performers, if I may so term them without disrespect, are concerned more with suppression, and so far their interest has dominated licensing policy. Remove the power to control the use of recordings at all levels, and this growing hierarchy of combinations in restraint of trade is deprived of its main *point d'appui*. That, as I see it, is the case for a simple amendment of the law designed to nullify the effects of the decision in the Carwardine case.

I have made a passing reference to broadcasting, and I must now consider very briefly a similar proposal which the BBC has put forward for the creation of broadcasters' rights analogous to copyright.

It will be convenient first of all to recall some of the actual words used by the BBC in memoranda submitted to the Beveridge Broadcasting Committee of 1949. When presenting a General Survey of the Broadcasting Service it stated that 'the history of the BBC has been the story of a steady liberation of the microphone. Some boycotts, bans and restrictions still remain. It is hoped the Committee will sustain the BBC in its fight to overcome them.' In framing its programmes, it 'seeks to provide for its listeners the widest range of broadcasting it is possible to achieve'. It submitted, however, to the same Committee, a further memorandum entitled 'A Copyright in Broadcasting. The urgent need to control the unauthorised use of broadcast programmes by third parties.' In this document it asked for legislation establishing a broadcaster's right as 'the only effective means of protecting its programmes against unauthorised use by third parties and exploitation for commercial gain, and thus enabling it to provide the best possible service to listeners'. The Corporation's right in its programmes would be analogous to the rights of the manufacturer of a gramophone record or the maker of a cinematographic film in their products, as these rights are additional to the right of the owner of any copyright works performed for the record or film.

The use of broadcast programmes by third parties may take two forms. The more simple form is the installation of an ordinary receiving set in a restaurant, or the public rooms of an hotel, or in business premises, or a hall of entertainment. Patrons and employees of these places may then enjoy, equally with listeners at home, the programmes which are broadcast. It is an additional amenity which some at least of those present may appreciate, at least some of the time. If, on balance, the service is generally favoured, the business firm which runs the premises may find the policy of installing the receiver remunerative. Patrons may increase, employees may be happier in their work, and it may even be possible to increase the charges made to customers. This is presumably one instance of exploitation of the broadcast programmes for commercial gain. The grant of a broadcaster's right to control these practices would give the BBC the power, if its aim was to make money, to license third parties to provide the service, in return for payment of the appropriate fee stated in its tariff of charges; or, if it wished to suppress the service, to refuse to grant a licence on any terms.

The other form of use by third parties is by making recordings or films from the broadcast programmes and giving performances subsequently in the same kinds of public place. Admission prices might be charged. A broadcaster's right might give to the broadcast authorities the sole power of authorising any recording of broadcast programmes.

The first question is whether the existing rights of performers are not adequate cover for their broadcasts. Performers are protected against unauthorised recording by the Act of 1925, and the broadcasting authority may presumably already require the performers who contract with it to take proceedings in appropriate cases. They have protection, but not copyright. It is of the essence of copyright that it must relate to works reduced to a recognisable material form, without which there cannot be certainty as to what is protected and what is not. Performances do not conform to this fundamental requirement. Each performance by an eminent actor or musician may embody a unique combination of artistic interpretation, skill and dexterity. He will hardly be content that it should be identical, even if he could make it so, with all his other performances of the same work. Coming to broadcasts, the diffusion of a performance through a microphone and broadcasting transmitter, so that it can be heard by an indefinitely large audience equipped with suitable receivers, does not endow it with any material form. It still remains purely a performance.

The performer's right to authorise a recording is ancillary to that of the author or composer. As regards copyright material, it is surely reasonable that the copyright owner should have the sole right to authorise a broadcast of his work. If he has already authorised a recording of it, he will have to take into account that, as the law stands, if he consents to a broadcast performance, then third parties will be free to make a recording of it. He is of course entitled to royalties on any sales of the records. But if he has not previously authorised a recording, then an authorised recording of the broadcast performance would be a breach of his copyright. The broadcasting authority might itself produce a record or a sound film of a performance, by arrangement with the copyright owners and performers concerned, and make its broadcasts from the record or film. In that case, again, copies made by third parties would constitute infringements, because films and records are copyright.

It would seem, therefore, that it is unnecessary in any case to create another broadcaster's right, since the protection already accorded by law to copyright owners and performers is adequate cover for their broadcasts.

All of this is no doubt better understood by the expert advisers of the BBC than by a mere professor of economics, and yet they advance the claim for a broadcaster's right. A clue to the reason may lie in the words 'exploitation of *its* programmes for commercial gain'. They are not satisfied with the protection of authors, composers and performers. The programmes are arranged by the BBC and the BBC needs more revenue. Power to control public performances would give it the opportunity to levy licence fees from hotels and Women's Institutes, from cinemas and industrial canteens – from café receivers here and now as well as from recorded performances hereafter. All of these places might be said, if we strain somewhat the normal meaning of words, to be exploiting BBC programmes for commercial gain. Yet it is reasonable to bear in mind that for large sections of the public, some permanently and many more occasionally resident in hotels, the sound and television receivers in the public rooms present the only opportunity to enjoy the advantages of the broadcast services, and it is the avowed aim of the BBC to provide the widest range of broadcasting service it is possible (not most profitable) to achieve. Is it really consonant with that laudable aim for the authority to seek to restrict access to its service in public places to the degree calculated to secure the greatest possible revenue from licences? Is the aim to provide a beneficial service, only on condition that the benefit is not material or pecuniary? A broadcasting monopoly surely needs to take special care that its arrangements cannot be criticised on the ground that they aim to monopolise for itself the exploitation of its service for commercial gain.

There is another very practical consideration that should be weighed. Suppose the broadcasting and television authority secured the right to control public performances and the kind of use to which its broadcasts are put, and then proceeded to exploit its power by fixing a scale of tariffs at which various classes of users would be franchised by licence. The experience of Phonographic Performances Limited indicates the sort of additional collective pressure to which it would then lay itself open from various organisations of performers and other suppliers of services, determined to share the proceeds. Experience shows that the demands would not rest there. It would be confronted by demands backed by threats of boycott that its licensing policy be framed, not to further the public interest, as the broadcasting authority might interpret it, or its own financial interest, as it saw it, but to protect and further the separate interests of these organisations *outside* the field of broadcasting, which the various collection organisations might consider likely to suffer damage from the full and unrestrained development of broadcasting services.

With the utmost deference, I suggest that the broadcasting authority would be best advised, on all grounds, to put behind it the temptations of envy and cupidity, and to continue to cast its programmes upon the ether for the full enjoyment of all subscribers, without discrimination between domestic and public reception. Because of new technological advances already emerging from the experimental stage, virtue may soon have its reward.

There can be no doubt that the major obstacle standing in the way of development and improvement of television broadcasting is finance. Its appetite for valuable material, always scarce, costly and laborious to prepare, is incessant and insatiable. It is a voracious consuming animal, without much of a hump and with very little capacity to keep going by chewing its own cud. Its service has hitherto been heavily subsidised throughout the world, in America by sponsoring patrons, in this country by the licensed listeners to sound broadcasting, and it is quite unable to provide the type of programme, and the incessant change of programme, for which so many viewers are clamouring. One or two nation-wide broadcasts may exhaust most of the value put into an expensive production. A new feature film costing hundreds of thousands of pounds could be seen in a single television showing by many millions of viewers in this country and by precisely the classes of the public who make up the bulk of the cinema attendances. The television authority has not the money to compensate the film producers for the sacrifice in cinema receipts which a 'first release' television performance would entail. Not only cinema showings of the same films, but contemporaneous cinema performances of other films would be affected, as well as rival forms of entertainment. The promoters of outstanding sporting events are in like case: even if their own televised events remain supported to full capacity by those who prefer to see them on the spot, minor fixtures catering for the same interests elsewhere at the same time would be affected.

Television can barely afford to begin to meet, from its present sources of revenue, the insatiable demands for services of these kinds, and no upward adjustment of the annual viewers' licence fee which is practical politics will provide the solution.

I will not waste your time with a discussion of the merits of a large State subsidy. However useful as a weapon for attacking an existing government such a demand might be to a party in opposition, no forward-looking, shadow Chancellor of the Exchequer is likely to allow such a proposal to figure high on an election programme.

So long as we continue in this country to finance the television, or indeed the sound broadcasting service, solely on the basis of annual licence fees payable by the owners of receiving sets, no solution to the problem will be found. I do not doubt that this system was appropriate, in fact the only one practicable, when the new service was first taken over from the manufacturers of radio equipment who launched it and demonstrated its vast potentialities. Nor can one doubt that it will remain for the foreseeable future the most appropriate and convenient system for financing the essential minimum services which the community will wish to be made available to everybody, without additional charge. But beyond these somewhat rigid limits, it has already shown itself to be inconvenient and inequitable, and above all incapable of meeting the costs of various types of new service which very many sections of the public desire and which many would be prepared to pay for, if faced with the alternative that they must otherwise go without them. It is the universal experience of organisations, such as clubs, which exist to provide a combination of expensive and inexpensive services, freely obtainable at call by individual members, that they cannot afford to go far in providing the more expensive amenities for which the demand is at all elastic. A social club which charges an annual subscription must confine the amenities available to its members without specific charge to those which are in reasonably equal demand by all and which it would be highly inconvenient to price separately. Meals and drinks, for instance, are paid for as members choose to take them.

Technological developments have already indicated the way in which specially expensive programmes, and in particular those which do not make an equally strong appeal all the time to all owners of broadcast receivers, can be made available through ordinary receivers only to those who are prepared to pay their estimated share of the costs involved. In a tentative and experimental way, the 'scrambler' system of diffusion, long in use for confidential telephonic communication, has now been applied to commercial television and sound broadcasting services. A particular programme is broadcast in a 'scrambled' or confused form, which when picked up becomes intelligible *en clair* only to those recipients who go through the prescribed operations to clear it. It may be 'unscrambled' for a controlled period by the deposit of the right number of the right coins in a slot: it may be cleared on credit account by the attachment of an audition or television time-meter to the receiving set, recording the times and wave bands on which the set has been operating: it can be cleared centrally on request over the telephone and charged accordingly.

I feel confident that if the authorities now directed the appropriate technologists to concentrate their attention, as a matter of urgency, on the perfection of contrivances to be applied to ordinary broadcast transmission and receiving equipment, inexpensive and efficient systems would be quickly forthcoming. The allocation of a separate wave-band avoids interruptions of the programmes concurrently available for all without charge. The scrambled service is an additional or alternative programme. The fees charged for each programme provide the fund from which the broadcasting authority buys the right to broadcast it. A charge of, say, five shillings would enable family gatherings to view the latest feature film or the Cup Final in their own home, and permit the offer of an acceptable fee to the film producer or sports organisation. Bulk charges can be arranged for halls and hotels in which 'public performances' take place. It may be objected that my argument here is inconsistent, in that it would seem to be necessary to give the authority the right to control the use made of its programmes in order that it might make a bulk charge. Yet technical changes already taking place suggest that this need not be so. Even in the case of sports events, convenience alone, and the need to edit televised versions, have already led to the practice of filming a spectacle and diffusing the broadcast version from the film. The delay is a matter of minutes only. It is likely that specially expensive television programmes will, in any event, be broadcast from film. Films are copyright, and their reproduction is protected. And I confine the proposal to the supplementary service for which specific charges are levied on all viewers. Without venturing to pronounce upon legal questions, I suggest that no drastic amendments of existing copyright law need be involved. The technologists may themselves devise the complete solution.

If there were a competitive television broadcast service, the negotiation of fees for broadcast rights would be fixed in the market by the competition of rival suppliers and rival broadcasting stations, and the finance of an improved service, including the determination of the appropriate charge to receivers of the scrambled service, would be a normal business venture. It should not be beyond the capacity of a public monopoly to proceed on similar lines. It would be highly regrettable if, wherever broadcasting remained a public monopoly, the service provided lagged in quality and flexibility behind that which alternative systems now have it within their means to provide.

I have already detained you far too long, and your patience must be more than exhausted. Yet I have been able only to touch upon a few aspects of the subject in a selective and superficial way. I trust I have, at any rate, satisfied you that this highly technical field of inquiry merits closer and more continuous study by economists. It has not been entirely neglected in this University. At the close of last century, during the period of his Chancellorship of the University, Lord Herschell introduced into the House of Lords a Bill to consolidate and amend the Copyright Law, and the Quain Professor of Law at University College delivered, in 1898, eighteen lectures on the general subject. Seven – the 'more popular' of them – were published. He was exceptionally well qualified – one of Her Majesty's Counsel, a member of Parliament, destined later to become a Minister of the Crown, and a master of elegant prose. I cannot better the closing words penned then by Professor Augustine Birrell: 'I may conclude . . . in the gracious language so often employed by the Crown in addressing Parliament, by commending these weighty matters to your experienced judgment.'

PART THREE

# Economic Processes at Work

It seems to me that this preface should give some sort of explanation of the thinking behind two related decisions: what to include and what topics to leave out altogether. For instance, I have included nothing on transport. In the 1930s I wrote a good deal on 'co-ordination and competition' in road and rail transport, in both passenger and freight transport services, but apart from one early paper delivered to the Institute of Transport these were mainly short articles written for the weekly journals. Government Committees were issuing provocative reports, transport control legislation was being enacted, transport undertakings were demanding privileged concessions, and there was much to debate as the course of events unfolded. These articles would have been useful material for a History of British Passenger and Freight Transport in the 1930s, but I had no such project in hand.

On Customs Tariffs I have frankly hesitated longer before deciding not to include any of my articles. In 1925 the South African government adopted a protective tariff, which I examined in a paper delivered to the Economic Society of South Africa. Four years later, I read a paper to the 1929 British Association meeting in Cape Town on 'The anti-dumping regulations of the South African tariff'. In *Economica* for February 1933 I reprinted an anonymous tract which I had come across, entitled 'Letter on the true principles of advantageous exportation'. The anti-dumping article has been printed in the *Journal of the Economic Society of South Africa*, as well as in *Tariffs: The Case Examined*, edited by Beveridge.

On the other hand, an article on Hayek has been included. This article, 'Homage to Hayek' (the title is new), was written at the invitation of Mr Denis Thomas, editor of *Economic Age*, and published at the beginning of 1970, as a review of *Roads to Freedom – Essays in Honour of Friedrich A. von Hayek*, which was published in 1969 by Routledge

& Kegan Paul. Readers of this present volume who have not seen my review in *Economic Age* now have another opportunity to do so.

It might be of interest for me to mention two papers which would have been the next to be chosen for reprinting had the decision on overall length of the contents of Part III relating to 'Economic processes at work' permitted. The first is the annual lecture which I delivered to the Library Association on 21 September 1950, the year in which the Public Libraries Centenary, 1850–1950, was celebrated, at a London conference. The title I chose was 'Are libraries businesslike?' My father was a pioneer public librarian who was in his time a well-known member of the Library Association; at the London School of Economics the Deputy Librarian in 1950 was my sister Marjorie Plant, D.Sc. (Econ.), FLA. The address was printed by the Library Association in the *Proceedings* of the Centenary Conference.

The second paper excluded was one of six contributed to the *University of Toronto Quarterly* for July 1957 in a symposium on the University and Business, the six contributors being drawn from Toronto, the Harvard Graduate School, the *Harvard Business Review* and myself as Professor of Commerce, University of London. My paper was entitled 'Universities and the making of business men' (pp. 520–34).

I should say a few words about the reprinting here of my UNESCO paper on the economics of nuclear energy. Early in 1957, if I remember correctly, I was invited by UNESCO to undertake the preparation of a paper on that subject. This was required as part of the documentation to be presented at an inter-disciplinary conference on the peaceful uses of nuclear energy planned to take place in Paris in the third week of September 1958. After the conference, UNESCO authorised the preparation of a report on the upshot of the discussions, and entrusted its publication to Otto Knineberg as editor. Various experts who had presented papers were asked to bring figures up to date. I did so, using the spring of 1960 as the dead-line. In the event the report was not finished for publication until 1964. These facts are made clear in a footnote at the beginning of Chapter 6 of the report in which my paper 'The economics of nuclear energy' is printed.

A. P.

CHAPTER 6

# The substance and the shadow – reflections on prosperity*

We in this country enjoy today a precarious prosperity. That is, we live in testing times: for prosperity permits indulgence in light-headed foolishness. So long as we feel there is a lot of ruin in the country before it is finally overtaken by bankruptcy and disaster, we are tempted to pursue shadows. In one of his essays on Heroes and Hero-Worship, Carlyle observed that 'adversity is sometimes hard upon a man: but for one man who can stand prosperity, there are a hundred that will stand adversity'. That is not a conclusive argument for preferring a slump but rather a hint as to how to sustain a boom. The last war sobered us, as a people; the immediate danger past, some of us are still loath to admit that it is now time armistice celebrations were over and done with.

Each of us is entitled to put his own interpretation on prosperity, or well-being, and, subject only to allowing similar freedom to others, to try to lead the sort of life that he prefers. Some people set great store on working only when they feel like it, and only in the place where they prefer to live. They may have sufficient independent means. In modern society very few people who have to work for their living are in that fortunate position – one calls to mind people like successful free-lance writers and artists and craftsmen whose works are sought out by eager buyers and who decline contractual engagements which would commit them to a working time-table. They are exceptional. Most self-employed workers and family concerns find it necessary to be available to do business with others at pre-arranged times. They have to face the fact that they are members, however occasional, of a

* The third Fawley University Lecture 1956, delivered at the University of Southampton on 31 May 1956. Published by the University of Southampton.

team; that consideration must be accorded to the wishes and convenience of other parties with whom they wish to maintain business relations, and that they must, therefore, make some concessions by way of adjustment of their own behaviour. Even those who are able to do their specialised work at home, on a family farm or in a domestic workplace, must consent to reside in locations within reaching distance, without incurring excessive transport costs, of those with whom they must transact business. Special skills are frequently wanted only in special places, and people who possess them and wish to exploit them must locate themselves where there is sufficient demand. In times of exceptionally serious unemployment in particular distressed areas, in advanced communities which will not allow the workless to starve or their homes to be broken up, the rest of the community, it is true, may acquiesce in making special and sometimes costly arrangements to transfer work to them. They will do so, so long as they can afford it, if, taking all the circumstances into account, that appears for the time to be, from the standpoint of the whole community, the most convenient and least costly arrangement. Normally, however, it is unlikely that a democratic community, in which most people do not feel any too well off themselves, will consent to continue these unusual arrangements on a permanent basis. They will demand that the same treatment be extended to other areas, and if it becomes clear that the cost of generalising the system would be too great, or the whole concept would then become nonsensical, or its general application would undermine the strength of the economy, they are likely to press for its abandonment.

The Special Areas, more recently re-named the Development Areas of this country, are a case in point. When the Special Areas legislation was passed in the' thirties, roughly 40 per cent of the insured population in the four areas designated were out of work. Under the Distribution of Industry Act of 1945 these four areas were enlarged, and in the next three years five more areas were added, so that they now include nearly one-fifth of the working population of the country. The legislation authorised the central government to give assistance to industrial development in the scheduled areas by a variety of measures which were not applicable to the rest of the country. Factories have been built with public money, amounting to about £60 millions, and leased out at subsidised rentals for a term of years. Grants or loans have been made to finance factory removals from other areas. Industrial development elsewhere has been prohibited by the withholding of licences in areas of so-called industrial congestion, with the intention of diverting it to the Development Areas. For an area to be included in the Schedule it must be deemed to be subject to a 'special danger of unemployment" and more recently it has been laid down that there must be first a persistently high average rate of unemployment, and secondly a high aggregate number of people unemployed in the district. The legislation also provides that where the special danger of unemployment no longer exists in any area or part of an area, that district can be removed from the Schedule. No district has in fact yet been removed. This year, the Select Committee on Estimates investigated and reported on the working of this legislation (2nd Report, 1955–6, Development Areas). It found that the percentage of unemployment in the Development Areas was now below the figure which is generally accepted as full employment. It clearly had formed the impression that at least some quite large districts no longer fulfilled the conditions for continuing designation, and that others not at present scheduled but with higher unemployment might be in greater need of any Government financial assistance that was going. It raised doubts whether, in the event of a severe depression, this particular fifth of the total working population of the country were any longer all in a 'special danger of unemployment' compared with at least some of the remaining four-fifths. It concluded that it was clear that the powers taken under the Acts were being used to a great extent for a purpose different from that originally envisaged when the powers were granted. In fact, the rest of the community is beginning to ask, in Parliament, whether the special reason for the levy which the legislation has imposed upon them has not disappeared.

Certain kinds of work such as mining must be performed in what to many of us are relatively uncongenial surroundings. Particular industrial processes cannot be economically carried on in garden cities, if these places are to remain garden cities. During the War, when munitions factories were particularly vulnerable to air attack, we learned that industrial operations, or the production of small parts and components, and the sub-assembly of components, can be successfully dispersed over hundreds or thousands of homes and small workshops. The Swiss and the Germans have long demonstrated that the dispersal of precision tasks over highly skilled workers in scattered domestic households, with power appliances laid on as necessary, often fits better into the pattern of their economy than the assembly of skilled workers into single factories, and enables them to compete most successfully in the world market for precision instruments. None the less, it remains generally the case that transport costs necessitate the assembly of workers in factories for most industrial operations that have to be performed in series. The convenience of the individual must be subordinated to the convenience of the team. Group production which requires expensive equipment and a balanced flow of work means regular attendance at fixed times for fixed periods, if it is to be economic, and the individual worker cannot expect to be allowed by the rest of the team to absent himself at will. Some industrial processes, because of their technological character or the high cost of the plant, must be continuously manned night and day, week in and week out, if they are to be undertaken at all; and some at any rate of the people who want that kind of work must accept shift-working. And to round off the catalogue, there are some services which by their nature must be carried on when the great majority of the community are asleep or otherwise enjoying themselves. It is to some of us a sad fact that an increasing proportion of the leisure occupations of the population seem to require that others shall be on duty at the same time. Those who work while others play must be content to forego, perhaps, the most popular television programme or football match or all those funs of the fair which are only laid on when large numbers are free to enjoy them. However, not everyone wants to spend his free time in a crowd. In a free market the differential rewards offered for these special tasks reflect the willingness of sufficient people to undertake them wherever and whenever they are wanted. That is why widely differential wage rates are essential in an egalitarian society.

People, then, differ widely in the values they set on the various constituents of well-being; and the economic system, the pattern of productive activity, the structure and technology of industry are moulded and re-moulded accordingly. Lord Snowden, you may recall, once remarked that it was a mistake to assume that the people of this country would be satisfied with full employment, guaranteed food and shelter, and an adequate medical service: that was proved by their almost universal anxiety to keep out of Dartmoor, where the State had offered those amenities over a long term of years. In the economically more backward, and in many cases under-developed, regions of the world, governments and business men, who from their differing motives are united in joint efforts to raise productivity and standards of life, are faced by this same fact. Some primitive peoples are content with the low level of existence which natural conditions afford in predominantly subsistence economies with rudimentary localised trade. The appearance of a white man fills some of them with apprehension: he wants them to go to work, they want to be left alone. His coming interferes with their mode of living. It may not be possible to allow them to go on entirely as before, if their old habits prevent others among them from seizing the new opportunities of a higher standard of life. Communal herds must be segregated, communal land tenure adjusted, public and veterinary medical services imposed, and so on. But beyond these minimal requirements, public opinion and policy, at least in the British dependencies, now frown upon attempts to compel subject peoples to go out to work by imposing poll taxes and other obligations designed to make non-compliance intolerable. The emphasis is now placed on the offer of positive incentives, calculated to arouse a wider and more eager appreciation of the attractions of a higher standard of life. Nevertheless, the introduction of an advanced exchange economy brings hazards of its own. Primitive peoples are often eager to learn to operate industrial machinery, and are quick in acquiring dexterity. The modern exchange economy, however, is co-extensive with the entire community which it serves. The individual is in touch with no more than a minute member of the whole mechanism: the remainder is intangible. The relation between effort, in terms of current output, and ultimate reward, measured in ambitions realised, may be far from obvious. To the untutored mind, there may appear to be no connection between the work done in helping to construct the permanent way for a new railroad, along which the worker sees no likelihood of ever travelling himself, or a new hydro-electric generating plant which is never likely to light his own hut, and the greater abundance of domestic utensils, clothing, shoes and bicycles which he subsequently enjoys after the capital works have been completed. Ignorance is a fertile soil in which mischief-makers, who choose to work for the overthrow of the Western form of economy, can plant jealousy and suspicion. Where extremely wide differences exist between the levels of understanding of the various participants in an exchange economy, special precautions against the infiltration of political saboteurs become indispensable.

I have allowed myself to be carried away: it is time I returned to my main theme. I began with a statement that we enjoy in this country a precarious prosperity. It is certainly precarious, compared with the conditions which our immediate forefathers enjoyed and which the older ones among us remember. How far are we in this country responsible for the deterioration? We cannot accept all of the blame. In common with all countries whose internal prosperity depends on favourable external opportunities for the exchange of goods and services, and far more so for us than for most, the maintenance of our living standards depends on the level of prosperity throughout the world of trading peoples, and we are particularly vulnerable when other countries so conduct their own affairs as to reduce the opportunities for international business. When successive governments of one country lack the courage and the power to correct serious maladjustments in their internal economic arrangements, and resort to measures calculated, rightly or wrongly, to export the resultant depression to other parts of the world, they should not be surprised or pained that the governments of other countries copy their example and take first similar defensive, and later perhaps even more damaging offensive measures by way of retaliation. We cannot pretend that our own behaviour in these respects has not in large measure created difficulties for other countries which have provided them with a bad example to imitate and an excuse to retaliate with even more damaging expedients. To many of them, the consequential damage in the long run is less than it is to us, in so far as their domestic economies are less dependent than ours on maintaining a large and expanding volume of multilateral international business. The measures which have been adopted – competitive devaluations of national currencies, consequential exchange controls, selective import restrictions, trade licensing and quotas, export subsidies and limitations on travellers' currency requirements – could hardly have been more damaging to the economic life of this country if they had been imposed internally, on a county basis. The more backward, largely self-sufficing counties would have suffered least, the more advanced inter-dependent counties most.

Without attempting to apportion blame between countries, I am convinced that our failure in this country to take the necessary measures, however unpleasant, to maintain since the war a reasonable measure of stability in the purchasing power of the £ sterling has been the largest brick that we have thrown into the international economic pool. For upwards of a century, justifiable confidence throughout the trading world in sterling as an acceptable medium for multilateral exchange and as the most reliable standard of value has been the mainstay of international commerce. Our continuing prosperity will not be assured until that confidence has been restored.

Other countries have not yet lost their interest in Britain as a market. We are still able to buy our supplies for sterling from about as many countries as there are counties in England. Overseas business men still accept sterling arising from multifarious kinds of transactions. Much thought and great subtlety have been directed by monetary authorities and experts in this country in recent years to the introduction of ingenious new devices designed to maintain and strengthen their willingness to go on doing so. We have attached distinguishing labels to different varieties of sterling, each according to its provenance, in order to permit foreign recipients to get rid of some of them on more acceptable terms. For the purposes of a wide range of current transactions which enjoy governmental approval, a sort of *de facto* convertibility has been established. But in the foreign exchange game, sterling is still an old maid in the pack. What we have so far failed to do is to restore in the minds of enough people either at home or abroad the firm belief that sterling is once again worth holding, as a reliable store of value, for what it will fetch in the future. Instead of stopping inflation, we have frittered away precious years in inventing palliatives which in varying degrees insulate particular commitments and activities from its most damaging effects while allowing the evil itself to continue. These expedients are sometimes given the euphonious title of 'controlled inflation'.

The varieties of uses to which the word 'inflation' is now applied have themselves become so unduly inflated that the term itself is in danger of losing much of its value in current discussion. From various sides we are urged to distinguish monetary inflation from credit inflation, price inflation from cost inflation, and wage inflation from all the rest. There is great confusion here between cause and effect. At the risk of being written-off myself as obsolete and old-fashioned, I propose to revert to the meaning that was generally accepted during and immediately after the First World War, when currency note issues in many parts of Europe were grossly increased by Governments which printed notes as the most convenient method of taxing the holders of currency and favouring debtors (including of course themselves) at the expense of creditors. The effect was, of course, to set in train a rise in prices which induced an acceleration of the note-printing presses in the attempt to keep ahead of the continuing rise in prices which resulted from that acceleration. In those days the late Lord Keynes was content to define inflation as an expansion in the supply of money to spend relatively to the supply of things to purchase, and in this particular context I am happy to stop with him at this point in the evolution of his acute and restless mind.

I myself have no doubt at all, and I earnestly hope that this audience will agree, that all of our troubles arising from our present inflationary position will cease as soon as a Government of this country decides to accept the full responsibility of its position as the sole controller of currency issues. One certain way to arrest the continuing inflation is for the Treasury to instruct the Bank of England that in any year from now on it must not increase the fiduciary currency note circulation above the peak figure of the previous year. The control exercised through the Bank of England over the power of banks to extend their credits depends ultimately upon the expansion of the currency. I am fully aware that credit expansion brings with it, somewhat later, a consequential inflation of notes. So long as the commercial banks are led to expect that the requisite notes will be forthcoming, they are relieved of the unpleasant task of endeavouring to discriminate between different credit-worthy offers of business or alternatively of rationing them all. But, by and large, commercial bankers know their business; and if they are clearly warned that they must themselves arrange the timing of their loans and investments in such a manner as will enable them to meet seasonal peak demands for cash or short-term advances from their own reserves, they are expert enough to conduct their business accordingly.

I detect an alarming tendency in some quarters to regard people who believe that the government should pay as much attention to maintaining a sound currency – a reliable £ sterling – as it does to enforcing a standard pound avoirdupois or a standard yard, as religious cranks or extremists. There is no valid analogy between moderate indulgence in alcoholic liquor as compared with total abstinence and moderate indulgence in inflation. We need to be on our guard against the temperance movement in the field of monetary inflation.

It is worth while pausing to reflect a little on some of the long-term consequences of continuing with the alternative policy of allowing the fall in the purchasing power of sterling to go on, even assuming that the cleverest minds are applied to 'controlling the inflation'. Consider first the effect of individual saving. Most prudent people wish to save when their earning power is at its peak, if only in the sense of spreading their expenditure more rationally over their whole life. We are officially exhorted to save more of our current incomes. If we can save, it is in present circumstances most prudent, however, to save more in kind than we would if prices were stable; to buy now more durable commodities which will provide a continuing flow of services over a long period. Why, by the way, should it be thought to be anti-social for people to buy durable household equipment (say a wardrobe) on hire-purchase but not to buy their house (with perhaps a fitted wardrobe included) on the instalment plan? Yet purchase taxes seem designed to discriminate against saving in kind, the rates of tax in general being higher than on articles which need more frequent replacement and possibly absorb a larger aggregate share of our scarce productive resources. The ordinary man is urged to save in sterling, to buy savings certificates and bonds on which interest will be paid in sterling. With the prospect of continually rising prices, he is at a loss to see the sense in this advice. If he suspects a confidence trick, what is the right answer to give him? Who among us does not prefer more goods for his money today to fewer goods for the same money plus interest in a year's time, and still fewer as far ahead as he can see – even though the choice of goods available today is not precisely that which he would prefer to buy later on, if only it were prudent to wait? Arrest the rise in prices and many people, rich and poor alike, who have hitherto been spending out of income or capital more than they would otherwise prefer to do, will soon begin to take a different view. Sterling will cease to be too hot to hold: and the proportion of saving to spending on immediate consumption will rise.

I turn now to some of the effects of inflation on the conduct of business. I will say nothing about rising costs and recurrent demands for higher wages, but will confine my observations to the effects of constantly rising prices on the already thorny question of ascertaining what are real profits for purposes of tax. We are all indebted to the experts who constituted the Royal Commission on Taxation of Profits and Income, which presented its most able Final Report (Command 9474 of June 1955) a year ago. The Royal Commission devoted more than four years to the study of voluminous evidence and the most thorough consideration of the new difficulties which have resulted from recent trends in our economic life. It is highly significant that they felt bound to say at the outset of their Report that, with regard to inflation, 'any discussion of the topic of savings (whether by an individual or by a business) is a mere deployment of words unless it can take as its basis the assumption that a reasonable stability in the purchasing power of money is a fixed canon of public policy'.

I select three topics, viz.

1 Allowances for depreciation on wasting assets, when ascertaining real profit for purposes of income tax.
2 Stock in trade and the computation of profits.
3 The differential profits tax on distributed and non-distributed profits.

There are two reasonable approaches to the problem of depreciation allowances on wasting assets. One conceives of a business as having an indefinite but not perpetual life, and regards its capital as sums of money which are invested at different times in varying kinds of assets. On this view, depreciation allowances are required only to the extent necessary to keep money capital intact. The fall in the purchasing power of money affects businesses no more than other taxpayers. If the trader decides to continue in business with a new and more expensive asset (though it may be identical with the cheaper one which it replaces) he must venture that much more capital and hope to receive from its use a correspondingly larger monetary return under the new conditions.

The alternative conception regards the trader's capital as consisting of the actual physical assets that belong to the business, the money capital having been expended once for all on their acquisition. It is the assets that waste in the course of trading and the depreciation allowances are the measure of the deterioration in the value of the assets concerned during the period of the account. According to this view, a business is a continuous and permanent activity, and profits have not been correctly computed unless they have been charged with as much as may turn out at the end of the life of each asset to be required to replace it as before. Clearly in the existing inflationary conditions this concept has a strong appeal to those concerned with existing businesses. The Royal Commission considered three alternative proposals designed to implement this latter concept, and rejected them all. The first was a revaluation scheme which would write up the depreciation allowance by reference to a general index of prices of an appropriate selection of commodities. The objection found to this was that it would introduce an undesirable discrimination between different classes of taxpayers, and would also be inequitable since the fall in the value of money has been going on for a considerable time and retrospective adjustments would be quite impracticable. The second suggestion was a Replacement allowance, chargeable when the wasted asset was actually replaced, equivalent to the change in price of the new asset compared with the old one. The objection to this also was that it could not be made retrospective and would favour particular businesses. The third suggestion, an Initial Investment Allowance on renewals, was rejected on the ground that it would be impossible to separate improvements from replacements.

Secondly, on stock in trade, the problem which arises is that when identical commodities are bought for stock at various times, while prices are changing, the value placed upon the cost of stock sold affects the computation of profits.

The debate concerning the relative appropriateness of LIFO (last in first out) and FIFO (first in first out) is a familiar one which I do not need to discuss here. What is of interest to the consideration of tax rules in times of inflationary movements of prices is that the Royal Commission which considered the problem came to the conclusion that there would be no advantage in requiring all businesses to use a single method, provided that the cost assigned to an item of stock was a real figure and not an arbitrary or fictitious estimate, and provided secondly that businesses should be required to use consistently over a number of years whichever system they elected to employ, and not be allowed to dodge from one to another to minimise tax. They considered it practicable to frame rules on these lines 'if effect is given to the principle that despite rising prices, there is no permanent exclusion from taxable income of an element to reflect the fall in the purchasing power of money'. They recognised, however, that if general prices continued to rise, the result might be a heavy reduction in the yield of tax.

These two examples exhibit the impossibility of combating a continuing inflation, from the standpoint of insulating desirable business enterprise from its damaging consequences, by modifying tax arrangements, particularly if reasonable regard is had to preserving equity between different classes of taxpayer. The proposals examined by the Royal Commission all conflicted with the general proposition (and I quote words used in 1944 by Viscount Waverley when he was Chancellor of the Exchequer) that the taxable profits of industry should be 'real profits in the sense that those profits should be struck only after making all proper deductions and allowances for the amortisation of money expended on assets which are used up in the making of the profits'.

The third example, profits tax, has a double interest for me in the context of this address, first as part of the inadequate armoury for 'restraining' or 'controlling' inflationary tendencies in the economy, and secondly because of its more general and far-reaching effects in encouraging the adoption of a pattern of business structure which does not appear to me to be the most suitable for a country as fully exposed as ours to the full vigour of international competition. I shall revert later to this second question. The Profits Tax, which differentiates between distributed and non-distributed profits, was first introduced in 1947. The differential element is introduced by imposing tax at the full rate on all the chargeable profits in each accounting period and then granting substantial relief from the full rate in respect of that part of the profits which is not distributed. There are most complicated provisions designed to prevent profits not distributed, and granted relief in one period, from reaching shareholders subsequently in any form without an additional tax charge being made; so that companies go on from year to year accumulating a heavy potential charge, the amount of which can never be ascertained and communicated to the shareholders in the annual accounts, since the conditions in which some part of it will later on be converted into an actual tax demand cannot be predicted. The profits tax is inequitable as between different businesses, and between one taxpayer and another, because it fails to allow for differences in capital structure. A business with preference shares must pay the preference dividend in full, although these dividends are distributed profits on which the full rate of profits tax is charged. These tax payments in respect of the preference dividends are therefore an additional charge on the equity of the business, and the ordinary shareholders may reasonably complain that the profits available for them ought not to be charged with tax on profits paid out to somebody else. Because of differences in capital structure, businesses which are equally free to make profits are not treated on an equal basis when it comes to distributing them. So long as this continues, new companies will be encouraged in the future to vary their capital structure from what would otherwise be the most economical method of attracting capital. Taken by itself, this cannot be wise.

The introduction of the differential treatment of distributed and non-distributed profits was intended partly to raise tax revenues, and partly to act as a deterrent against 'inflationary spending' by ordinary shareholders. Whether company expenditure by ploughing back profits contributes any less to the general rise in prices than the expenditure or outside investment of the same amount of money by shareholders, had the profits been distributed, is in itself debatable. Retained profits may or may not be ploughed back, dependent upon the company's view of economic prospects for its kind of business. Other factors, such as purchase taxes levied on its products, may seriously reduce its opportunities for profitably expanding the scale of the activities which it was established to engage upon. It cannot in any case be assumed that further expansion of a particular business is the best use to which individual shareholders would devote the profits. Mere retention of the undistributed profit is no solution: if the company cannot put them to fruitful use, let alone the most fruitful use, it is clearly better that they be distributed. There would then be at least a chance that they will not be wasted.

Just as the rise in prices caused by monetary inflation deters money saving, so also the differential profits tax discourages saving for investment. Market values of shares are depressed and the reduced return on investment makes the general public less willing to supply additional capital. The Royal Commission recommended a year ago that the differential rates should be brought to an end. In his wisdom, and in his desire to continue the attempt to restrain inflation rather than stop it, the Chancellor has in his recent Budget raised both the profits tax on distributed profits from 27½ to 30 per cent and the much lower tax on undistributed profits from 2½ to 3 per cent. A company which maintains its former dividend, in the hope of encouraging the public to save and invest more capital in it, now has less itself to plough back than before.

The profits tax accentuates an anomaly which has been present in our system of taxing business enterprise ever since the introduction of highly progressive scales of income tax and surtax. The profits tax applies only to companies (with profits in excess of £2000), and not at all to individual businesses. That in itself may have a distorting influence, however slight, on business structure. On the other hand, individual proprietors of a business who are liable to surtax and who wish to retain part of their profits in the business must bear not only income tax (as of course do companies) but also surtax on the amount retained. A company can set aside out of profits for developing its business as much as it likes without any question of surtax arising. The result is that equity shareholders who are substantial surtax payers have a special incentive to acquiesce in the progressive expansion of the range and scale of activity of existing businesses in which they hold shares, rather than insist on a larger distribution in order that they might re-invest profits earned in one company in other new or more promising enterprises. They are encouraged to keep more and more eggs in existing baskets – or, should I say, in existing but expanding incubators. As the incubators expand, does as large a proportion of the eggs hatch out, and do the larger broods of chickens develop into the most useful and vigorous kinds of birds?

The ordinary shareholder who pays a high rate of surtax will be left with a very small amount of his share of the profits if they are distributed, and his main concern is to see that the resultant gain in capital appreciation of his holdings when the profits are retained for use in the company is at least greater than that amount. From his standpoint, comparison of the profitability of the use of retained profits with what it might have been if the same amount could have been distributed and wholly invested elsewhere is irrelevant; the surtax liability rules that possibility out. Company taxation coupled with highly progressive taxation on personal incomes may therefore have led to serious waste of scarce capital by encouraging an overall misdirection of investment. Differential profits tax, by adding a further potent deterrent to distribution, greatly increases the danger of maldistribution of scarce capital by extending the same indifference as to where it is invested to all ordinary shareholders, irrespective of whether or not they are liable to high rates of surtax. A serious doubt therefore arises whether all of the spectacular growth of existing companies and their satellites, relative to the multiplication of independent companies and individual businesses, has really promoted the overall and continuing prosperity of the country. As regards transfers of profits between associated companies, I do not at the moment remember, if indeed I was ever entirely clear, how the highly complex tax rules determine liability to the full rate of profits as affecting wholly owned subidiaries of a single group, subsidiaries with minority interests of independent shareholders, subsidiaries jointly owned, or mainly owned, by two or more groups, and so on; but by and large the profits tax undoubtedly encourages concentration of the control of a growing proportion of the business enterprise of this country in fewer hands than hitherto.

It seems to me therefore very desirable that we should keep clear in our minds the conditions in which the continued expansion of large existing businesses contributes to the increase in national prosperity and the conditions in which it is unlikely to do so.

The governing consideration is the gains from specialisation through the division of labour, both between individuals and between business concerns. They have been generally exploited, though not universally understood, for thousands of years. The Greeks wrote about them. They were set out, two centuries before Christ, by the Jewish writer Ben-Sira in a charming, if undemocratic, passage in Chapter 38 of *Ecclesiasticus*, preserved for us in the *Apocrypha*. The most notable formal analysis and exposition is still that with which Adam Smith opened his *Inquiry into the Nature and Causes of the Wealth of Nations* (Chapters I–IV). The first sentence of Chapter I of Book I reads: 'The greatest improvement in the productive powers of labour, and the greater part of the skill, dexterity and judgment with which it is anywhere directed, or applied, seem to be the effects of the division of labour.' Adam Smith believed that too much of the differences in capacity and achievement of different people in their prime is attributed to differences in their natural talents; that they are, much more generally than is commonly supposed, the effects rather than the cause of the division of labour. That is the materialist case for supporting the democratic insistence on equality of opportunity. He showed that the division of labour arises from the human propensity to trade, and is facilitated by the existence of a monetary unit which people will accept as a convenient medium of exchange and a dependable store of value. He explained how the breaking down of production into specialised operations simplifies the introduction of mechanical aids to labour, and the application of power-driven appliances. But he showed also that it is limited by the extent of the market, that is, of the opportunity to trade.

Every art is perfected by practice, which means constant repetition of appropriate routine, concentration of the faculties on a limited range of tasks, and the conscious decision to adopt suitable habits of work.

What begins as arduous effort, requiring close concentration, ends in the almost effortless mastery of an acquired skill or dexterity. Habit overcomes fatigue, promotes infallibility within the range of its context, and releases strain. The art of administration and management, at whatever level, is no exception: skill in these arts depends largely on appropriate specialisation, and on adopting and developing the appropriate habits of work.

The normal condition for the sustained and profitable growth of business concerns is specialisation. It allows the exploitation of the very considerable internal economies of scale, and these economies permit penetration into more distant markets, in order to secure the requisite volume of turnover, by more than offsetting the transport costs of distribution. These internal economies are dependent on specialisation of personnel and equipment, which involves high 'indivisible' costs, and they frequently depend not only on specialisation, but also on standardisation of the product. To take only one example, probably the main economy introduced by the great multiple-store concerns is the cost of buying standardised stock. When market surveying reveals a strong probability that a vast section of the consuming public will prefer a standard article, provided that its price is sufficiently low, the trading concern may be able to spread the costs of studying the market, determining the standard and organising the supply over millions instead of hundreds of units. The additional cost of the expensive buying department becomes infinitesimal, per unit sold, and is far outweighed by overall economy obtained.

Standardisation of products of course imports new risks of its own, risks of expensive errors due to miscalculation of the market situation and of the alertness of competitors. In a well-developed market, these risks can be shared by contractual arrangements between the many specialist concerns which normally participate in the various aspects and stages of production and distribution of the commodity.

I am well aware that some people will maintain that these broad generalisations are too simple and no longer square with the facts. It may be objected, for instance, that the acceleration in the speed of technological change, coupled with the vast scale of capital investment which is now necessary in specific plant and equipment, have so increased the magnitude of the risks due to obsolescence and changing demand, that financial prudence alone requires many industrial concerns to reject narrow specialisation in favour of the deliberate diversification not merely of their investments, as in the case of investment trusts, but also of their production. And notable examples will be instanced which apparently uphold the objection.

For my own part, I am satisfied with the adequacy of the classical explanation. Adam Smith provided a master key which still unlocks many doors and admits the light of better understanding. Specialisation, he said, is limited by the extent of the market; and the market is neither ubiquitous nor homogeneous. External economies are not equally available to a concern whenever it has to operate, either in the product markets or in the markets for the factors of production. For that reason, concerns with branch establishments in relatively undeveloped areas must often be content to be much more self-sufficient, or integrated, in those regions, if they are to do business there at all, than they need to be elsewhere; and their unit costs will be so much greater. The scale of output which, from the standpoint of unit costs, best suits the main activity of a concern may, for instance, be much too small for the most efficient production of many components or ancillary requirements. Many engineering firms, for instance, prefer not to have to operate their own steel foundry, and very few would wish to make standard nuts and bolts. In some regions they may have to do more than they wish, until the local market is sufficiently developed to permit specialist component manufacturers to operate on a larger scale and at lower costs, relieve them of these preoccupations and enable them to concentrate more fully on their main activity.

Similar reasoning, I believe, adequately explains the behaviour of some large industrial concerns which integrate under their control a large range of discrete and separable activities. On the one hand, they engage in the manufacture of specialised and often standardised products, which constitutes their main revenue-earning activity. On this side, the markets for production factors and components, and for the sale of products in perhaps a semi-finished condition to be worked up by other concerns, are sufficiently developed to allow them to specialise on the tasks which can be combined at the optimum scale of output from the standpoint of cost minimisation. On the other side of their activities, however, they are looking to their own future: developing new products whose potential applications are still uncertain and whose technological specifications have still to reveal themselves in a reasonably stabilised condition. Until these uncertainties are ironed out the market arrangements which allow specialisation are usually non-existent, and the concern promoting the new development may find it necessary to cumber itself with the manufacture of components and special supplies at one end, and the working up of its product into various new forms of final commodities at the other end, until such time as the production process is established and the new product is reasonably assured. Thereafter the concern will normally encourage independent manufacturers to assist by taking over all the functions which are better performed on a different scale from that which is appropriate to its own preferred specialisation. The appropriate market organisation emerges. That at any rate seems to have been the course of evolution in the motor-car, aluminium, radio, television, chemical and similar industries.

On this occasion I must, for more than one reason, content myself by doing no more than mention, for the sake of completeness, a third consideration which leads some concerns to expand by continually integrating new activities into their sphere of interests. It is the belief, mistaken or otherwise, that it will pay them to obtain a dominating status in a section of the economy, even at the cost of foregoing the advantages of specialisation. They may aim at securing and maintaining for themselves a degree of monopoly power to control the supplies and prices of what they sell or buy. The things done by such concerns, as a result of, or for the purpose of preserving these powers, are matters which affect the public interest, and are at this time of great interest to the Government. They are, moreover, matters on which party politicians are apt to take opposing views. As I myself am not one of those who believes that professorial duties mix well with active participation in party politics, and since in any case this is not an appropriate occasion to attempt the experiment, I will merely echo in this context some words of Thomas Carlyle, 'Brothers, I am sorry I have got no Morrison's Pill for curing the maladies of society.'

I conclude, therefore, that because the effects of our taxation arrangements are to encourage the concentration of control of a growing proportion of business enterprise in fewer hands, and that they do so by promoting further integration rather than specialisation of the expanding concerns, the result is a tendency to reduced overall efficiency. Even in highly specialised businesses, when they exceed a certain size, the boards of directors and committees of top executives have difficulty in finding time to give adequate consideration to all the matters which ought not to be delegated, and on which early decisions must be reached. The more 'integrated' the affairs of the concern, the greater the number of discrete questions which require attention at the top level; and, the more varied the problems, the slower and the more fallible the decisions. The load on the management is increased and its efficiency impaired. The agenda paper becomes over-congested, and important decisions have to be left to the discretion of subordinates. That is abdication from control. An element of mitigation but no ultimate solution is afforded by the creation of subsidiary companies, for there will frequently be conflict between the interests of the parent company and the aspirations of the subsidiaries, and between the interests of subsidiaries themselves. Restrictions imposed by the parent, in its own interest, on developments which would be profitable to a subsidiary are frustrating to those who manage the subsidiary and who are naturally anxious to exploit its potentialities and market opportunities to the full. Once the representatives of dependencies are unanimously agreed that their reasonable aspirations are being frustrated, self-government and independence are usually not long delayed. So also with business subsidiaries; when the relations between the back-seat driver and the man at the wheel become intolerable to both, it may be better that they should separate before they cease to be friends, so that each can be free to go his own way. Unfortunately, our tax arrangements, although they do not forbid divorce, make it very expensive to contemplate. They therefore tend to put a premium on business inefficiency, and on the wasteful investment of new capital saved from profits. It is high time they were reviewed by the tax authorities, from the standpoint of their effect on the administration of business.

CHAPTER 7

# Engineering in an expanding economy*

As an economist, and particularly as one of the Honorary Secretaries of the Royal Economic Society, I greatly appreciate the honour of the invitation to deliver the 1959 Graham Clark Lecture, instituted under the combined auspices of the three great Institutions of Civil, Mechanical, and Electrical Engineers. As a person, I am very conscious of my unworthiness, for although my first years of gainful employment were spent in the management of two mechanical engineering concerns (both of which still happily survive) I am in fact a renegade from the ranks of engineering, having allowed myself to be lured away by the appeal of that even deeper mystery, the science of economics. Subsequent to my desertion, I discovered that I had merely followed a trail blazed over the past century or more by a number of far more illustrious predecessors.

We economists should indeed remember with gratitude the contributions to the development of analytical economics made during the nineteenth century by mathematicians, natural scientists, and engineers. The debt is substantial. The expansion of the economy of Western Europe was accompanied by a rapid increase in specialisation in many walks of life, at the cost of a growing separation between the worlds of business and scholarship, and between scholars themselves. As knowledge increased, and methods of investigation and research were refined, study in depth became more immediately rewarding to the intellect, newly equipped with specific tools designed for particular rather than general application, than the vain endeavour to attain universal or all-embracing omniscience. The growing danger, then as now, was excessive inbreeding and insufficient cross-fertilisation.

* Fifth Graham Clark Lecture, Institution of Mechanical Engineers, 1959.

Engineers – I refer solely to their intellectual activity – are a virile and lusty body of men, with a marked propensity for cross-fertilisation, and political economy is not alone among the new sciences, which sprang from the old schools of moral and natural philosophy, in the enrichment it owes to the attentions of roving engineers. The founders of the science of political economy were for the most part University scholars, men of high intellectual attainment reared in the traditional schools of moral philosophy, jurisprudence, the classics and history, rather than of natural philosophy and mathematics. In the spirit of their age, they were fired by noble aspirations for the material and social amelioration of common people. A new era of material progress in the rapidly expanding exchange economy was being ushered in by the industrial revolution and the quickening and cheapening of transport; and the political economists of the classical school sought to interpret the significant changes taking place by analysing the conditions and causes which influence and determine wealth, the level of individual and communal well-being. Their success in establishing the new science on broadly unassailable general principles can perhaps be attributed to three main factors: their remarkable subtlety and intellectual power in the field of logical analysis, their compelling elegance and skill in the art of literary exposition, and the collaboration of knowledgeable men of business and affairs, like David Ricardo, who were able and eager to apply their time and minds to the elaboration of basic theory relevant to their fields of economic activity. The political economists were not content merely to establish the unassailable laws of their new science. They were also enthusiastic propagandists for the reform of market institutions and national economic policy. Their analysis demonstrated conclusively that the rapid expansion of the exchange economy was conducive to general betterment, and yet that expansion was so hampered by sectional resistance and ill-founded national economic policy that the economists conceived it to be an inescapable part of their public duty to expose the logical errors underlying prevailing misconceptions. In the sphere of political reform, the utilitarian criterion of the attainment of the greatest happiness of the greatest number provided an attractive banner under which to rally the men of goodwill who were not content to allow sectional privilege to stand in the way of general material and social amelioration. By the middle of the nineteenth century the political philosophy to which the economists gave their scientific support had won the day. The more egregious errors of illogical reasoning on economic problems had been exposed, and the old obstacles to material advance of the common man largely removed by legislative reforms and by the general recognition of the benefits already accruing from freer and wider markets. Eminent economists began to express the view that little fundamental new work remained to be done in establishing the basic principles of their science. The truth rather was that the tools of the political economists were no longer adequate, except in the hands of men with quite unusual insight and imagination, for the fundamental work that still remained to be tackled.

> . . . All was not light.
> It did not last. The Devil howling 'Ho!
> Let Einstein be' restored the status quo.

The devil's disciples were mathematicians, natural scientists and, not least, engineers. They became interested in the economic laws of supply and demand, which are essentially quantitative, at least in the sense of being concerned with relative magnitudes, with things being greater or less; and, being what they were, they found the existing literary expositions of these laws both lacking in precision and unduly prolix. They proceeded to analyse economic relationships afresh, using mathematical symbols and methods.

I trust that this audience will be a little interested in a brief account of some of the outstanding men who were responsible for this development, and of what they achieved. Academic economists were slow to follow the lead with sufficient enthusiasm, and this failure is the more regrettable because they had gladly accepted assistance in the 1830s from an eminent precursor, the mathematician and mechanician Charles Babbage, who devoted so much of his life to the construction of machines for calculating and printing mathematical tables, and to devising an analytical punched-card machine to evaluate automatically any mathematical formula. To economists his name continues to be revered for three things: First, for his book *On the Economy of Machinery and Manufactures*, published in 1832, which is still read as a model analytical and descriptive account of the emerging structure of British industry. Second, it is mainly to his timely initiative and cheerful contravention of standing orders and the formal rules of procedure of the British Association for the Advancement of Science, at the Cambridge meeting in 1833, that economists and statisticians owe the creation of what is now Section F, covering Economic Science and Statistics. Third, he was one of the leading promoters in 1834 of the London Statistical Society, now the Royal Statistical Society. His enthusiasm for the collection and analysis of statistical data stimulated the trend towards quantitative economic research by attracting to this field a new type of scholar who possessed the requisite specialist aptitude and training.

The application of mathematical methods of analysis in the field of economic theory was a European rather than solely British development. The outstanding pioneer was undoubtedly Augustin A. Cournot, a French professor of mathematics at Lyons and subsequent Rector of the Academies of Grenoble and Dijon, who in 1838, at the age of 37, published his *Researches into the Mathematical Principles of the Theory of Wealth*. He had no intention of questioning the overall benefits accruing from an expanding economy.

> The progress of nations in the commercial system is a fact in which all discussion of its desirability becomes idle. . . . Experience unquestionably shows that this is true, in most cases, since, in general, an incontestable improvement in the condition of the people has kept pace with an equally incontestable increase in the sum total of wealth in circulation.

Unfortunately, economic theory at the stage it had then reached 'is unable to explain why this usually happens and is still less able to demonstrate that it must always continue to occur'. What troubled him as a mathematical scientist was the possibility that the *first effect* of the creation of a wider exchange economy might be, by reducing the aggregate incomes hitherto accruing to monopolists in regions previously isolated, to diminish the mass values in circulation in those regions. He therefore urged:

> Let us avoid confounding what is in the domain of accurate reasoning with what is the object of a more or less happy guess; what is rational with what is empirical. It is enough to have to guard against errors in logic on the first score; let us avoid encountering passionate declamations and insoluble questions on the other.

Cournot proceeded in his book to apply to the theory of wealth the forms and symbols of mathematical analysis. He foresaw that by doing so he was likely at the outset to draw on himself the condemnation of theorists of repute, but he urged that their aversion to mathematics arose from a misapprehension of the nature of the applications of mathematical analysis. They imagined that the use of symbols and formulas could only lead to numerical calculations, and they knew that the subject was not suited to such a numerical determination of value by theory alone. 'But,' said Cournot, 'those skilled in mathematical analysis know that its object is not simply to calculate numbers, but that it is also employed to find the relations between magnitudes which cannot be expressed in numbers and between *functions* whose law is not capable of algebraic expression.' In his book he set out to show that the solution of the general questions which arise from the theory of wealth depends essentially on that branch of analysis which comprises arbitrary functions, which are merely restricted to satisfying certain conditions; and for his purpose the first principles of the differential and integral calculus sufficed. His final prefatory remarks will commend themselves to many professional economists in our own time:

> I am far from having thought of writing in support of any system, and from joining the banners of any party; I believe that there is an immense step in passing from theory to governmental applications; I believe that theory loses none of its value in thus remaining preserved from contact with impassioned polemics; and I believe, if this essay is of any practical value, it will be chiefly in making clear how far we are from being able to solve, with full knowledge of the case, a multitude of questions which are boldly decided every day.

In brief, what Cournot did in his book was to exhibit mathematically the theory of value in an exchange economy, proceeding from the most simple to progressively more complex conditions. He began with a single monopoly situation, with one seller of a natural product which involved no costs of production. Second, he made the monopoly subject to taxation. Third, he introduced a second independent competing monopolist offering the same natural product. He demonstrated how profits are maximised, fourth, when producers are offering different products and have to incur production costs; and fifth, when an expanding economy brings into communication markets which were previously isolated from each other. Finally, he sought to establish what can be accurately said about the determinants of social incomes, and of variations in social incomes, inside an economic system. The conclusions reached by his mathematical analysis were set out in literary form, and an appendix exhibited in ten sets of curves the first graphical representations which we possess of demand and supply phenomena as revealed by his analysis.

For a generation the work of Cournot made no impact on the orthodox economists in any country. In France, indeed, almost a century passed before he was generally recognised as a prophet, so that we English may derive some relative satisfaction from the knowledge that our own pioneers in the application of mathematical methods to economic analysis were only one generation behind Cournot. English economists, however, are bound to admit that the two pioneer Englishmen were an eminent engineer and a student of mathematics and natural science who turned to political economy. The engineer was Henry Charles Fleeming Jenkin (1833–85), Professor of Engineering in University College, London (1865), and in Edinburgh (from 1868). Fleeming Jenkin makes no reference to Cournot, and there is no evidence that he knew of Cournot's economic writings: but it must be recorded that he lived in Paris as a boy and went to school there, at the time of the 1848 revolution, and moved on with his family to Genoa, where he studied natural sciences at the University. While at Edinburgh, between 1868 and the time of his death, he completed five papers on aspects of political economy, the most significant being that published in 1870 under the title 'The graphical representation of the laws of supply and demand, and their application to labour'. Both the underlying philosophy and the content of this essay are strongly reminiscent of Cournot. I will quote only the opening sentences:

> Recent discussions on the laws determining the price of commodities seem to show that these laws are neither so well understood nor so clearly expressed in the writings of economists as is sometimes supposed. Men are too much in the habit of speaking of laws of political economy, without attaching to the word law the same rigid meaning which it bears in physical sciences. There are, however, some truths concerning the subjects treated by the economist which do deserve the name of laws, and admit of being stated as accurately, and defined in the same manner, as any mathematical laws affecting quantities of any description.
>
> The following essay is an attempt to state in this rigorous

manner some propositions concerning the market price of commodities, using what is known as the graphic method of curves to illustrate the laws and propositions as they arise.

Fleeming Jenkin's contribution was to clarify by graphical representation the concept of quantities offered – the supply – and quantities demanded – the demand – being 'functions of the price', supply and demand both probably varying with the price; and he drew illustrative demand and supply curves. He developed three propositions: first, that the market price of a commodity is that at which the supply and demand curves cut; second, that changes in supply and in demand conditions will have different effects on market price; and third, that in the case of manufactured products the *price* in the long run is chiefly determined by the cost of production, and the *quantity* manufactured is chiefly determined by the demand at that price.

A year later, in a paper published in the Proceedings of the Royal Society of Edinburgh (1871–2), Fleeming Jenkin applied similar graphical methods to elucidate 'The incidence of taxes', and ventured to fortify his reasoning with a little recourse to algebra and the calculus. In extenuation he made reference to the 'much more complex algebraic representation' and integration curves which W. Stanley Jevons had used in his *Theory of Political Economy*, published in 1871. Jevons had studied mathematics and natural science at University College, London, but had migrated to Owen's College, Manchester, as Professor of Political Economy. He was the first professor of economics to insist on the need to develop economics as a mathematical science. He used mathematical analysis mainly to explore the implications for general theory of the concept of diminishing utility derived by the individual from successive increments of physically similar units of wealth. That concept had provided Tom Paine, as early as 1792, with the foundation for his proposal, in Part II of *The Rights of Man*, for sharply progressive rates of income tax and estate duty, and had been explored by Jeremy Bentham in his adumbration of the 'maximisation' process as a key to human behaviour. The genius and scientific training of Jevons produced from it his final utility theory of value which became the starting point from which marginal analysis has developed.

I have by no means done with my theme of the responsibility which engineers and natural scientists must share for making economics what it is today. As I have said, Cournot had been uneasy about the way in which the classical school of political economy had concentrated on the implications of competitive exchange in developed economies, and he used his mathematics to explore the transition from monopoly to competition. In active competition, as they defined it, a single price for a commodity applied equally to all buyers and sellers, since none of them operated on a sufficient scale to influence the ruling price. A manufacturer's receipts from sales were therefore proportionate to output – the marginal and the average revenues were identical. Similarly the consumer's outlays were strictly proportionate to the quantities he bought – his marginal and average expenditures were identical. Marginal changes were much more significant, however, in the behaviour of monopolists, and Cournot was not alone in being concerned about monopoly situations. Mathematically trained engineers were increasingly, in the nineteenth century, involved professionally in the administration of public utilities, of water supply, roads, canals and railways, all of which operated under conditions of continuing monopoly.

One such was A. J. Étienne-Juvénal Dupuit (1804–66), who held the government office in France of Inspecteur-Général des Ponts et Chaussées, and whose duties led him to reflect upon the utility of these services to the public and the means of measuring these benefits with precision, as a basis for ascertaining the prices to be charged. He published two papers, in the *Annales des Ponts et Chaussées*, one in 1844 on the 'Measurement of utility of public works', and the second 'On the influence of tolls on the utility of communication services', dealing with the special problem of pricing the services of public utilities with heavy fixed costs and low operating expenses. His conclusion was that a government, seeking a minimum return to meet fixed charges and concerned at the same time to ensure the maximum advantage to the public, would in general impose a different scale of charges from that levied by a monopoly aiming at a maximum aggregate net revenue. His contributions have greatly influenced subsequent economic analysis, and it must be confessed that little significant advance has been made on his own findings. His defence of mathematical analysis was sturdy: 'When one cannot know something, much is already achieved by realising one's ignorance.'

A second mathematician and natural scientist, at the time residing, for reasons of prudence, in Paris, was the prolific author Professor the Reverend Dionysius Lardner (1793–1859), a scholar of Trinity College,

Dublin, who had occupied the Chair of Natural Philosophy at University College, London. In 1850 he published a treatise on Railway Economy, in which he devoted two chapters (12 and 13) to the analysis of costs and the fixing of charges. He insisted on the need for separating fixed from variable costs, and attributing as precisely as possible to each distinguishable class of traffic that share of the expense for which the particular traffic is responsible. 'Although,' he wrote, '. . . it may not be expedient in all cases to exact from the various objects of traffic the same proportion of profit, yet . . . it can never be right, as a permanent measure, to transport any object of traffic at a loss. . . . Important as such an investigation is, it has never been attempted by the managers of English railways. We are indebted, however, to some foreign engineers and economists for inquiries on this subject'; and he gives an account of the publications of a number of French and Belgian railway engineers. On tariff policy, Lardner introduces mathematical reasoning and graphical presentation with originality and success. The problem as he saw it was to ascertain for each class of traffic the tariff which would yield maximum net profit, and it was therefore necessary to study the relation between variations in aggregate receipts and aggregate costs for each class. As regards gross receipts, he observed that if the unit charge were zero there would be much traffic but no revenue, while at the other extreme if the unit charge were prohibitive there would be no traffic and again no revenue. At some point to be ascertained, between these two extremes, aggregate receipts would be maximised. Turning to costs, he showed that these did not change at a constant rate as the volume of traffic changed. The optimum tariff for each class was therefore that which adjusted the volume of traffic to the point where the distance between the aggregate receipt curve and the aggregate cost curve was greatest, and he showed geometrically that this point was located where the tangents to the two curves were parallel. Lardner's methods became part of the standard equipment in the 'tool box' of economists of later years, and he has good cause to be remembered also with gratitude by all monopolists.

A generation later another prominent engineer turned his attention to mathematical economics, this time in Germany. W. Launhardt was a railway engineer who had for many years been Director of the Technical High School at Hanover when he published, in 1885, his *Mathematical Foundations of Economics*. He also was primarily concerned to find a solution to the pricing problems of railways and public utilities. To that end he studied comprehensively the new contributions to the utility theory of value, from Cournot onwards. His own researches led him to reject the conclusion which Lardner had reached that the objective of railway and public utility pricing should be to maximise monopoly profits, and he sought to demonstrate that tariffs should be based on marginal costs, leaving any deficiency in the recoupment of the full costs incurred in installing fixed investments in equipment to be met by subsidies from taxation. After his treatise had appeared, the nature of the pricing problems involved in the administration of nationalised undertakings was at last clearly defined. We now know also that we do not know the answers.

I have said that Jevons, working in England in the 1860s and unacquainted with the publications of continental writers, was the first professional economist to use mathematics. It must, however, be acknowledged that he also was the son and grandson of engineers in business in Liverpool, and by education a mathematician and natural scientist, with five years of workshop experience when, as a very young man, he was employed as assayer in the Mint at Sydney, New South Wales. It seems to me to be no accident that Jevons's counterparts in Switzerland, the two renowned economists who established the worldwide reputation of the Lausanne School (in which general economic equilibrium analysis was systematised by the use of mathematical techniques) were also previously connected with railways. They were Leon Walras (1834–1910) and Vilfredo Pareto (1848–1923). Walras was educated in France as a mathematician and natural scientist, and it was due to the influence of his father, the economist Auguste Walras, who had been at school with Cournot, that Leon turned to economics. Unfortunately for him, the hostility to mathematical methods of the strongly entrenched classical political economists barred his way to academic appointment in France, and he worked for a time in railway administration. It was Lausanne which gave him his opportunity by appointing him, in 1870, to a newly created chair of political economy. Leon Walras's *Elements of Pure Political Economy* appeared in instalments in the years 1874–7. The task which he set himself was to provide a comprehensive mathematical analysis of a system of general equilibrium in a perfectly competitive market. His successor in the chair, when he retired in 1893 on account of ill-health, was Vilfredo Pareto, an Italian of noble birth. Pareto also had been a student of engineering, mathematics and natural sciences at the University of Turin before embarking on an industrial career in which he occupied an important administration post on the Italian railways. Under the influence of the Italian professor of economics, Pantaleoni, a somewhat younger contemporary, he was attracted to the field of mathematical economics and to the theory of general equilibrium which Leon Walras was engaged upon. His *Course in Political Economy* appeared in 1896 and his *Manual* in 1909.

By the turn of the century, mathematical analysis was generally accepted as the most precise and convenient technique for the investigation of some important branches of economic theory. In England the attitude of professional economists had changed in thirty years from opposition to acceptance and, in notable instances, to enthusiastic conversion. The giants who had wrought this change, following Jevons, were P. H. Wicksteed, F. Y. Edgeworth and, greatest of all, Alfred Marshall. Jevons's *Theory* irritated Marshall in the early 1870s, but Marshall was too good a mathematician and too dedicated a scientist to allow prejudice to warp his fine mind and judgment to the extent of rejecting tools which he was particularly competent to use. The mathematical appendices and footnotes to his *Principles of Economics*, first published in 1890, were analytically of great significance, and his development of the concepts of marginal revenue and marginal expenses of production in these sections of subsequent editions are the main source of the ideas on which later English economists have based their own contributions. Yet Marshall apparently retained to the end the opinion which he expressed in 1872 that, with scarcely an exception, all that is important in the reasoning and results which we owe to mathematical economists was capable of being expressed in ordinary language, and neither mathematics nor graphical representation was ever allowed to intrude into the main body of the text of his *Principles*. For that reason, his immediate personal influence as a teacher was far wider, despite a certain prolixity of style, than that of either Walras or Pareto.

And now I really have done with this theme. I have not wished to attempt to communicate to you the findings of economics, but only to persuade you that engineers in the past century have played a notable part in making the science what it is. I have done so partly to acknowledge a debt, but partly also in the hope of rallying your strong support for the joint efforts which economists and engineers are now making on both sides of the Atlantic, in University graduate schools and institutes of research, to organise a unified attack on the current problems of industrial dynamics. I shall return to this topic later on.

## Relation between changes in material prosperity and activity in engineering and allied industries

Bearing in mind the title of my address, it is time I now invited you to reflect for a while on the relation between changes in general material prosperity and the level of activity in the engineering and allied industries. I assume that an expanding economy normally means an increase in the average real income per head of the population. In a free economy a rising *per capita* income normally results in an increase in consumption of goods and services, which in turn generates an increased demand for engineering products. Even at the level of final consumption, however, the situation can be complicated. A given rate of expansion overall does not necessarily imply the same proportionate change throughout all sections of the economy. When we say that the standard of life in this country can be doubled in a generation, we do not mean that our children will each want two coffins instead of one, or twice as many kitchen ovens, or even twice the size of helping at their Christmas dinner. The size of population is not likely to remain constant, and if it did the age distribution is likely to change, so that even if old and young did not change their wants, the pattern of aggregate demand would vary. In fact, consumption tastes do change drastically over time in the same locality. Moreover, an economy which expands by bringing overseas territories within the orbit of the free exchange system will throw up a very different consumption pattern from that of the population of Britain. In many regions, a higher income per head will certainly mean that more children will survive, whatever happens to the numbers born, and the population will grow, with more dependants to be supported by each earner of income. In some regions there may be earlier marriages, more separate households, and a larger demand for durable household equipment, which will interest engineering concerns. An increase in *per capita* income can therefore mean large variations in the relative demands for the various objects of consumption, according to what is called the income elasticity of demand for each class in each community. All of this keeps market surveying people quite busy trying to forecast for their industrial clients the probable aggregate demand for domestic installations, for public utility services, and for out-of-home facilities such as transport vehicles and services, schools, hospitals, shops, restaurants, entertainments, and so on.

Many of the engineering products acquired or used by the general public are capable of being shared, which means that habits of life affect appreciably the numbers and the types required. Households may acquire cars or rely on public transport; they may install washing machines or use a laundrette service, home television sets or cinemas. Each household may have its own heating equipment, or, in blocks of flats, be served by one central installation. A rising *per capita* income may mean that more people will prefer the convenience of owning rather than sharing some kinds of equipment, particularly if instalment purchase facilities are not controlled, and the equipment makers will sell more units to meet a given aggregate user.

Of perhaps greater importance to the engineering industry is the fact that its products sold to the general public are mainly consumers' durable equipment. Many consumers' goods, such as a match or a glass of beer, are completely destroyed by the act of consumption; so that a steady continuing demand means that replacement orders are identical with the volume of consumption plus, in the case of perishables, normal distribution and storage wastages. Durable equipment is capable of yielding a flow of service throughout its productive life. A new durable commodity, such as a television set, which quickly becomes a necessity in many homes, can easily spell boom conditions for the concerns which produce it, lasting perhaps until most of the potential users are equipped; but the greater the durability of the equipment, the greater also will be the fall in annual demand when the saturation point is reached and orders are confined mainly to replacements. Moreover, in the case of consumers' durable equipment, the rate of replacement is in general likely to be much slower than in the case of industrial equipment. Competitive forces compel many producers to replace deteriorating equipment before it is completely worn out, and still more to install more efficient types which reduce unit costs of production or give a service of better quality, and, as they use the equipment for business purposes, they can often look to increased sales to finance the replacement and cover the costs of obsolescence. The general public who acquire durable equipment are under no such compulsion and may cling affectionately to antiquated types so long as their inefficiency can be tolerated. The installation of a new or better replacement would no doubt give greater satisfaction, but it often does nothing to increase the flow of disposable income of the householder. It therefore usually involves him in additional outlay which cannot be recovered. If times are hard, replacement of consumers' durables may be postponed indefinitely, failing a complete breakdown. The fluctuations in the orders received by the suppliers can therefore be very wide. To counter this tendency, high-pressure salesmanship may press suppliers to introduce fashion changes from time to time, and they have some success so far as the public life of the general public is concerned. Smith may wish to keep up with the Joneses in expenditure which is conspicuous to the Joneses, the Browns and the Robinsons – a frequent change of car, or of the interior decoration of the more public rooms in his home; but generally speaking the introduction of fashion changes in the field of consumers' durable equipment is hardly likely to achieve more than increase the rate of penetration into the poorer households through the medium of the second-hand market.

In recent times, it is probably true that consumers' durables have grown in importance relatively to producers' equipment in the aggregate sales of engineering and allied concerns, and this has provided a welcome stabilising influence on the fortunes of the concerns which have participated in this new business. The demand for machinery and other equipment used by industrial firms fluctuates more widely than that for the consumers' goods which the machinery enables them to produce. Concerns which produce things like cigarettes, newspapers, motor-spirit, soap or foodstuffs in mass quantities may use very durable specialised plant which provides a good deal of business for engineering and allied firms during the stage of initial installation, but thereafter, so long as the demand for these consumer goods remains steady, the replacement orders for plant and equipment will fall to the relatively small proportion of the total installed capacity determined by its average life. Wearing parts may on average require replacement every ten years, and complete machines much less frequently. If the industry expanded rapidly to the market saturation level, there will be a disturbing replacement cycle of orders to the extent that the initial installations fall due for renewal at about the same time, with relatively few orders passing back to the machinery makers in the intervening years. If, on the other hand, the initial expansion was more gradual, replacement orders will be more evenly spread, but will still be small in relation to the total installed capacity, because of its durability. For equipment with an average life of forty years, the annual replacement demand is 2½ per cent. In a competitive industry, each industrial concern will prefer to operate on a scale which minimises its unit costs of production and will seek to keep its equipment reasonably fully employed.

Consider, however, what may well happen when the demand for a final product increases quickly by, say, 10 per cent. The increased demand may be due to an expansion of the whole market served, or to an increase in disposable incomes of buyers in the existing market, or to a change of taste which alters the pattern of consumers' outlays from a constant income. If the existing capacity of the producers is fully employed, they may between them place orders for additional plant equivalent to 10 per cent of the total installed equipment. If the normal replacement demand is 2½ per cent, this would mean a fivefold once-for-all increase in the order books of the equipment manufacturers, generated by a rise of only 10 per cent in the demand for the final product.

An equivalent fall in the level of final consumption can be even more disturbing. It might be caused by a general recession throughout the market, or by the failure of consumers' real incomes to keep pace with inflation, or by the closing of an existing market, or simply by a change of taste. A 10 per cent fall in demand will render that amount of the installed capacity idle, and it will no longer be necessary or worth while to replace equipment which wears out. For four successive years the engineering industry might receive no orders even for renewals.

I have said that all this may happen. Of course there may be a good deal of backlash in the chain. Some concerns will wait to see whether an increase in demand is likely to persist, and in the meantime will build up a backlog of unfulfilled orders, or resort to costly 'over-full' capacity working of their plant. Some may have reserve capacity which they can bring in. Similarly, if orders fall off, they may prefer to run all the plant for a period on short time and continue to renew it at the normal rate, until the future position is clear. Equipment suppliers themselves when they receive a flood of new orders may build up a backlog and keep their clients waiting; and when their orders fall off they may run down their backlog of unfilled orders and keep up their normal rate of production as long as they can. But the wide fluctuation in orders for equipment is undeniable, however delayed the response may be down the line. We certainly seem to have here at least part of the explanation why fluctuations in the order books of the industrial machinery makers, and behind them of the machine-tool makers, and behind them again of some specialised branches of the steel industry which cater for the needs of the machine-tool industry, magnify in a highly geared chain the amplitude of a relatively small change in the level of demand for a final consumers' commodity.

There are often compensating fluctuations within the engineering industry itself, taken as a whole. For instance, a reduction in demand for one consumers' product, which is due merely to a change in taste in favour of another durable product, may throw up countervailing orders for new additional equipment in another section of industry which will increase activity in some branches of the machinery construction business by more than the decline in replacement orders for the section adversely affected. The evolution of the structure of the engineering and allied industries in this country probably reflects the influence of these circumstances. The many different production functions involved in making specialised machinery are widely distributed over large numbers of collaborating concerns, some large and some small, and this serves to concentrate the main impact of an adverse market movement on to the relatively few specialist firms closely and specially concerned with it. Generally speaking, these concerns have so organised their production arrangements that fluctuations can be absorbed with minimum overall disturbance. There is as much subcontracting as can perhaps be conveniently arranged throughout the industry. Castings and forgings, rolled sections, extrusions, a wide range of components, machine power-units, transmission gearing, couplings and so on can usually be bought in, either to special specification or of standard dimensions and types, from concerns which serve a large variety of specialist machinery makers. The result is that the subcontractors jointly concerned in producing complete installations can enjoy a much steadier aggregate demand for their particular products. They are concerned with a wide range of manufacture of equipment and are not in general over-dependent on the fluctuating fortunes of particular specialists. Viewed as a whole, the industry is reasonably well organised in this way to secure the economy of massed reserves of capacity, and the various specialist plant makers can draw on the common pool to a greater or less extent as circumstances require. This structure makes for an overall better utilisation of aggregate capacity and for flexibility of adjustment to changing market conditions.

The engineering industries, located as it were in the back-axle, have thus introduced a sort of 'differential box' of their own, to accommodate themselves more comfortably to changes in direction. Whether or not the whole production machine is going forward or backward, if one rear wheel has to slow down, the other quickens in sympathy. Between the back-axle and the engines are gear ratios at the various stages, each ratio fixed by the average durability of the equipment used. But the main influence which determines whether the entire machine runs steadily, or changes speed up or down, is the strength of consumer demand which provides the motive power in the engine, and we are bound to admit that the throttle is only to a very limited extent under human control. Agricultural and pastoral producers still make up a large proportion of the world's population, and their aggregate disposable income is largely and unpredictably affected by the fickleness of nature, by climatic upsets and strange epidemics, producing alternations of famine and glut and spreading disturbance throughout the economic system. The natural and applied scientists who study these elemental forces of nature have made great progress in containing them, by developing resistant strains and by laying the scientific foundations for elaborate and vast regional schemes and organisations for drought, flood and pest control and the like; but we must face the obvious fact that the level of prosperity in the world at large is still liable in the foreseeable future to be suddenly undermined by forces which are beyond human control.

Nevertheless, we have only ourselves to blame if we do not push on, while recognising our limitations, to eliminate or mitigate as fast as we can, by national action and international collaboration, the obstacles to expansion which are clearly ascribable to human folly and to nice calculations of short-term sectional advantage. It is on expansion of the whole economy that the engineering industries depend for their prosperity. An upward trend of *per capita* income need not in itself generate additional instability if national authorities work and plan together, and particularly if the governments of the richer countries in the world economy are scrupulously careful, in their economic relations with the less developed territories, to assist and not hinder the general march of progress.

It seems clear, first, that, if the poorer countries wish above all else to raise the real incomes of their people, the best general policy for most of them will be, for some time to come, to expand their production of staple commodities for export. By so doing they are far more likely to obtain by exchange more, and a wider and more diversified choice, of all the other things they need for a richer and fuller life. It is, however, true that the world prices of their exports of primary products fluctuate more widely than the world prices of their imports of manufactured goods. If the richer countries are from now on likely to be more successful than hitherto in reducing the amplitude of their own internal industrial trade cycle – and there are reasonably good grounds for the belief that they will be more successful – it seems to me to be of cardinal importance that they should, both nationally and by common international agreement, take parallel steps to stabilise as far as they can their imports of primary produce. In the world economy, the long-term interests of the richer countries are bound up with the fortunes of the poorer members, and in times of threatening recession they should at least resist the temptation to improve their own short-run prospects, at the expense of the rest, by imposing restrictions on imports, with the object of exporting their own recession to the other members of the world economy. The richer countries should no longer lay themselves open to the old charge that, whenever the United States, or Western Europe or the United Kingdom sneezes, they see to it that the rest of the world catches pneumonia.

Second, because of the dependence of the standards of life in the poorer communities on the aggregate value of their exports of primary produce, it is not surprising that they and their governments should seek to obtain greater internal stability by diversifying not only their exports but their whole economies, beginning to manufacture for themselves some of the commodities which they have hitherto imported. So long as there is a continual danger that the terms of external trade will turn sharply against them, a measure of added stability of living standards may well be preferable to precarious opulence. The richer countries should, in my view, accept the consequences of this trend and adapt their own economies to it, rather than actively hinder it by restricting the free flow of capital which would otherwise be willingly invested in these poorer territories; or, worse still, attempt to cripple the growth of these nascent industries by adopting an aggressive and subsidised selling policy against them.

Third, Britain should keep the interests of the poorer communities continually in mind when framing its own policy in relation to the newly created European Common Market. There cannot be any question that the decision to merge the six countries which signed the Rome Treaty into a closer and freer exchange economy is a great step forward, not only for their own prosperity but ultimately for the rest of the free world which trades with them. It is nevertheless very regrettable that the strenuous efforts made by the other countries of Western Europe, including the United Kingdom, to establish at the same time a Free Trade Area, which would have extended the range of that free economy and incidentally greatly enriched it, have not so far been allowed to come to fruition. The single point which I wish to make is that the alternative proposal that Britain should now itself seek to enter the Common Market (a proposal which may not commend itself to all of the Rome Treaty powers) is not one which is clearly compatible with our wider obligations and responsibilities *vis à vis* the rest of the free world in which we buy and sell. Over the past centuries our close economic ties with the Rome Treaty countries have added great strength to our own internal economy, and today one-seventh of our external trade is done with them. If we remain outside the Common Market, that mutually beneficial exchange will be impaired to the extent that the new common customs tariff surrounding the six countries is higher than it was. But the alternative of entering it, and being required to apply the same common tariff against all the rest of the world, including the poorer countries who look to us as an important export market for their primary products, would in my view be a retrograde step. The issue might be sharply described as a choice between encouraging, to the fullest extent of our power, the expansion of the wider economy of the free world as a whole, including in particular its poorest members, or sheltering inside a select European club of some of the richer countries, indifferent to the consequences of our action on the rest. There is, however, another policy open to Britain. Behind their common tariff the populations of each of the six countries will benefit from freer access to each other's products, as their internal tariffs are gradually eliminated, and their discrimination could result in their diverting to each other some exports which Britain and the rest of the outside world have been glad to continue to receive. We can prevent that diversion, so far as Britain is concerned, by behaving in that respect as though we were in the Common Market, lowering our own tariffs in line with the reductions which the six countries are committed to make to each other. At the same time we can abstain from erecting new barriers between ourselves and the rest of the world, which full membership of the Common Market would require us to do. The prospect of being on the wrong side of the tariff wall surrounding the Common Market is a regrettable change of climate in our intercourse with the Rome Treaty countries, so far as our export business is concerned, but we need not make matters even worse by not taking steps to preserve equal access to their products.

In their efforts to develop industries of their own, the poorer countries have an advantage which was not available to the richer communities when they themselves set out on the same road. They have access to the accumulated scientific and technical knowledge which the more developed countries have built up, and have already largely exploited. Moreover, as contrasted with conditions a century ago, they may draw on the experience and supplies of many different industrialised countries, and not merely of Britain and Germany. Some of the other suppliers have first-hand experience of conditions not dissimilar from those obtaining today in the newly developing regions, and their standard machinery and equipment may suit those conditions better than British models of the type which best meet the requirements of our home market. Machine and plant designs need to be adapted to the circumstances of the locality in which they are to be installed: to environmental conditions such as climate, to the peculiarities of the qualities of local materials to be processed, to the qualities of the local labour force, and to the availability of capital for industrial development. This being obviously so, it follows that it cannot always be safe for British machine producers to regard export business as an additional outlet for standard products manufactured expressly to suit the requirements of the home market. A great proportion of the export trade is likely, if it is to be fully successful, to be of custom-built machines specifically adapted to the working conditions in each localised market. For example, in many parts of Africa, industrial factories have to be manned, in the main, by migrant peasant workers who are not likely to stay for more than a few months, and who may not be counted on to return to the factory, or even to other urban employment. In such circumstances, the machines must be of a type which can be profitably operated by 'green' labour. Other industrial countries already have first-hand experience at home of problems similar to this. As regards the availability of capital, I will observe only that interest rates are very high in the poorer countries, and that less durable equipment, which is capable of a given rate of output, is usually cheaper than equipment with a longer life but only the same output rate. Faced with an acute scarcity of capital, industrialists in these poorer regions will prefer more machines with a short life to fewer of greater durability.

Britain's share of the business will depend on the readiness of our machinery producers to make a thorough study of the conditions in each market and to design and produce what is most acceptable. As I have already said, the structure of the British engineering and allied industries seems to me to be well adapted to meet the need. There are many specialist firms, well organised to give intensive high-level attention to all-important questions of detail.

## The engineer-administrator in the expanding economy

I come now to my concluding topic. Preoccupation with the dynamic problems of the expanding economy has given new and important emphasis to much current economic thinking, research and teaching. The field of static economics – the study of the process of economic adjustment in an exchange economy towards a position of general equilibrium – has, with the aid of marginal analysis, been reduced in its main essential elements to order and precision by the efforts of the logicians and mathematicians. New aids to investigation and research have now made possible a co-ordinated and systematic attack on the phenomena of economic growth. Dynamic economics is concerned with analysing the effects on the stability of an expanding economy of changes in population and in its tastes; of changes in income or output per head, due for instance to technological advance; and of changes in capital saving and investment.

The techniques of research, including the construction of simulation models, the study of 'closed circuit' or 'feed-back systems', the use of electronic computers and similar new aids, embody elements which are by no means limited in interest to, if indeed they were originated in any significant degree by, economic analysts. Mathematical engineers who participate in these economic inquiries feel, with good reason, that they are 'playing on their home ground'. It is no accident that, in the main graduate schools of the social sciences in Britain and the United States of America the leading groups of research workers and teachers concentrating in this field comprise men with basic training in mathematics and engineering as well as economics.

This new field of economic research has great significance and interest for industrial administrators. In the first place, the economic, political and social environment in which industrial concerns have to operate today is characterised by continual complex and interrelated changes of overall pattern. The administrator needs to discern quickly, interpret correctly and assess as accurately as he can this changing pattern of general trends which influence his markets, both for the sale of his products and for access to the productive resources that he requires. In the macro-economic field, economists are analysing the overall processes of economic growth and fluctuations, endeavouring to detect and isolate the elements in growth which generate fluctuations, and seeking for the criteria of human intervention which will enable these fluctuations to be eliminated, or corrected, or contained, without arresting the secular upward trend. Progress in this field holds out to the business administrator the prospect of a more equable and agreeable climate of operations, in which the quality and dependability of the economic intelligence presented to him by his market analysts will more certainly justify its cost.

In the second place, industrial administrators can look to dynamic research in the micro-economic field for great assistance in tracing the causation of endogenous fluctuations, generated within the retail, wholesale and producer chain-relationship of an industry, or within a single integrated concern, and consequent upon a single once-for-all external change such as a sudden increase in consumer-buying. Systematic quantitative research has already revealed the extent to which typical manufacturing and distributional practices generate inside an industry or concern large fluctuations in production loads, stock accumulation, instability of employment, overloading or running-down of supply pipelines, delays in delivery, and sharp reversals of the flow and magnitude of trade orders; all of which disturbances have traditionally been ascribed to external instability. In consequence inappropriate corrective measures, such as large advertising and price-discount changes have been resorted to, which have added additional cyclical disturbance, and expansions of factory plant have been put in hand, creating serious excess capacity, because of failure to realise that the wide fluctuations in machine loading were due to endogenous causes, such as internal weaknesses of organisation, structure and communications, and not to changes in external market conditions.

In the third place, graduate schools of administration are evolving a valuable analytical approach to the theory of administration within typical concerns, based on the contributions made by investigators of individual and group behaviour into motivation, influence procedure, communication processes; and projected into the problems of functional and operating relationships, the decision-making process and the arrangements and organisations by which decisions can most effectively be implemented.

I must resist the temptation to dwell on this topic, and will content myself with two simple illustrations: In planning a new engineering business to produce a standard product in mass quantities, three main sets of problems fall within the province of different specialist divisions, which somehow or other have to be induced and organised to work as one harmonious group, to produce the best overall plan. They are the product designers, who are concerned with its breakdown into component parts for production and assembly; the production engineers who plan how the many operations shall be performed and distributed over what kinds of machines, operated by what kinds of labour; and the works superintendents who are concerned with factory layout. Each specialist division can make the work of each other division more or less difficult and costly, unless the arrangements for co-ordination and securing group agreement at every stage of planning work effectively and smoothly. Much guidance and instruction can be derived from a critical and comparative analysis of detailed case studies of the organisational and planning procedures adopted in particular concerns. The second illustration is the works-management and progressing procedure of multi-product engineering concerns engaged in manufacturing large machine installations on a bespoke, individual contract basis; committed to delivery dates, and concerned to secure the best use of its wide range of common-user plant, and the greatest possible economy of working capital locked up in work-in-progress. Here again much can be learnt by graduate students from detailed examination of case studies of progressing arrangements. How successful are they in ensuring that, from the standpoint of profit maximisation, every job from the drawing office to the material acquisition, the machining and the final assembly and test is done at the last possible moment consistent with punctual delivery, while at the same time securing a steady flow of remunerative work for the most expensive plant and the most efficient and skilled workers? My own limited experience in works management was derived in a medium-size mechanical engineering business, and I well recollect the lessons I learnt about my own field when I had the opportunity to examine in detail the programming and progressing procedure adopted by an office-construction concern in clearing a congested site in the City of London and erecting a large block of offices, with very little space for the assembly of material and severe police limitations on the hours during which access of delivery trucks to the site could be permitted. Case studies drawn from a wide range of experience can provide excellent material for organised graduate training, and particularly so if they are both compiled and used by competent and expert instructors, if the numbers participating in seminar discussion are kept small enough to promote full student participation, and if each of the members of the group has had ample time to study the case thoroughly and think about it before the seminar meets.

I have at last got round, as some of you who know my background will have expected me to do, to the topic of the further education and training of young engineers in the top flight for careers in industrial administration and management. I hope that many of you share my view that the problems of the expanding economy present a challenge to some of our finest intellects, not only those concerned with matters of public policy but also those on whom the responsibility rests for directing industrial concerns. I hope also that you will agree that the education and training which engineers undergo fits them particularly for work in this field, and that the work is worthy of the attention of some of the best men coming forward, scarce and valuable as good engineers always are. Many of them are attracted by the idea of making a career eventually in general management, and readily avail themselves of the opportunities now afforded them, in the final stages of their undergraduate education, to acquire some understanding of the basic economic, administrative, social and legal problems with which industrial management has to deal. At that stage in their education as engineers there is no time, nor would it be wise, to attempt to do more than instil awareness, awaken interest and stimulate the imagination; but some of the best men are fired with a determination, after fully qualifying as engineers, to go on to further study, research and training in business administration. In many fields of industry, a high level of professional competence in engineering is an invaluable, if not indispensable, qualification for some high posts in general management, just as in others a parallel qualification in one of the applied sciences may be equally desirable. There are others in which even a first-class man educated in the humanities can make his way. All of them, however, will be better administrators if they are enabled to prepare themselves as seriously for these special duties as they were able to do in their undergraduate course of study.

Since I am personally engaged in helping to provide a graduate course of education and training for business administration, you will perhaps allow me to say briefly what our arrangements are at the London School of Economics in the University of London. We do it there because a graduate course of this kind needs to draw on a wide range of specialists in the relevant social sciences for research and teaching, and the School has a large academic staff specialising in the different fields of analytical and applied economics, in statistics and operational research, in accounting, law, labour relations, sociology and so on. We offer a somewhat rigorous and integrated full-time Graduate Course in Business Administration, extending over one academic year. Its size is strictly limited to the numbers who, apart from syndicate work in small groups, can participate fully in seminars conducted by senior specialist teachers. We take great pains in selecting graduate students, looking for high intellectual quality and attainment, a good balance of the various academic disciplines – engineers, natural scientists, lawyers, economists, the humanities – appropriate personal qualities, a firm resolve to make a career in management, and lastly a good spread of regional background – men from Britain particularly, but also from the Dominions, the United States, Western Europe and so on. Our main deficiencies are, at the student level, not a high enough proportion of good men from Britain, and the necessity to limit the total number admitted each year, because of the high costs and other difficulties of duplicating the staff of really competent specialists, and our determination not to allow standards to fall.

The engineers who take this Course do so as part of, or immediately following their period of graduate apprenticeship training. In the USA, the leading graduate schools of business and industrial administration are of course richly endowed and generously financed by business, and the numbers of engineering graduates who turn to administration and are encouraged and assisted by their employers to attend these institutions for one or two years of full-time study or research, in preparation for senior management appointments, are in striking contrast to the situation which has hitherto prevailed in Britain. Since the Second World War, a steady stream of Canadian engineering graduates has come each year to the United Kingdom, under the Athlone Fellowship scheme, to gain practical experience in engineering and industrial concerns and to undergo further advanced courses in universities on this side, and we have been glad to welcome a considerable number of them to spend one of their two years in the Graduate Course in Business Administration at the London School of Economics. But whereas British industrialists have been far-sighted in encouraging and assisting their engineering and other technological staff to attend university graduate courses for further advanced study and research in the field of their undergraduate specialisation, and have generously endowed the provision in the Universities of adequate facilities and specialist staff to conduct these advanced courses, there has been so far very little recognition by British industry of the urgent need for parallel encouragement and assistance to engineers and applied scientists to prepare themselves for posts on the higher managerial and administrative side of business.

I am happy, however, to end on a brighter note. At the last Annual Conference of the Institute of Directors held in London a few months ago, the President of the Institute, Lord Chandos, made a strong plea for support for a business course in a school of a great university, though not for a specialised course which neglected the humanities. 'Of the qualifications for the profession, avocation, occupation or distinction of being a director, the first might possibly be', he suggested, 'the fundamental or theoretical knowledge of business.' Nobody, he said, who was exercising the simplest function of management in peace, or command in war, without a theoretical knowledge of his profession, could do it as well as those who had. He announced that the Institute's Council intended to pursue the subject further. I am still happier to be able to add that, apart from the action contemplated by the Institute itself, Lord Chandos in his capacity as Chairman of Associated Electrical Industries Ltd has resolved to give a lead by sending to the Graduate Course in Business Administration at the London School of Economics each year, on completing their professional training, a number of the most promising graduate engineering apprentices to whom it is decided to offer a permanent appointment in the concern.

On the academic side, engineers and economists are, I suggest, now well equipped to collaborate in a combined attack on the problems of improving industrial efficiency in the expanding economy. It is for business to decide, following the authoritative lead of Lord Chandos and other like-minded industrialists, how quickly, by a parallel collaboration between industry and university, we in the United Kingdom can create, and set to work, this new profession of the engineer-administrator.

# CHAPTER 8

# Homage to Hayek*

Friedrich August von Hayek was 70 on 8 May 1969. One of the achievements of this many-sided scholar was to found the Mont Pèlerin Society, whose members have gathered annually for many years as (I quote his own words) an international group of economists, historians, and social philosophers, to discuss the problems of the preservation of a free society against the totalitarian threat. Fritz Hayek is the Honorary President of this Society, and it is in this capacity that *Roads to Freedom* has been planned by its four editors to honour him. The contributors are confined to certain members of the Society and a very few old friends, and the presentation to Hayek was made at the meeting of the Mont Pèlerin Society following his seventieth birthday. We are told by the organising editor, Erich Streissler, in his introduction, that the title of the volume was suggested by one of the fourteen contributors, Sir Karl Popper. Hayek became world famous with his *The Road to Serfdom*, and the editors chose 'the plural "Roads" to denote that, while Serfdom is by its compulsive nature conformist, liberals must always allow a plurality of approaches; and that such a plurality is demonstrated in an exemplary fashion in Hayek's own work'. An admirable suggestion and an appropriate choice.

The year 1971 will mark a centenary which the organisers of this *Festschrift* will also wish to celebrate, for it was in 1871 that Carl Menger published his *Grundsätze der Volkswirtschaftslehre* and thereby, in the judgment of most historians of economic analysis, founded the Austrian School of economists. That book stimulated Böhm-Bawerk and Wieser to produce their own treatise on capital, interest and the theory of value during the 1880s and 1890s. By the turn of the century

* Review of *Roads to Freedom: Essays in honour of Friedrich A. von Hayek*, ed. Erich Streissler and others, London, Routledge & Kegan Paul, 1970. This essay was first published in *Economic Age,* Jan.–Feb. 1970.

economists the world over were aware that these three pioneers and their students and followers in Vienna had established and were developing a distinctive and important contribution to economic theory and public finance. Hayek, a young Austrian army officer in the later stages of the First World War, returned to Vienna to study economics in the University. Böhm-Bawerk had died in 1914, Menger had retired, but Hayek was in time to sit at the feet of Wieser and to learn and dispute with the second generation of the Austrian School, in particular Ludwig von Mises, whose output of contributions was in full flood.

In the last quarter of the nineteenth century the significance of the essentially Austrian contribution to economic analysis was only exceptionally realised by leading economists in this country. William Smart in Glasgow was the outstanding exception. He translated and appraised Böhm-Bawerk's *Capital and Interest* (1890) and his *Positive Theory of Capital* (1891), and arranged for and edited a translation of Wieser's *Natural Value* (1893). In 1891 Smart published *An Introduction to the Theory of Value on the lines of Menger, Wieser and Böhm-Bawerk*. A sentence from the preface is worth quoting here: 'I do not consider that the last word on value has been said by the Austrian School, but that seems to me no reason why the principles of the new theory should remain any longer beyond the reach of the ordinary English student.' All of these books by Smart were published by Macmillan's: they made the main ideas of the Austrian School easily accessible to English-speaking economists who read German only with difficulty, if at all, and provoked those with sufficient German and intellectual curiosity to extend their reading to the widening stream of important publications by the Austrian School not yet available in English translations. Vienna agreed with Smart: the Austrian School had by no means said, in 1891, their last word on the Theory of Value. Communications were much improved in the years immediately preceding the outbreak of war in 1914.

As an example, the writings of Mises on monetary theory and practice were closely studied by some English economists, and his major work in this field, *Theorie des Geldes und der Umlaufsmittel*, published in 1912, whetted English appetites for more intimate collaboration when the fighting ceased. T. E. Gregory (now Sir Theodore) and senior students at the London School of Economics began to visit Mises in Vienna in the early 1920s, and the discussions with the younger economists there stimulated contacts with members of Swedish, Swiss and Italian schools of economics who, because of the absence of linguistic impediments, already enjoyed much closer collaboration and amicable debate with the Austrian economists.

Hayek's *Geldtheorie und Konjunkturtheorie* appeared in 1929, the year in which Robbins returned from Oxford to occupy the Chair of Economics at the London School. The interest shown in this book (LSE and Cambridge economists had been collaborating since 1924 in providing 'The London and Cambridge Economic Service' under the lead of Bowley) led to an invitation to Hayek to deliver a course of lectures at LSE in the first half of 1931. The success of this course of lectures (which formed the basis of his *Prices and Production* published in the same year) led to the revival of a University of London chair – the Tooke Professorship of Economic Science and Statistics – tenable at LSE, and Hayek returned to London as professor in the autumn of 1931.

I can testify from personal experience to the immense stimulus and direction which Hayek's migration to this country gave to economic research in the 1930s, not only in London and economics faculties throughout the United Kingdom, but also in the international world of scholarship. The focus was Robbins's Economics seminar at LSE, which became the forum for timeless discussion of Hayek's ideas on monetary influences on the structure of production and industrial fluctuations, and their many-sided implications throughout the field of economic, social and political policy.

I myself had returned to LSE in the middle of 1930 after six years at the University of Cape Town, where I had developed a special interest in the scope and functions of property and ownership, both private and public. It was a delight to find Hayek as well seized of the economic significance of the ramifications of property law as I was myself. I recall his excitement when I called his attention to the profound discussion of these matters in David Hume's *Inquiry concerning the Principles of Morals*: section III, 'Of Justice', and my own gratitude to him for his influence on my own thinking about so-called intellectual and industrial property law.

I was by no means alone in benefiting from the impact of Hayek's receptive and imaginative mind. Few of those who attended the seminars and lectures failed to be impressed by the welcome he gave to criticisms of his attempts to clarify the concepts of the effects of divergencies between the monetary and the 'natural' rates of interest on economic structure of production, and of 'neutral money'. Hayek's 1929 book was translated by Nicholas Kaldor and the late Honor Croome for publication in 1933 under the title *Monetary Theory and the Trade Cycle*.

As I have said, Hayek's presence added great strength to the magnetic attraction of Robbins's seminar. Senior economists on the move between the old and the new world planned their itineraries to include a visit to LSE. Economists elsewhere were perhaps a little envious of one's own privileges as a member of the London faculty. I remember passing through Germany in the spring of 1933 on my way to deliver some lectures in Copenhagen. Hitler had become Chancellor on 30 January, and following the Reichstag fire on 27 February had suspended civil liberties and the freedom of the press. On 23 March an enabling law gave him dictatorial powers for four years. A few days later I visited the economists at the Institute at Kiel for discussions of their research plans and to hear about their personal anxieties. Their academic freedom was more than threatened, and several were planning to emigrate. I suppose, said one, that LSE will have no vacancy for me, now that you have become 'ein Vorort von Wien' – a suburb of Vienna. Fortunately, economists in Denmark and Sweden were free from such personal problems at that time, and international contacts were well established because of their fluency in English. I found Heckscher looking forward to the publication of his *Mercantilism* in its English translation in 1935.

Robbins in these years was pushing ahead with his translation plans. Mises's *Theory of Money and Credit* (1912) appeared in its English translation by Batson in 1934, and his *Die Gemeinwirtschaft* (1912), as later revised, was issued in 1936 in the translation of the late J. Kahane as *Socialism: An Economic and Sociological Analysis*. In that same year the translation by two London economists, Stonier and Benham, of Haberler's *Theory of International Trade* (1933) was also published. Robbins himself edited in 1934 and 1935 the two volumes of Wicksell's *Lectures in Political Economy* (of 1901 and 1906). One of Hayek's research students, Vera Smith (Mrs Lutz), translated Machlup's *The Stock Market, Credit and Capital Formation* (which first appeared while he was in Vienna in 1931) for publication in 1940 with the author's revisions. By the outbreak of war in 1939 the 'liberal' economists of Austria and Germany were dispersed throughout the non-Hitlerised world, making their contributions to international scholarship mainly in English rather than German, aided in their teaching by the published translations and collected reprints of their illustrious forebears and teachers. Hayek was an outstanding compiler of editions of *Gesammelte Werke*.

This brings me once more to *Roads to Freedom*. The co-editors with Streissler are Gottfried Haberler and Fritz Machlup, both intimate contemporaries with Hayek in the Vienna of the 1920s, and Friedrich Lutz, who was the President of the Mont Pèlerin Society at the time when the volume was conceived. All the four editors contribute essays, and Streissler also provides a ten-page introduction in which he highlights the main details of Hayek's distinguished career and proceeds in a charming and ingenious way to review the 14 contributions so as to show with considerable skill that each acknowledges or reveals evidence of Hayekian influence on its content, or at least of parallelism in analytical method. The last section of the book should enable readers to make up their minds whether to be content to keep a copy borrowed from a library on their desk for as long as they decently or indecently can, or to purchase their own copy for their shelves; and to decide in favour of ownership. It is a complete bibliography of Hayek's published writings extending over 45 years down to at least the early months of 1969. Not that there are any signs at present of any slowing-down or weakening in the intellectual quality and range of output from this youthful mind.

This bibliography lists, with date and place of publication, fourteen complete books, ten more edited by Hayek and containing contributions from his pen, eight pamphlets, and at an estimate about 130 articles not included elsewhere. The relative length of these works is not a reliable measure of their comparative importance, or of the penetrative power of the light they throw on fundamental problems. Often Hayek's great service has been to rescue from almost complete oblivion a paper by another scholar and make it widely accessible in one of his edited collections of miscellaneous writings on a common theme.

We each no doubt have our particular favourites: one of mine is the paper on 'The treatment of capitalism by historians' read by the late Professor T. S. Ashton to a meeting of the Mont Pèlerin Society in September 1951, and preserved for a much wider public in Hayek's *Capitalism and the Historians*, 1954. My only regret is that in a normally busy life I cannot re-read it often enough for my own pleasure and profit. Both professors and unfortunate examinees are quoted to emphasise the woolliness of much contemporary writing. The examinee who produced for Ashton the profound remark, 'In earlier centuries agriculture was widespread in England. Today it is confined to the rural areas', reminds me of the other examinee whom one of my teachers, Professor Lilian Knowles, alleged to have written for her the sentence: 'In times of dearth the Irish peasant falls back upon his pig, and vice versa'.

One of the most notable signs of progress in our own time is the writing of economic history by economists like Ashton and Sayers. In the 1930s, J. R. Hicks was one of the outstanding regular attenders at the Robbins-Hayek seminar: in 1969 Sir John's latest publication is *A Theory of Economic History*. In his Preface he tells us that he has long been interested in economic history. 'I wandered away, and I am myself surprised to find that I have come back. I am sure I would not have done so had it not been for T. S. Ashton.' In my own case, I am fairly sure that my essays into problems of applied economics show frequent traces of the fact that as an undergraduate (1920–3) I fortunately elected to specialise in economic history under Lilian Knowles, Harry Tawney and Eileen Power.

Readers of this essay on the background to *Roads to Freedom* will wish to know at least who the contributors are. In addition to the four editors they are Jacques Rueff, member of the Académie Française; Emeritus Professors Sir Karl Popper and Frank Paish, and Professor Peter Bauer of London; Professor James M. Buchanan and Professor Gordon Tullock of the Virginia Polytechnic Institute; Professor George Halm of Tufts University, Massachusetts; Professor Ludwig Lachmann of the University of the Witwatersrand, Johannesburg; Professor Michael Polanyi, formerly of the University of Manchester; and Professor Günter Schmölders of Cologne.

It is not easy to separate the contributions into clear-cut categories. That by Jacques Rueff is *sui generis* – a short, moving tribute to the timely publication by Hayek in December 1943 of 'un livre magistral', *The Road to Serfdom*. Rueff's tribute is entitled 'Laudatio: un message pour le siècle'. Sir Karl Popper, who in 1960 dedicated to Hayek his own *Conjectures and Refutations*, writes on 'A pluralist approach to the philosophy of history'. Machlup (Professor at Princeton), mindful of the rational and non-emotional search by Hayek for clear and unambiguous definitions of such words as 'liberty' and 'freedom', in his monumental *Constitution of Liberty* (1960), examines the woolliness of conflicting popular usages of 'liberalism' and 'freedom' by politicians and social reformers. Streissler (Professor in Vienna) and Bauer both show that Hayek's early analyses of business fluctuations were in essence important precursors to the Theory of Growth, both in economically advanced and so-called 'under-developed' communities. Lachmann, Schmölders, Tullock and Lutz (Professor at Zürich) concern themselves with the market economy, monetary theory, corporations and the concept of 'neutral' money. Paish and Haberler (Professor at Harvard) write on macro-economic problems, the one on Governmental Control of Demand and the other on Wage Push Inflation. Halm examines the fundamental gulf between market and planned economies. Polanyi compares the administrative problems of totalitarian economies under State ownership with those of private enterprise, and argues that in practice the central authority cannot exercise more effective control over its various enterprises than would emerge if investment in each section were private and the managers appointed by directors elected by shareholders. Buchanan examines the usefulness for meaningful analysis of describing economics as the Science of Choice.

We have chosen in this appreciation to portray the role which Fritz Hayek has played over the last forty years in promoting international collaboration among economists. Contrary to ill-informed critics of his ideas, his contributions to academic discussion have been characterised by a sober attempt at rational persuasion. Those whose advocacy of social change is powered by strong emotion have often been repelled by the cold-blooded nature of his purely intellectual approach. They would do well to reflect that they would not wish a surgeon to operate upon them while his hands were trembling with emotion.

CHAPTER 9

# Centralise or decentralise?*

The problem of determining the appropriate scope of central and regional, as of superior and subordinate, authorities is as old as empires and governments, and has been much discussed by political scientists and students of public administration. Precisely similar questions arise continually in business, but the criteria of success and the penalties of error are very different in the field of business administration, and particularly so in firms which are exposed to an environment of inflexible market prices. For that reason a paper may well be devoted to a statement in the most simple terms of the underlying principles of successful delegation on the one hand and centralisation on the other, and to a survey of current business practice in the light of that analysis.

A modern business firm is constantly confronted, as its transactions change in character and volume, by the problem whether or not to centralise some functions which are at the moment dispersed among several members, and also whether or not to allow the delegation of other functions which are at that time reserved to a central authority. A given change in market conditions may involve opposite treatment of different functions at the same time. It will nevertheless be convenient in this paper, making for greater clarity without sacrificing realism, if the two sets of conditions are considered separately.

Imagine first of all a firm with a growing volume of business reaching the stage at which further expansion will be possible only on condition that the volume of work falling upon a particular person does not increase. Either he must be duplicated, or he must delegate part of his work to a subordinate and concentrate upon the remainder. Is the character of the business such that either expedient is possible, or has the limit of expansion been reached? If the latter of the two expedients – delegation – is feasible, what can most wisely be delegated? A very

* From *Some Modern Business Problems*, Longmans, Green, 1937.

simple underlying principle which suggests itself when the question is approached in this way explains much of the behaviour of successful business men and throws light upon the failure of others to make the most of their opportunities.

If we then pass on to consider the other kind of business situation, in which an opportunity or need presents itself for centralising part of the activities of a number of departments in a firm, or of a number of firms in an amalgamation, the same kind of question arises. For which functions, if any, is centralisation feasible and likely to be profitable, and for which is it likely to be most profitable? Once again a very simple generalisation will be found to explain much of the success and failure of contemporary business practice.

In neither case is perfect conformity to be expected between principle and practice. There are bound to be instances of spectacular business successes attended by trends in centralisation or delegation which are completely contrary to expectation. Considerations of strategy, if not of tactics, will generally be found to explain these aberrations from theory. The academic economist does not concern himself with questions of tactics. He does not wish – or expect – the business man to say to him, in the words of the 119th Psalm, 'Thy word is a lantern unto my feet'; he does not pretend to predict short-period movements. His prognostications are most reliable when they relate to trends; he is content if business men look to them to throw light upon their path.

## 1 The major and minor advantages of delegation

Let us therefore begin with a very simple case, and imagine a one-man firm which secures a growing volume of varied business, demanding a combination of different aptitudes, training, and experience. He needs assistance. Which functions shall he devolve upon assistants? There are two main reasons for delegating a function. The first and more obvious one is that the task which is devolved may thereby be better performed. As we shall see later, that reason serves also to explain why a function may be surrendered to a central authority by associated firms or departments. The second reason – more fundamental and possibly more usual – is that the delegation of one function will enable other functions which are reserved and not delegated to be better performed.

### (a) THE MAJOR ADVANTAGE IS THE BETTER PERFORMANCE OF THE RESERVED FUNCTIONS

If any excuse were needed for dwelling upon this second reason, I would put forward the conviction that many business people whose behaviour actually conforms with it do not always clearly perceive the reason why they should behave as they do, and in consequence they subject themselves to a good deal of unnecessary and anxious concern. Every student of elementary economics is taught, and many of them indeed learn, that it is not a necessary condition for wise co-operation and profitable exchange that a task which one leaves to others shall be better performed than if one did it for oneself. The principle of 'comparative costs' which is often invoked to explain trade between nations applies equally to the delegation of functions inside a business. A country will grow new potatoes for export, and import wheat which it could have grown more cheaply than the wheat-producing country, if the profit from applying its scarce productive resources to potato growing is greater than it would have been from producing its own wheat.

In the same way, a film actress, no matter how seductive her voice, may well decide to leave her less intimate telephoning to a secretary far less seductive than herself, so that she may conserve her own attractions for still more profitable employment. A sales manager, although possibly a better salesman than any of his own staff, may wisely delegate the interviewing of clients to teams of inferior salesmen, if it is still more profitable for his firm that he should concentrate his own energy upon the direction of policy at headquarters. Many such people would sleep better at night if they would put away vain regret, realising that because their time and energy are limited and valuable it is sound business to conserve them for those fields of employment in which the *net* contribution which they can make to receipts is greatest; taking into account, that is, not only the enhanced receipts from the 'reserved functions' which they continue to perform but any loss in value of the devolved services now performed by other workers.

Even if a business man has an equal natural superiority in two functions, it will pay him to concentrate upon one and devolve the other, if specialisation results in a gain in his 'dexterity', as measured by rate and quality of output, and in a saving of the time and energy involved in changing continually from the one function to the other and in keeping abreast of new developments in both, sufficient at least to offset any loss arising from delegating the other function to a less competent person. In professional work of a kind that cannot be delegated, it is precisely this gain from the introduction of some degree of specialisation which makes it profitable for men to form a partnership, instead of each establishing a separate practice. If the volume of specialised work is not sufficient to warrant complete specialisation, doctors, for example, with general experience, but specialist aptitude or inclination, may by working in partnership give greater satisfaction to their clients and secure better results for themselves. Such conditions are well exemplified again by the accountancy profession, in which partners frequently combine general practice with a large measure of specialisation, as for instance upon problems of taxation.

Recourse may be made to this same principle to explain the whole of the successful delegation which obtains down the hierarchy of workers in each of the separate divisions of a modern complex business. At each grade in the hierarchy it will pay to devolve certain functions still further, in order that the worker at that grade shall be enabled to concentrate on the duties which represent the highest net contribution of which he is capable to the receipts of the business. The standard of performance of the devolved function may deteriorate steadily as it is transferred farther and farther down the hierarchy, and yet delegation may still be worth while. The limit to which it may be taken is determined in each case by the minimum quality of performance of that function which will be tolerated by the buyers in the market, and their tolerance is determined by the amount and quality of substitute service offered by other suppliers. The increment of value contributed by this minimum quality of performance is similarly determined by the price at which acceptable substitutes are offered by other firms.

The availability of substitutes determines minima, but a particular firm may rightly decide to concentrate on furnishing the buying public with consistently better qualities than the minima with which some of them would be content, and it will continue to do so if the additional receipts from the better quality of service offset the additional costs of providing it. For instance, a department store manager might wisely decide to employ educated lift girls of superior presence and cultured accent if the additional costs, as compared with ordinary attendants or purely automatic mechanism, were likely to be more than offset by an increase in receipts due to improved patronage of the store.

### (b) A MINOR ADVANTAGE IS THAT THE DELEGATED FUNCTIONS MAY BE BETTER PERFORMED

In this way delegation of work may pay even when the standard of performance of the delegated function is lowered by the change. The second and more obvious reason that may explain the transference of work to other persons is that the transferred work will itself be better performed. In some instances this is a fortunate concomitant of delegation necessitated by other considerations: in others the position is simply that there is an opportunity for profitable specialisation, the gains accruing being sufficient to outweigh any increased costs due to new problems of co-ordination. Human beings are not homogeneous concoctions of abilities, training and experience combined in fixed proportions; the heads of businesses are not uniformly superior to their employees in all aspects of the work to be performed. Natural endowments vary, and so does the capacity to learn. The business man who dictates his letters might be a better typist than his secretary, but it is unlikely; for the sake of the typing, as well as for the sake of his other work, he is generally wise to leave the typing to her. The commissionaire who combines dignity with efficiency in keeping small boys from the door undoubtedly performs that task more effectively, as well as more cheaply, than would the average managing director. The gains from specialisation need no emphasis: more detailed study can be made of functional and regional differences, and specialists will moreover have the knowledge to appreciate their significance. They can make more decisions, and more appropriate decisions, than a single central authority. And it is important to remember also the possible psychological gain, reflected in the intensity and quality of effort which may be evoked in subordinates by the delegation of responsibility for initiative, for management and for actual performance of functions.

## 2 The conditions for successful delegation obtain less frequently in professional work

This bare recital of some of the obvious gains from specialisation itself suggests the answer to the question of the extent to which decentralisation is possible. The opportunities will be least where the success of the firm depends mainly upon the personal qualities of the central authority. We are all familiar with the situation portrayed in *The*

*Doctor's Dilemma*, in which Mr George Bernard Shaw throws upon an eminent medical practitioner the responsibility for deciding whether to cure a distinguished artist of unstable moral character or an undistinguished poor man's doctor imbued with a strong social purpose; for lack of time and other resources the specialist could not take both patients. His personal attention was vital to success: delegation was technically impracticable. In cases such as this, the size of a business is for technical reasons strictly limited. In professional work, that is, the pyramid of practicable control has a very acute angle at the apex. An eminent professor is reputed to have remarked that, whereas a University teacher may effectively advise a considerable number of research *students* in the conduct of their research and the preparation of their dissertations, he will not normally be able effectively to superintend the work of more than two personal research *assistants*; for, in the first case, the responsibility for the work done lies with the student, and in the second the responsibility for the results obtained lies with the professor himself, and he will find it expedient to rework laboriously and scrutinise critically most of the work which his assistants will have done. The influence of his teaching and inspiration may be widespread in the work of his students, but the output of work for which he is personally responsible must remain severely limited in quantity. Surgeons and artists may have their menial assistants; writers may employ 'devils' for that part of their journalistic output which they regard as 'pot-boiling', but such delegation on a large scale is hazardous to their reputation.

### (a) IS ACCOUNTANCY A SPECIAL CASE?

In recent decades we have witnessed in the field of accountancy what might be thought to be an important departure from this simple rule. It has become usual for large joint stock companies to employ as their professional accountants and auditors one of a fairly small number of professional firms. With this growing demand for their professional services some of the firms in question have expanded their scale of operations until they now maintain large subordinate staffs, engaged in clerical functions, and in the voluminous checking work involved in the periodic audit of their clients' accounts. Their leading principals may have found it necessary on occasion to delegate even important professional decisions to teams of technically qualified assistants. But it would clearly be wrong hastily to conclude that these firms of professional accountants would claim to invest the work of their subordinate staff with the reputation of their principals. A different degree of authority attaches to the work personally performed by the leading principals of these firms and the more anonymous professional services which the firms render in a more collective way. To be selected as an assistant or junior partner in such a firm undoubtedly extends to the professional man an added *cachet*; he is specially recommended by the eminent principals with whom he becomes associated – he receives, as it were, a higher degree in addition to his professional qualification – and the principal is entitled to charge for this middleman service. But it would be clearly erroneous for the general public to suppose that these professional firms, in extending their scale of operation by decentralisation, are able to extend indefinitely over a wider and wider field the strictly limited capacity of their eminent principals for exceptional personal service. The special professional reputations remain attached to the personal services of the people concerned.

### (b) THE IMPLICATIONS OF STANDING ORDERS

From this apparent digression it becomes clear that the dominating condition for effective decentralisation is that part of the decisions taken at the centre may be generally applicable to the work which is devolved. If the market in which the firm operates is highly heterogeneous in kind, so that each transaction, or a large proportion of the transactions, involves separate attention, further decentralisation will soon become impracticable and a limit be set to expansion. If, on the other hand, a decision once taken can become a precedent, or standing order, governing a volume of future transactions, then one central decision will suffice for an expanding volume of work of that kind. This criterion must be applied to decisions upon all matters affecting the profitability of the main activities of the firm. In a manufacturing business where alternative materials can be substituted one for the other (as in the charging of a steel converter with pig iron or scrap, or the charging of carding machines in cotton spinning with cotton fibres of different staples) and the prices of these alternative materials do not vary together, then the exercise of the buying function and its co-ordination with the planning of production are fundamental to the profitability of the operations of the firm and are matters involving much attention from the central authority. Yet if all the variables can be gathered together into a generalised expression, then its practicable interpretation and application may safely be delegated to minor executives, subject to withdrawal of the delegated authority on clearly pre-defined contingencies. If, on the other hand, the technique of production is also constantly changing, production planning will inevitably absorb much of the time of the central authority. And similarly, of course, with variations in the demand for the product. The size of firms engaged in the manufacture of women's dresses, if they are style goods, is severely limited by the number of functions which cannot safely be delegated. When styles become fashions a larger output, in fact mass production output, may be controlled with as little strain on the central authority. The essential conditions here are the practicability of standardisation of output during the short period of life of the fashion, the possibility of organising production on easily adaptable machinery, and the application of speed and resource in changing the nature of the output.

The dominating fact throughout is the limit to the working day of the head of the business. He may secure some relief, and be enabled to take more and better decisions, if part of the work involved can be delegated. Much of his time is taken up in ascertaining the really relevant facts concerning each situation which demands a new decision, and in pondering the probable effects of alternative policies. In both of these matters relief will be sought at an early stage. It was the view of Francis Bacon over three hundred years ago that if decisions are urgent the first of these responsibilities cannot be widely diffused with advantage, whereas the second can. 'There be three parts of business', he wrote in his essay on Dispatch, 'the preparation; the debate, or examination; and the perfection. Whereof, if you look for dispatch, let the middle only be the work of many, and the first and last the work of few.' In the multitude of counsel there will be celerity as well as wisdom – on the whole, time is not wasted in conference – but the work of ascertaining the nature of a problem, of marshalling the evidence into a form in which debate will be profitable, must be concentrated upon a few persons, although it may be delegated. If this be true, the risks of expansion are great, if it involves extensive delegation of the function of fact-finding. If time does not allow the head of a business to collate the reports of many investigators, he will need great faith in his fact-finders if he is to rely upon their evidence in making decisions. If the work is highly complex, and the number of decisions large in relation to the volume of business undertaken, the time will soon come when a limit will be placed upon the delegation of fact-finding. Such business men, like scientific workers, cannot effectively multiply the number of their research assistants. If they wish to expand their scale of operations, they must abandon the complex business which cannot safely be delegated; they must specialise upon functions and types of business which can more safely be standardised.

Still more is this the case when further expansion of the business involves the delegation of part of the 'debate' on policy from the conference of major executive officials to committees of minor officials, and when responsibility for taking important decisions must be similarly devolved. A harness of generalised instructions, of standing orders, has to be improvised to control the exercise of delegated discretion. In a rapidly changing market, a growing business finds itself upon the horns of a dilemma. If the standing orders are left standing, they cease to be appropriate to changed conditions; if they are changed with great frequency confusion and misunderstanding will almost certainly arise. Relevant changes in other orders will not invariably be made as one is altered, for standing orders breed multitudes of regulations lower down the hierarchy as functions are further devolved. Many of us are familiar with the books of regulations issued to new-comers in large concerns, amply interleaved for corrections, frequently conflicting in themselves and still more frequently honoured by heroes in the breach in the valiant endeavour to avert the spread of *rigor mortis*. For if precedents continue to be applied after the conditions which justified them have changed, a firm will either tend to refuse business which it should accept, or continue to accept business which in the changed circumstances it ought to refuse. To avoid disaster in active competition, such large firms are compelled to concentrate more and more upon the kind of output which can most safely be standardised.

### (c) THE LIMITATIONS OF MECHANICAL AID IN MANAGEMENT

It is of course recognised that this fundamental problem of control has not been by any means ignored in large and expanding businesses. A wealth of talent and ingenuity has been lavished upon it in recent years. The most able administrators have turned their minds to it, and immense strides have been made. Large-scale operation has its advantages as well as its weaknesses; it alone, for instance, has made possible the emergence of a new race of professional specialists in management who have raised appreciably the standard of performance of their particular functions. But the new problem of internal co-ordination has thereby been created. Where standardisation of output is feasible, firms with large but highly specialised output avoid many of the internal problems of the more diversified business because they submit to the co-ordination imposed upon their activities by the price mechanism of the market. The more complex the business, the earlier will it need, as it expands, to devise new techniques and mechanism which will amplify the eyes and ears and other sense-organs of the central authority. Standing regulations for the harnessing of delegated discretion, statistical devices for the planning and measurement of a complex output which can no longer be supervised directly, elaborate costing systems with impressive names which scarcely suffice to conceal their inadequacy, all of these and similar pieces of machinery certainly serve with a greater or less degree of perfection and promptitude, on the one hand to broadcast more widely throughout the large concern the intentions of its central administration, and on the other to imprint more voluminously upon the central nervous system a record of what is actually performed at the extremities. It would be preposterous to belittle in any way the achievements of management technicians, with the aid of office mechanisation. The department of business administration at the London School of Economics, indeed, devotes itself largely to the study of their contribution, and of their potentiality, and they form the subject of some of the papers in this present series. But it is one thing to increase the speed and range of contacts within a firm, and quite another to evoke indefinitely a greater and greater volume of response from the (still only human) organism which endeavours to direct the business from the centre. The time and energy of the central authority is strictly limited. As business grows, and problems grow with business, the time approaches when the capacity of the co-operating specialists in the firm to serve its clients will be greater if the attempt at maintaining a central 'co-ordination' of all of their activities is abandoned, and parts of the firm are disintegrated into more easily manageable units.

Rigid standing orders may be honoured by loyal executives in the breach. A still greater danger is that they breed in themselves a new race of officials, timorously anxious to obey the letter and ignore the spirit of obsolete instructions. A hundred years ago Sir Henry Taylor wrote bitterly in the *Statesman* against precisely this failing in some of the officials in Government departments. Men whose activities have long been ruled by precedent and drilled into conformity with voluminous regulations learn to suppress their imaginative faculties. The qualities required for rapid and appropriate response to a changing environment become atrophied. Large firms for these reasons have been faced in recent decades with the urgent problem of devising special machinery for securing men of vision, and training them, freed from excessive routine duties, for managerial posts.

The trend of development of the department store type of organisation in the field of retail distribution provides a good example of the two alternatives open, centralisation and standardisation of merchandise on the one hand, decentralisation and individuality on the other. Department stores have to draw their customers from a wide area; their merchandise in consequence must possess an individuality and quality that will attract shoppers from the small specialist shops in their habitual market area. To maintain such standards, specialist departmental buyers have proved essential, and the general managers have found it expedient to allow them wide discretion. The more specialised their merchandise, the greater the reliance which has to be placed upon their judgment. The more profitable their operations, or the greater the 'drawing-power' of their department, the greater the measure of independence from central control that the buyers may exact. Their contracts with the management reflect the personal character of their relations, the terms in extreme cases amounting to a virtual leasing of the department from the firm, which may be content to draw a relatively fixed income from the receipts from its operation while the buyer's remuneration will vary directly with his success. The general management will normally be content to limit its interference with the conduct of such departments to the necessary co-ordination of finance through the common budget, and of the planning of special features in accordance with the staffing, publicity and space requirements of other sections of the business. In such cases it is a very short step to the complete 'disintegration' of the risk by the actual leasing of departments as independent businesses. On the other hand, as we shall see later, the attractions of the economy in buying costs which accrues when a centralised office buys in bulk for a number of similar departments in a chain of stores have led to a contrary trend, dependent for success upon the trade being capable of standardisation upon a large scale.

It would be easy to multiply examples in other spheres of business of this same necessity for extensive delegation as the price of growth of complex businesses, and of the tendency to abandon particular types of business if retaining them implies carrying the risk as before but relinquishing the control. It is not accidental that motor-car manufacturers in this country, whose businesses rapidly expand, generally tend at the same time to 'buy in' more and more parts, instead of continuing to make them for themselves.[1]

## 3 The advantages of centralisation, and the conditions for their attainment

It will now be convenient to come to the second standpoint, from which I suggested at the outset that this whole question may be reviewed, and ask whether, when firms are brought together by amalgamation or by some looser form of association, it will pay them to centralise any of their functions; and if so, which? Decentralisation passes certain tasks down the hierarchy, centralisation passes tasks up the hierarchy if the net earnings of the business are thereby increased. Looking at the matter first as one of decentralisation, we found the principle at work to be, in its most simplified form, that of comparative cost. Is there a parallel principle to explain wise and profitable centralisation?

### (a) THE ACQUISITION OF POWER TO CONTROL MARKET PRICES

Approaching the problem from this standpoint, I wish to refer first of all to a gain from centralisation which is of prime importance, but upon which I do not propose to dwell here; although in itself it undoubtedly provides, by increasing receipts or reducing particular costs, an adequate justification for a great deal of centralisation which is in other respects cost-raising and inefficient. That is the opportunity which is afforded by growth in the scale of operation for the exercise of monopoly power to control prices, either of what is sold or of what is bought. The larger the share of the output of commodities, for which no easily obtainable substitute exists, which is controlled by a central marketing authority, the greater the power to control the price by regulating the supply. If the cartel controls the sale of the entire output, it may increase profit still further by charging different prices on different occasions. The desire to attain to such powers has in all ages provided the motive for much of the centralisation of selling, or complete amalgamation, which has taken place. Combines, cartels, trade unions, central marketing boards, the transformation of private businesses into public utility concerns all reflect that desire to a greater or less extent. Less frequently, similar associations have centralised buying in order to reduce the prices at which raw materials and labour are sold to them, by restricting the amount of their purchases. These important reasons for centralising are a fascinating topic upon which many volumes have been and are still to be written. I shall, however, confine my discussion in this paper to those increases of receipts and reductions in cost, brought about by centralisation, which do not depend upon the acquisition of power to influence prices.

### (b) SPECIALISATION OF STAFF WHICH IS NOT OTHERWISE ATTAINABLE

Neglecting this aspect of the question, centralisation is the means by which the collaborating enterprises secure the advantage of specialised services or equipment which would not otherwise be available to them on such favourable terms, if at all. If the service or merchandise in question is freely bought and sold on any scale in a well-organised market, there will be no need for centralisation of firms. It is the absence of a well-organised market which may justify firms in pooling their requirements.

Consider first of all the gain which accrues to a firm from the specialisation of staff. As we have seen, decentralisation may result in the work decentralised being better done by a subordinate; 'devolution upward', in which associated firms relinquish particular functions to a centralised specialist, is justified in precisely the same way. Decentralisation is forced by the pressure of business on the central authority; centralisation is imposed by competitive market forces upon the associated businesses. The gains from specialisation staff have already been touched upon. To secure these advantages to the full there must be a sufficient volume of specialised work available for the specialist to undertake. The minimum annual cost of the specialist must be spread over a sufficiently large output, if he is to pay his way, to leave a net gain to the organisation which employs him. Centralisation, or the pooling of the service, may serve to make this possible.

## ILLUSTRATIONS FROM VARIOUS FIELDS

### (*i*) *Finance*

I need hardly dwell for long upon examples. Take, for instance, finance. There are undoubted advantages to be gained from concentrating financial work in the hands of a specialist officer, and firms which are large enough will centralise their financial operations under a treasurer's or comptroller's department. The financial market is of course well organised in some of its branches, and small firms may be able to buy various kinds of financial service on terms which may leave little incentive to further centralisation with other institutions. Nevertheless, the holding company form of association, and chain grouping of retail shops, may conveniently combine certain parts of what we may call banking business, for the service of their constituent enterprises. Specialist accountant service is usually easily acquired in the open market from professional firms; but here again, there may be an economy to the larger firm or amalgamation which can offer full-time specialised employment to a professional accountant.

### (*ii*) *Production technique*

When we come to production technique, in many fields, the market is probably not so well organised on a consultant basis. The small firm is unable to secure the part-time assistance of as many and varied specialists as its larger competitors can maintain in full employment, and in consequence, the small firm is inevitably deprived to some extent of that quality of service which only highly specialised workers can render. We have witnessed in recent years the amalgamation of small electricity companies, for instance, into groups which can maintain a team of full-time specialist technicians. In the gas industry the larger associations possess this advantage already, and smaller concerns are steadily becoming associated together by the development of holding companies which maintain a similar team of specialists at their disposal for consulting purposes.

It is important to realise that standardisation of product, or of technical processes, is an essential condition for the attainment of many of these economies, and that the size of unit must remain small where individuality of service is the essential condition for successful operation. The firm which employs its own specialist is limited by his limitations. If it 'buys in' its specialist advice it may take advantage of the specialisation among specialists.

### (*iii*) *Sales promotion*

If we look at the work of sales promotion, the necessity for centralisation is clearly less than it would otherwise be, on account of the firms of professional consultant advertising practitioners who place their specialist services at the disposal of firms, large and small. Firms extending the area over which they do business will often be wise to proceed cautiously in undertaking the financial costs of maintaining branch offices. They will begin by operating through independent middlemen whom they may nominate as agents: they may subsequently take the risk of limiting the range of their appeal by appointing a *sole* agent for an area, if countervailing gains of better service seem likely to emerge, and eventually they may go to the point of establishing a branch office at their own risk if the consequential further increase in volume of business seems likely to outweigh the additional costs of maintenance and central control. And as we have seen, effective central control of scattered premises is no easy task.

### (*iv*) *Personnel*

Consider, again, the merits of specialist departments to handle matters of personnel. The owner of a small business will take care to keep the appointment of staff, the fixing of salaries and of wages, and the responsibility for dismissals in his own hands, but as his firm grows he will be compelled to leave much of this work to subordinates, so far as the lower grades of staff are concerned. It is unlikely that the delegated work will continue to be as well performed. Efficiency will suffer. He will soon be aware that his labour costs are high compared with those of his larger competitors whose scale of operations is sufficient to justify a specialist personnel department. The medium-sized firm may be able, with a reasonable degree of precision, to define the qualities of labour that it needs, but the market in human effort is not yet so well organised that the qualities of workers offering themselves for employment can be accurately and expeditiously tested except by specialists. Opportunities exist, therefore, for improvement in selection by employing a team of specialists in personnel work, and the centralising of staff recruitment may enable this to be done. Moreover, where organised labour is strong enough to insist that higher posts be filled by promotion from within the firm, a new advantage is offered by amalgamations. For if an important position has to be filled, the chance of finding someone already on the staff who will compare favourably with outside applicants will be the greater, the larger is the number from which the selection has to be made. Businesses like banks, insurance companies, railway companies, or public utility corporations, which have made this concession to their staff organisations in the interests of harmonious relations will therefore secure by amalgamation a wider field of choice, a closer approximation to the conditions of the open market. But against this gain must be set the new problem of organising and staffing the central control of the amalgamation itself.

### (*v*) *Buying*

One of the clearest cases of the economy to be derived from specialisation of staff is that which is made possible by centralising the buying function in a trading or manufacturing business. The larger the amount of buying that can be brought under one specialist, the better the quality of buyer that can be afforded, and the more continuously can he specialise upon that work. Evidence of better buying may be spread right through the firm's trading accounts. If better buying increases the sales of the business, the higher salary of a more skilled buyer may not represent a higher expense, measured as a percentage of the increased turnover. Even if the percentage expense of better buying is greater, net profit may still be increased on account of consequential reductions in other expenses, such as mark-downs on inappropriate merchandise, and interest and warehousing charges on idle stock. If the improvement in buying takes the form of securing the same merchandise at a lower aggregate cost, the firm is free either to increase its gross margin of profit, or to lower its selling prices while keeping the percentage of gross profit constant, according to its view of the market situation. The greatest of the economies secured by chains of shops arises out of their ability, with a large volume of buying, to employ highly skilled buyers and keep them continuously employed on that function. Yet the full economies of bulk purchase can be secured only if the merchandise bought for resale in the various shops or branches can safely be standardised sufficiently to enable one set of negotiations and one order to take the place of several. (I deliberately exclude from this discussion, it will be remembered, the concessions which 'important' buyers may for a time secure from sellers, out of relation to actual cost differences. To the extent that markets are not highly competitive, these advantages of large-scale buying organisations are responsible in large measure for the amalgamations and growth of large chains which have occurred.) If local shops rely for their turnover in part upon merchandise that can be so standardised (proprietary articles provide an extreme example), but also in part upon the individual appeal which they may make to a section of their customers by stocking 'something different' – whether as a continuous feature or by sporadically displaying special lines – then the centralisation of buying which may be imposed after amalgamation into a chain may well lead to a loss of goodwill and of business. Great significance therefore attaches to the development over the last fifty years in the USA, and more recently in this country, of loose associations of independent retailers for the purpose of co-operative purchase of merchandise. Each co-operating trader preserves by this method his ability to cater independently for the idiosyncrasies of his own customers, while benefiting from the advantages of bulk buying of standard merchandise. He may still continue to purchase small quantities of special goods which would not interest the central buying department of a chain, preoccupied as it rightly is with securing the full economies of bulk ordering. The question may well be asked why these co-operative buying associations can offer terms better than those of established wholesalers. The answer would appear to be that their opportunity is greatest where the wholesalers distribute a highly heterogeneous range of merchandise to a mixed body of retailers, and fail to relieve that part of their business which is standard, regular and apparently certain, of the extra costs incurred by the other parts which are diverse, irregular and uncertain. Unless they improve their cost accounting and refine their pricing system they must face the gradual loss to the new buying associations of the trade which provides the subsidy and expansion of that part which receives it.

### (*vi*) *Warehousing of stock*

There is, in addition, an important indirect economy which may result from central buying, and which is a fundamental cause of much amalgamation. In the open market, retailers may come into existence because they actually lower final prices, if the cost of carrying stock, which would have to be incurred in their absence, is taken into account. The retailer centralises the carrying of stock, and the amount that he needs to hold, to meet all requirements, is less than the aggregate value of stock which his customers would otherwise have to carry in their homes. The interest, depreciation, and storage charges which each of them has to bear may consequently be reduced. Collective action for the purchase of merchandise may afford similar opportunities for economy by the centralising of stocks. A central reserve of merchandise held at the disposal of a number of consuming or distributing units is smaller in aggregate than it would be necessary to hold if each unit were independent and carried its own. The centralisation of reserves of cash held at the head office of a commercial banking system, or at a reserve bank, produces a precisely parallel saving in interest charges. In the case of merchandise other than cash there is, at least in times of stable currencies, an additional saving in 'mark-downs' on depreciated stock. Where central buying can be accompanied by centralisation of stocks, therefore, as in the case of chain stores, these further savings may be important.

### (c) ACCESS TO SPECIALISED EQUIPMENT NOT OTHERWISE OBTAINABLE

So far in this discussion of the gains from centralisation I have concentrated upon those accruing from the specialisation of staff. The same considerations apply to the use of specialised equipment. The initial obstacle to its employment is the outlay involved, in view of which a minimum volume of output will be necessary before it will be cheaper than alternative methods. If the market is active and highly competitive, it may be possible for a small firm to secure the same economy by putting out the work to a specialist firm. That is conceivable, for instance, in office work involving duplicating or tabulating machinery. Alternatively the equipment may be available on hire for short periods: taxi-cabs are more frequently cheaper than owned cars than car-owners are willing to admit. Hiring and buying-in, however, are not always practicable, and amalgamations may make possible the advantageous use of specialised equipment. A good example is afforded by the fleets of delivery vehicles by which chains of department stores may offer frequent delivery over large areas. One fleet may often serve a number of stores operating in the same area, and if the merchandise is standardised the vans may be loaded from a centralised stock. No doubt if there were an open market, the delivery function would frequently be better disintegrated to specialist haulage contractors, but the Rail and Road Traffic Act of 1933 has put an end to the open market in road goods transport services; and large firms which centralise their delivery service secure an economy of pooling which their smaller competitors cannot share. Where the large undertaking consists of an amalgamation of trading firms which find it expedient to continue to trade under their old names, we have here a good reason for deliveries of merchandise being made 'in plain vans'.

(d) WILL THE NECESSARY STANDARDISATION PAY?

It is an important condition for securing these economies of centralisation by amalgamation that the joint demands of the collaborating firms aggregate together in such a way as to utilise 'surplus capacity'. Seasonal variations may not dovetail into each other. With completely standardised merchandise a buyer can place an order for twenty shops at least as cheaply as for one, but without standardisation one buyer may be able to buy for many shops only if the demand of each fits into the 'valley periods', when he would otherwise be idle. Department stores which have centralised buying have found on occasion that the economy from standardisation has led to 'trading down', i.e. lowering the grade of merchandise handled. If the central office is to make the reorganisations necessary for 'trading-up' once more, by reintroducing the wider varieties of merchandise which that policy involves, then these department stores have had to engage more and more specialist buyers at the centre. The economy ceases to be so impressive.

What has just been said applies also in spheres other than buying. The degree of standardisation necessary for economical centralisation may not be in the interests of efficiency in particular sections of the business. Personnel departments will, it has been said, improve efficiency, in filling vacancies from within a business, by widening the area of selection as far as possible. To facilitate comparisons and transfers between departments they will rightly seek to standardise the grading of staff within them. In particular departments the consequential changes in existing grades is frequently resented, and it is quite possible that the section will be right in protesting that its own special grading has been carefully devised to meet the peculiar needs of the staff it employs. A change in the interests of uniformity will impair efficiency. Similarly, in the field of banking central advance departments created as the outcome of amalgamations of small banks may provide safeguards and ensure prudent lending, but the standardisation of loan conditions necessary to enable a central office to consider a large volume of applications may also prove unsuited to the special circumstances of a particular region, or type of business. The advance business may in that way be unduly curtailed, and conceivably, in some cases, unduly extended. Again, in buying stores or raw materials for manufacturing concerns, after amalgamation a central purchasing office will be tempted to standardise the requirements of different sections, in order to squeeze the last economy out of bulk buying, but not all the variations in the requirements of particular departments are unreasonable. If the differences in grade of material insisted upon have important technical justifications (as, for instance, in the case of the many different grades of flour which may be necessary for the manufacture of different kinds of biscuits), then the central economy in purchasing from eliminating these differences must be weighed against the loss in efficiency, and possibly in sales, of the departments adversely affected.

The standardisation which would pay all sections of a business or association of businesses, if costs alone are considered, may or may not be acceptable to the public, and receipts may suffer. In some cases, however, the public will pay more for standardised articles, as, for instance, for the guarantee of interchangeability of spares, even if higher costs and higher prices are involved. More generally, standardisation involves a sacrifice to the public that prefers variety and a price concession will be necessary on that count alone, if standardisation takes place. Savings in cost will not necessarily, therefore, be a *net* gain to the concerns which centralise at the price of standardisation. But these considerations of public preference will not arise where the effects of centralisation are not discernible in the product or service rendered.

## 4 The attractions of discretionary centralisation

The dangers which I have just stressed lend a particular attraction to the possibility of making more general the looser form of co-operation in which individual sections of firms may contract out and dispense with centralisation, where their own particular interest would not thereby be served. At least one large chain of department stores in this country today 'co-ordinates' its buying instead of centralising it, so that the buyers in the separate stores may collaborate where they are convinced that an economy is likely to emerge, or when an experiment in standardisation is, in their view, worth making, but leaving them free to abstain from such co-operation, on their own responsibility, if they believe that independent action will be more appropriate to their department. No doubt useful centralisation does not on that count proceed as fast as it might, but, on the other hand, where individuality of appeal is fundamental to the maintenance of trade, the risk of serious loss of goodwill is thereby avoided, and the wholehearted co-operation of departmental heads is moreover ensured. In all amalgamations, whether formal or through the agency of a holding company, the danger to the individual unit is that a majority decision will adversely affect its future. There would seem, therefore, to be great scope in the future for development of new machinery of co-ordination, somewhat perhaps on the lines of the loose associations for co-operative retail buying, in which minorities are free to abstain from any collective action with which they are not in agreement. Illustrations of what is possible are provided by some of the useful co-operation between firms which results from trade association activity. For example, annually now for six years department stores in this country have been enabled to pool to their mutual advantage the most intimate details of their operating cost experience, the statistical returns and their analysis being entrusted to Mr R. F. Fowler, and myself, in the Department of Business Administration at the London School of Economics, anonymity being ensured by coding through the co-operation of the Retail Distributors' Association and the statistical section of the Bank of England. Department stores may participate or not as they please, and over a hundred have chosen to do so each year.

## 5 Considerations involving strategy

### (a) KEEPING UP APPEARANCES

When the rigid standardisation imposed by complete centralisation appears likely to involve so great a loss to an important part of the organisation that the aggregate net receipts of the whole concern would be reduced, endeavours will obviously be made to maintain the necessary local variations. It is not difficult to find examples. There is the question whether it will be expedient for newly associated enterprises to operate under a common name. If they are not catering for the same class of public, then those sections which concentrate upon the lower grades of merchandise will stand to benefit from the adoption of a name that implies a guarantee of a minimum standard of quality and service; but the use of the same name by the other sections which do a better class of business might be construed by the public as an indication that qualities would be allowed to descend to that minimum. In these organisations, care is usually taken to avoid such public emphasis upon the amalgamation as would damage the select reputation of important sections. Former trading names which carry valuable regional goodwill are preserved, and others which are better forgotten will be superseded, when firms which deal with the general public are amalgamated. Postwar amalgamations of department stores and of chains of grocery shops provide illustrations. In the same way, there are considerable economies to be secured from operating as one unit whole chains of hotels and restaurants, although they cater for very different classes of the public in different establishments. A single name for such chains will be emphasised prominently as a guarantee of quality and purity in the lower grades, but will be used less and less in the upper reaches in which select exclusiveness is more appreciated. The necessity for maintaining separate trade marks or house names for those parts of a business which it is desired that the public shall keep distinct in its mind may thus impose limits upon the extent of practicable centralisation. On the other hand, the general public is not always appreciative of the finer points of successful business policy, particularly where the advantages of specialisation are concerned; and a firm's prestige may be enhanced if the public imagines its activities to be more widespread, its central control more far-reaching, than is either practicable or desirable from the aspect of profitability. Food preparations, fruit preserves and the like may enjoy a wider sale if the public imagines the manufacturer to be so unusual in his business methods as to rely on his own farms for his supplies of materials, and the model farms which are prominently located adjacent to main railway lines and trunk roads may incidentally serve therefore as a business-like concession to popular superstition.

### (b) APPARENT CONTRADICTIONS IN BUSINESS PRACTICE

It will be observed that these concluding remarks relate in part to considerations of business strategy. Firms whose controllers are under no illusion as to what their ultimate objective should be, whether towards a greater degree of centralisation or of decentralisation, nevertheless appear all around us, in spite of the similarity of their needs, to be travelling in different directions. In what has been said we have, I believe, sufficient explanations of these apparent contradictions. If individuality of service appears fundamental to the trading success of a unit business in an amalgamation, we may expect that concern to be cautious in the imposition of extensive centralisation. If, on the other hand, standardisation is likely to be acceptable to the public, this same hesitation need not hold back the attainment of substantial economies. Department store chains will centralise the buying of linens, but continue to allow their fashion buyers in each store almost unfettered discretion. Strategy enters in the determination of the rate at which progress shall be made in one direction or the other. An amalgamated railway, absorbing several important local systems, may be so harassed by new road competition that substantial economies must be secured quickly, unimpeded by the parochial loyalties of former officials of the constituent concerns. A department store chain in which it has been decided to concentrate on the lower class of trade may decide to ignore the protests of buyers whose departmental policy is thereby reversed, in the interests of the general trend. An amalgamation of banks in each of which loan policy has with varying degrees of success been determined in the past by considerations peculiar to the district or to the special class of business upon which particular units may have concentrated, may decide that for a term of years the maintenance of a supply of local officers competent to continue that same diverse policy, without grave risk of loss, may present insuperable difficulty, and that the only alternative is a rigid centralisation of all important loan decisions by a central advance department. Yet in these cases what in the long run would prove to be excessive centralisation may well be the inevitable condition for securing in the short run other conditions which are essential to the success of the amalgamation; as, for example, a realisation of common interest, the eradication of losses due to local inefficiency, the achievement of a major economy. Once these objects have been realised a reverse process of decentralisation may well be set in train. A new race of officials may be recruited and trained upon whom discretion can more safely be delegated. A new trade may be redeveloped, in merchandise such as fashion goods, which can be handled only by specialists with local discretion. An organisation may be created which will provide staff of a calibre sufficient to carry greater responsibility. Central personnel departments may tend more and more to leave the ultimate choice of staff to the departmental manager under whom it will have to work, the central department merely holding its advice and its facilities at the disposal of the section. Bank advances may be left more freely to the discretion of local or specialised persons, free, within the confines dictated by central policy, to accept or reject (on their own responsibility) the views of a central advisory advance department. In brief, contrary trends at present discernible in the various spheres of business may be merely the safest road for vehicles of different construction to take towards the same ultimate destination.

Our picture would be seriously incomplete if it were to omit the political considerations which affect the degree of centralisation or decentralisation that exists in those business enterprises directly affected by Governmental activity. In such fields, the scale of operations may not be within the control of the administration of the business, but imposed from outside by the conditions of Government instruction. For that reason the size of unit may be far from the optimum that would be dictated by considerations of administrative efficiency alone, and the opportunities for profitable centralisation and decentralisation may in like manner be subject to severe limitation. Municipal enterprise springs at once to mind as an example of these imposed difficulties of centralisation, for amalgamations of municipal undertakings may not be easy of attainment. In like manner undertakings which must be operated on a national scale may be denied the opportunities for profitable decentralisation that are open to similar enterprises which are free from Government control. But to dwell here upon these aspects of the problem would be to become involved in a discussion of the limits of central economic planning. The title of our paper has already been strained enough.

## Note

1 In the prosperous conditions of 1927, long before acute depression enforced drastic reorganisation throughout American business, a vice-president of the General Motors Corporation – Mr Donaldson Brown – contributed some very acute remarks upon this question in a paper (entitled 'Decentralised operations and responsibilities with co-ordinated control') read before the American Management

Association. 'If the executive committee [acting for the board of directors] be composed of department heads, or men actively engaged in the administrative management, it is usually advantageous because of their intimate knowledge of the problems of the business. On the other hand, this circumstance makes it difficult at times to distinguish between those questions requiring executive committee action and those questions which, in the interest of individual initiative, had better be left to administrative control. It should be recognised that the function of any individual as a member of the executive committee is quite different from his function as an executive officer. Committee action is by majority vote; executive action is by individual choice. The executive may seek the counsel and advice of any number of men on a given problem, but the decision is his.' In the General Motors organisation, which consists (1927) of many operating units which are each capable of being run as independent businesses, 'each one of these operating units, known as divisions, is entirely self-contained, with a general manager and complete jurisdiction and responsibility established. . . . Obviously it is humanly and physically impossible for the Executive Committee of General Motors to maintain the same kind of intimate contact with the details of its business as would be practicable in the case of a very much less diversified business. Still the responsibility to stock-holders is exactly the same, and the proper organisation of control has been forced by absolute necessity. Otherwise, the business were better split up into various units with separate ownership, even at the sacrifice of the great advantages of the existing combination, so that the stock-holders of each unit respectively could elect a board of directors capable of assuming the usual responsibilities. . . . The head of each division should be qualified in every way to hold the position of president were its business owned and operated by an independent Company. . . .'

Clearly in such an organisation a decision on policy made by the executive committee may subordinate the interests of one division to that of others. It may be expected to yield a net advantage to the corporation as a whole; and yet the division which is penalised may well find its future completely jeopardised if it is not allowed to adjust its operations as freely as may its competitors to changing conditions. That is not always desirable. When decentralisation reaches this stage there may be a strong case for maintaining a more loose alliance between divisions, which would still secure to each the advantages of association, at its discretion, but would leave them free to 'contract out' and make their own arrangements if they can do better independently.

CHAPTER 10

# The distribution of proprietary articles*

This paper is concerned with the trade in branded goods. To economists the term 'proprietary article' may be ambiguous. In the full sense it applies in our economy to all articles of value, for none remain for long unappropriated. In a much narrower sense it may be confined to products such as copyright books or patented inventions, in the case of which the right to reproduce or multiply the supply is a property right conferred by law upon certain persons. In ordinary trade practice, however, proprietary articles are branded goods, distinguished by a proprietary label or trade-mark, and it is to the special aspects of the distribution of such goods that attention is here directed.

Because of its dependence upon prominent advertisement, the increase in the importance of branded merchandise in modern commerce has been one of the most obvious economic changes of our age. It has come about as a result of several contributing causes. For instance, the progress of industrial technique has made possible enormous reductions in manufacturing costs dependent upon mass production; improvements in means of communication, both of goods and of information, have enabled mass-produced products to be distributed over wide areas and yet remain within the range of purchasing power of a sufficiently large number of buyers to keep the mass production factories occupied; the population has enjoyed a considerable increase in purchasing power and has certainly shown itself open to suggestion as to the new objects upon which to disburse it, while the spread of literacy down to the most humble classes has enabled a national press to emerge largely upon the basis of lending its columns to the advertisement of such merchandise. The dependence of daily

* From *Some Modern Business Problems*, Longmans, Green, 1937.

newspapers in their present form upon the continuance of press advertising of branded goods is obvious; advertisers of financial propositions may pay more for their space, but they do not advertise so extensively or so regularly, and the annual appropriations for press publicity of the largest of our department stores barely approach those which are normal for a single branded article. And the newspaper press has by no means the monopoly of the publicity given to proprietary articles; advertisements of branded goods virtually monopolise the hoardings, they comprise an increasing proportion of our daily post, they are the topic of earnest conversation several times daily between our housemaids and their handsome young callers, they are insinuated into our radio entertainment, despite the purity of the BBC and the vigilance of the Import Duties Advisory Committee, and most recently of all they have begun to distract our attention skywards when we should be keeping our eyes on the traffic.

These latter developments have naturally been disapproved by those who are associated with the daily press, and disinterested observers of social trends have also found much to criticise in them. With much of this criticism we are not here concerned. It is not our present purpose to discuss matters of social policy, but to ask how far the business arrangements and business policies which have been evolved in connection with the distribution of branded merchandise have been well-conceived in the interests of those who participate in the trade.

## 1 To brand or not to brand? And who shall brand?

Consider first of all why merchandise is branded by a manufacturer. His purpose is clear; he wishes to expand the market for his product. Undoubtedly, branding is in many cases well advised. Frequently, indeed, it is the best method of attaining his end. But it is important to recognise that branding certainly is not the only way, and need not by any means be the best way to increase sales. Many manufacturers expand their business, and flourish, by supplying their goods without an identifying mark of any description to traders or other manufacturers. They prosper by maintaining quality and service, while quoting competitive prices. They have confidence in their ability to compete and to keep sufficiently abreast of changes in productive technique, and in the trend of demand, to secure repeat orders and a growing business. There may, indeed, be a good deal of weight attaching to the view that the introduction of brands implies a doubt in the mind of the manufacturer whether he can otherwise continuously hold the market. It suggests a fear that his products would not invariably be acceptable if offered anonymously on a strictly comparable basis, and a belief that it is advisable to enlist goodwill from past services in order to influence the buyer's choice. It is true and important, on the other hand, that consumers will often themselves welcome branding as a means of recognising and insisting upon what pleased them previously, as well as of avoiding in future what failed to please. The manufacturer may, again, have a justifiable concern to safeguard himself against domination by particular traders. If he allows his sales to be dependent upon the whim of a few dominating merchants, he may find himself suddenly cut off from his market, or he may give them the opportunity to drive unpleasantly hard bargains. His difficulty in finding alternative outlets quickly may enable them to compel him to increase his trade discount, under the threat of transferring their custom to other suppliers. The branding of his goods offers some protection; if he is able to build up 'consumer insistence' for his article, traders will be more chary about refusing to stock it. They will hesitate to use the threat of boycott in case their bluff is called and they have to choose between climbing down and disappointing their customers. These considerations have weight, but they clearly are not conclusive, and the creation of 'consumer insistence' may be an expensive process. There are, indeed, abundant examples of manufacturers who flourish on the basis of selling an anonymous product to many other manufacturers and traders, exercising continuous vigilance in framing their contracts to avoid placing themselves under the domination of any one buyer, or group of buyers. We shall do well, therefore, in the first place to notice that branding is not universally believed by manufacturers to be the best way of selling their output.

We may tend to think of branding as a device employed mainly by manufacturers of consumers' goods, but it is important to bear in mind that it may be adopted by intermediaries at many different stages between the preparation of raw materials and the final transfer of finished products to ultimate consumers. The purpose being to create 'consumer preference' or 'consumer insistence' for the branded product, it is necessary simply that the product shall remain identifiable until that stage is reached at which the publicity is intended to operate.

Raw materials may be successfully branded and advertised to the manufacturers who use them, although they may subsequently be so transformed by further elaboration of the product that they cease to remain identifiable. The branding serves its purpose if it creates sufficient insistence on the proprietary raw material by firms at an intermediate stage. In other cases, parts of a finished product which remain identifiable in the final product may be advertised direct to consumers, in order that they may insist upon the so-called 'manufacturers' of the final product incorporating the proprietary fitting in their assembled product. The tyres and carburettor and electric fittings of a motor-car suggest themselves as examples. On the other hand, the manufacturers who brand consumers' goods may, in certain cases, do little more than assemble finished parts which have been bought unbranded from a variety of suppliers. That may be the case, for instance, in the radio trade. In fact, in a competitive market the most astute manufacturers might endeavour to confine their operations to little more than trading, leaving the risky business of making fixed investments in specialised productive equipment as far as possible to other manufacturers.

There is, therefore, nothing peculiar in *dealers'* trade-marks. The store which buys skilfully, brands the products which it distributes, maintains the quality or grade of the branded goods by careful purchasing, while leaving itself free to vary the source of its supplies with changes in market conditions, acts in no way differently from the manufacturer. Its brand is in no sense spurious. Nevertheless, there is a natural tendency for branding of consumers' goods to be adopted mainly by the first manufacturer or middleman, in the chain between prime materials and final consumption, to pass on the product in a form and with a name which will be identifiable by the ultimate consumer. The trade-mark known to the buyer of a radio set is more likely to be that of the assembler of the component parts than of either the manufacturer of the condenser which it contains or the suburban retailer who ultimately sells it to him. But it is by no means invariably the case.

## 2 The scope for grading as a substitute for branding

The intermediary who brands the article may thus take but little part in its preparation for the market. How small a part is not of course realised by the great mass of consumers. The real function, if any, undertaken by the proprietor of the trade-mark is to hold himself out as responsible for taking care that so long as the brand exists the article shall conform to the expectations which the brand has created in the minds of the public. If the public's expectations are disappointed when they buy the product, the reputation of the brand is damaged.

From the consumers' point of view, therefore, the brand is essentially a grading device. The name on the article evokes expectations of a certain quality or specification. For that reason the consuming public is not likely to take much interest in trade-marks where products are already efficiently graded by other market organisations into those categories which the consumers desire to distinguish. It is conceivable, for example, that such movements as that sponsored by the department stores (which are not keenly interested in branded goods) in founding a Retail Trading Standards Association to promote greater accuracy in the description of merchandise, might tend to lessen public interest in trade-marks. The public function of branding, as distinct from the private interest of the brander, is to distinguish grades. Here arises a point of which the trade may need in time to take account. A grade distinguished by a trade-mark remains monopolised by the person or group owning the trade-mark. The owners can restrict the supply in their own interest. The public is, however, concerned simply to be assured that the articles it consumes conform with the expectations created by the branded name and not that it is the product of particular firms. (As has been said, no matter what the public thinks, most trade-marked goods are not by any means entirely the product of one particular factory.) On account of these considerations, the suggestion has recently been made that trade-marks after a term of years should be converted, as it were, into grades, in order that no one proprietor of a trade-mark should continue to have the power of restricting the supply of articles conforming with the implied grade. The Harvard economist, Professor Edward Chamberlin, the author of one of the most interesting volumes of recent years in the field of economic theory (*The Theory of Monopolistic Competition*), includes in it an Appendix E entitled 'Some arguments in favor of trade-mark infringement and "unfair trading"', in which he argues that any producer who wishes to put his capital and other productive resources to such use should be allowed to add to the production of any trade-marked product and to mingle his own output with the rest 'of that grade', subject only to a preliminary monopoly period, of say five years, on lines parallel to the existing law relating to patented inventions and copyright products.

There are obvious limitations to the extent to which well-defined grades might take the place of trade-marks. Agricultural produce and other primary materials are already largely graded, and little scope is left for further differentiation by trade-mark, provided that the grades are appropriately determined and continually adjusted to meet the requirements of buyers, and are scrupulously maintained. The buyer is indifferent as to the source of a particular grade of Manitoba wheat, provided that any consignment delivered under that grade conforms with the expectation created by the definition of that grade. The trade-marks which cannot so easily be superseded by grades are those attaching to those classes of consumers' goods for which the buying motives of the consumer are not capable of analysis in terms of a demand for clearly ascertainable and definable qualities. Technical equipment like sewing-machines, or vacuum cleaners, or radio sets might well be graded, but toilet preparations and merchandise bought rather for reasons of emulation than for their precise chemical content or standards of performance are in another category. One cannot easily imagine a grading system which would convey the satisfaction to be derived from a shaving soap similar to that habitually used by the ex-King of Ruritania. It is clear, however, that if this movement for placing a limit on the term of private property in trade-marks grows, its significance must be carefully weighed by business men before they make large irredeemable investments in 'goodwill' advertising.

## 3 The cost and problems of brand advertising

Successful branding may involve a very large investment in advertising. A decision whether or not to brand a product must, therefore, rest upon the estimated cost of establishing 'buyer preference' and the estimated increase in receipts which that additional expense would produce. The cost of creating a national demand may be covered by the additional receipts from one kind of product but not from another. There is a certain degree of what economists have termed 'indivisibility' about the expense of national advertising. A continuous press campaign to maintain the reputation for a consumers' good in popular demand in a national market, such as the United Kingdom, quite usually involves an expenditure of over £50,000 per year. Apparently a minimum 'acreage' and minimum frequency of insertions are necessary for success. £100,000 per year is not a very unusual figure, and as much as £200,000 may be spent annually upon the press advertisement of each of a number of brands of cigarette. If an effective campaign absorbs at least £50,000 per year, a large minimum turnover from sales will be required to finance it upon a lasting basis.

In the case of, let us suppose, motor-cars, it might well be that the increased turnover accruing on the average to each manufacturer who advertised on that scale would be sufficient not only to enable him to make an at least countervailing reduction in factory costs, but also to make the cost of advertising appear very reasonable to the buying public, when reckoned in terms of the number of cars sold. In the radio trade, on the other hand, the cost per set probably represents a much greater proportion of the total price, and for other articles which have a relatively small market despite a relatively low purchase price, the cost of establishing a national brand may well appear both prohibitive to the manufacturer and exorbitant to the public. Press campaigns clearly are not for all who aspire to national markets. There is, moreover, the difficulty of selectivity which arises in press advertising. The manufacturer is fortunate whose product is potentially of interest to all the persons comprising the 'net circulation' on the basis of which the cost of his advertising is calculated. He will usually have to pay the price of informing some classes of the public who will never buy his merchandise, and yet the press medium may still be more effective than any alternative available to him. Publishers' announcements on the review page may be a case in point.

It will be clear, in view of these two considerations, why the movement for group advertising, covering a number of comparable branded goods, has made more headway for some classes of merchandise than for others. It provides a means of reducing the total cost of advertising the comparable products without necessarily reducing their aggregate sales in the same proportion. On the other hand, the advertisers of cigarettes may well feel that they make a better use of their publicity appropriation in present circumstances by advertising one competing brand against another, than they would by collective advertising or by reducing the total advertisement appropriation and spending part of the saving on other things. In so far as the consuming public 'likes a change of brand' from time to time, manufacturers may even increase their aggregate net profits by maintaining more than one brand and advertising them all separately, thus retaining part of the custom when changes are made.

It must surely be concluded that existing conditions in the advertising of proprietary articles are far from stable, and that the trade must keep a vigilant eye upon current trends. The newspaper trade is naturally concerned to pursue a policy which will maintain its aggregate revenue from advertisements. To that end a censorship has been imposed upon advertisements in order to exclude any which might bring press advertising in general into disrepute. Presumably with an eye to the same end, they impose further limitations which are not so clearly in the interests either of particular advertisers of repute or indeed of the general public. For instance, it can hardly be doubted that it would be in the public interest that information should be broadcast relating to the results of impartial tests, scientifically conducted, into the relative merits of competing brands of merchandise, and the validity of the claims made on their behalf by their advertisers. Nor can it be doubted that a clear incentive exists for those advertisers who believe that their products would emerge successful from such tests to bear the expense involved in informing the public. Yet such 'knocking copy', as it is termed, is viewed at present with disapproval. The advertising experts are themselves divided upon the matter, for the legal position is not entirely clear, and since the effect upon advertisement revenue might in the short run be adverse, the public is kept in ignorance. Matters can hardly be left indefinitely as they stand. It seems probable that those concerned to safeguard the future of advertising will in the fairly near future secure such modifications of general policy as will permit the dissemination of information which is so clearly necessary to the public for the wise expenditure of its income. 'Consumer research' is almost certain to be inaugurated before long in this country, in one form or another, and it is hardly to be expected that the newspaper press will neglect its opportunities in that promising field.

## 4 The other costs of distribution

The prevalent impression that costs of distribution are inordinately high does not arise merely from consideration of the costs of advertising. Criticism concentrates rather upon the number of so-called middlemen engaged in the physical handling of finished products; and, as we shall see, that criticism may carry more weight in the peculiar conditions under which many proprietary articles are marketed than it does in the case of the trade in unbranded merchandise.

### (a) TWO SIMPLE FALLACIES

It is moreover far too frequently asserted in these days that the problem of factory production has been solved while that of distribution has not yet been faced. The fact is, of course, that manufacturers can make no claim at all to have shown greater concern about their costs than have their colleagues in the field of distribution, and it is perhaps necessary to correct one general impression which arises out of a simple statistical fallacy. It is sometimes alleged that the concentration of factory production in a centrally located works for the service of a whole national area has enormously reduced factory costs, but that distribution costs of the product have, in the meantime, risen, rather than fallen. It is a necessary condition for such reductions of factory costs that distribution costs should rise. So long as factory production took place at each consuming centre in a small works it was the raw materials which were distributed over the area, the distribution costs being concealed in the delivered prices of the materials at each works. The subsequent concentration of factory production at one centrally located works reduces the transport item in the delivered price of the materials, and merely transfers it to the distribution cost of the finished product from the more remote factory to all the consuming points. In so far as the final product weighs less than the raw materials, on account of factory waste, the distribution costs may actually be reduced, rather than raised, by this development; although it is possible that the discriminating rates on the railways, levying higher charges per ton mile on finished goods than on raw materials, may offset this saving. As the result of mass production the final delivered price of the finished product is lower than before, and the reduction in factory costs must be set against the consequential increase in the transport cost of the finished products.

It may be as well to exclude at this stage from the discussion of distribution costs a second very prevalent impression, that in spite of active competition (indeed, some would say on account of it) the final price of an article will be raised whenever an additional middleman succeeds in interposing himself between the factory and the final consumer. In truth, of course, the fact that the additional middleman can maintain his position in active competition indicates that the final price of the product is actually lowered thereby, as compared with what it would have been if the same goods were distributed to the same buyers at the same time without his aid. No one would argue that the 'middlemen' who stand side by side on the conveyor line in the assembly plant of a mass production motor-car factory each raise the price of a completed car, as compared with what it would have been if one mechanic performed every consecutive operation on each car. Specialisation of work enables each mechanic so to increase his output that the aggregate assembly costs when spread over the enormously greater production of cars is less per car than by any alternative method. That indeed is the purpose of distributing the work among so many specialist 'middlemen' mechanics. Precisely the same economies are secured in active competition when the middlemen functions to be performed *outside* the factory, before the finished product reaches the final consumer, are divided among a number of specialist 'middlemen'; and the advantages from specialisation accrue as certainly from dividing the risk between separate firms as from dividing the other functions between separate workers.

Apart from erroneous impressions such as these, there exist nevertheless more cogent reasons for the belief that distribution costs, particularly in the case of proprietary articles, are higher than they need be. Enlightened critics naturally concentrate their attack upon the central problem of the amount of trader's gross profit, measured as a percentage of the final retail selling price, which represents the cost of distribution and consists of the difference between what the consumer pays and what the manufacturer receives. In what conditions are there valid grounds for the contention that this gross margin is unnecessarily large?

### (b) LOW COST DISTRIBUTION OF A COMMODITY

A convenient approach to this whole question is provided by taking in the first place as simple a case of distribution as can be found, and then proceeding to ask what additional difficulties, involving additional costs, have to be met in the case of various categories of goods.

There is probably no branded good so simple to distribute as the postage stamp. The distributor of this nationally known article enjoys an established market; very little publicity expenditure is necessarily involved in maintaining it. It is a branded article which can be stocked with confidence that no fashion change will be allowed to destroy its value. Kings may change, but the King's head on the postage stamp need not be changed until existing stocks have been exhausted. The risks of pilferage, fire and tempest can easily be covered by precaution and insurance. It is bought because it is useful for paying to have letters delivered, and the sellers themselves can see to it that its utility persists. What gross profit should be allowed to the distributor who handles this agreeable commodity? Clearly it need not be large. In France, ordinary tobacconists' shops sell postage stamps with their other merchandise, and my information is that their gross profit is 1 per cent on the retail price, which we may compare with margins ranging from say 7½ per cent to 50 per cent over the many different kinds of proprietary articles on the market in this country.

It would be difficult, I imagine, to find many examples in the retail trade of a lower gross margin than that, and yet I am not aware that French tobacconists have refused to include this commodity on such terms in their stock-in-trade. I am assured upon excellent authority that the distribution costs in this country are not much higher, despite the much better service that is provided. It is not merely that many more convenient selling points are maintained here; the French tobacconist does not hesitate to keep up his rate of stock-turn of postage stamps by concentrating on a very few 'leading lines', meeting requests for multiples by strings of stamps of small denomination. No one surely would criticise the British Post Offices for reducing their rate of stock-turn by maintaining for the greater convenience of the stamp-licking public a large and varied stock of slowly-moving merchandise, which incidentally involves an economy in the production costs of paper and printing, and probably does not increase the interest charge on warehouse-stocks.

### (c) HIGH COST DISTRIBUTION OF A SIMILAR COMMODITY

How peculiarly simple and costless the retailing of postage stamps is, when compared with the trade even in other nationally advertised branded goods, will become abundantly clear if we stop to consider a branch of retailing which while physically almost identical is economically vastly different. I refer, of course, to a philatelist's business, the retailing of used and unused postage stamps to collectors rather than to correspondents. It would be difficult to make an exhaustive list of all the additional costs to be covered in this branch of the postage-stamp trade. He has firstly a buying expense which has no parallel in the case of the Post Office, for he needs to possess, or to employ someone with, competence in judging the value of a vast range of varieties of stamps, used and unused, piece by piece, and in estimating the likelihood of changes in their value. There can be few more difficult problems in the field of unit merchandise control. He has secondly to organise the selling of his stock over a large area, for it is not an article in universal demand on a national scale; he must seek out collectors and maintain a service for their information by catalogue, advertising and display. He has to pay interest on his stock, which must be protected from damage, and his rate of stock-turn is likely to be low. His turnover will depend upon maintaining an enormous variety of stock to attract customers to inspect his wares. Because of fluctuations in market prices, he must know what he holds, and be for ever overhauling his stock, eliminating by bargain-offers those slowly moving items which are in danger of depreciation, and retaining only those which are likely to appreciate by more than the cost of holding. Instead of 1 per cent, therefore, it would not be surprising to find that an average gross profit of more like 50 per cent is necessary to keep a philatelist's business going.

In selecting a philatelist's business I have, of course, taken an unusual example, but one which is nevertheless illustrative of the conditions in which much modern retailing has to be conducted. For many branded goods the nature of the demand, and the efforts of the manufacturer to maintain it, very greatly reduce the costs falling upon the retailer. Thus for packet-tea the rate of stock-turn may be so high that retailers may operate on a gross profit of as low as $7\frac{1}{2}$ to $12\frac{1}{2}$ per cent. The shop assistant for this type of product is in some areas in competition with the automatic slot-machine. For other kinds of merchandise one needs to add to the expense of the philatelist little more than the additional costs of warehousing and delivering more bulky stock, of occupying more central premises, and of arranging more elaborate window display. The larger the store, the greater also will be the central administration charges for direction, although buying costs will almost certainly fall.

### (d) INFLUENCE OF THE RATE OF STOCK-TURN ON COSTS

The rate of gross profit which must be secured if a retailing business is to continue permanently is clearly related to the rate of stock-turn which can be attained. A steady business will involve a certain minimum investment in stock-in-trade and a minimum outlay in warehouse space, shop rental, wages of sales staff and other expenses; but as the volume of business increases these expenses will not all rise proportionately. Customers will not frequent shops which do not display a minimum variety of stock, dependent upon the kind of business; but given that variety, the amount held at any one time need not expand greatly with the volume of trade, and the expenses which are associated with the amount of stock will not increase in proportion. A small shopkeeper will also be able to increase his sales within a fair range before he finds his wages bill for selling staff increasing proportionately with turnover. The aggregate costs of doing business, measured as a percentage of sales, will therefore vary from shop to shop according to the rate of stock-turn, and so will the gross margins necessary to cover those costs. Moreover, goods which are in universal demand may be so easily distributed at the retail stage that the process becomes quite automatic. So far as such merchandise is concerned, retail shopkeepers perform few functions which cannot be performed by the proprietors of automatic machines. For instance, postage stamps and small branded articles will tend to be sold in automatic machines whenever the density of demand for each type of product is sufficient to bring the cost, including the overhead cost of the machine, below that of alternative methods of retailing. Where this method is practicable the gross profit need not be so high as in regions in which the density of demand is much less. As we shall see later, this consideration is of the greatest importance when we are considering the policy of those manufacturers who attempt to fix the margin of gross profit obtainable on their products rigidly for all shops, irrespective of the differences in rate of stock-turn which can be achieved in different locations.

### (e) SHOP LOCATION AND THE CONVENIENCE OF THE PUBLIC

A special problem which confronts manufacturers of branded goods is that of supporting their direct advertising of the brand to the consuming public by measures to ensure that their goods shall be stocked at locations convenient to the buying public. What convenience means in terms of location will depend in part upon the nature of the goods, and also in part upon the shopping habits of the buying population. There is perhaps an undue tendency to regard the population that buys a particular brand of goods as a homogeneous class of persons possessing broadly similar shopping habits. It would seem a more reasonable assumption that different classes of people buying the same article may choose to regard it as convenient to secure their supplies in different ways. If they have implicit faith in brand advertising, they may go to the nearest shop, and insist upon the brand in which they believe most implicitly. If shopping is a nuisance to them, and they live in a sparsely frequented district in which other traders would be reluctant to open, they will readily pay a little more to a dealer who provides added convenience to them by maintaining a shop there. If they are keen shoppers, they will plan their purchases in advance, and go to a cheap market-place where they will expect to secure a price concession for the trouble they take, since it relieves the dealer of part of his expenses of operation. If, while interested in brand advertising, and influenced by it, they nevertheless desire to crystallise their buying decision by personal comparison of rival brands, they may either seek out a dealer who carries a varied stock, or take the trouble to visit a specialised market district, in which a number of dealers, or manufacturers' agents, have premises conveniently close to each other to facilitate these shopping and inspecting expeditions. It should be noted that when branded goods are price-maintained, it is generally convenient to have shops well distributed through the residential area; whereas, if prices and qualities are fluid, rival dealers congregate together at special market-places. Thus new books can be bought anywhere, prices being fixed for large zones, but buyers of second-hand and antiquarian books seek them in the special districts in which competing traders display their stocks of books at various prices and in various conditions. Currency used to be sold, when it varied in quality, comparing piece by piece at the same time, by dealers congregated in Lombard Street: today nationally advertised currency notes, no longer varying in value piece by piece at any one time, are usually bought at the local branch of one's bank.

Now it will be clear that the costs of operation incurred in conducting business in these different locations will differ widely on account of differences in rentals and other expenses, and in the turnover which can be secured from a given investment of resources. One shopper will pay more if he can secure additional convenience of service, while another will expect to be charged a lower price if he goes out of his way to reduce costs for the dealer; and one and the same shopper will, on some occasions, wish for added convenience at a higher price, and on others prefer to economise and do more for himself. That being so, it is normal to expect, even in the market for branded goods, that different prices will be charged at different places and at different times by different shopkeepers. The manufacturer who wishes to secure the full advantage from his publicity expenditure will be anxious not to lose any business because of failure to meet, whenever possible, the reasonable expectations of potential buyers. It is not merely the article by itself which customers desire from a shop they frequent. In addition to the other expectations which I have enumerated, a particular buyer, a housewife for example, may also attach great value to the courtesy of service, consideration, punctual delivery, not to say personal qualities of the shopkeeper and his sales assistants. A manufacturer who confines his business to a limited number of dealers runs considerable risks, therefore, of restricting his contacts with potential buyers. There is, therefore, much reason behind the efforts of many manufacturers of proprietary articles to have their articles stocked by as large as possible a number of shops in every area. Whether the method which many of them adopt in their effort to achieve this end is the right one is another question, to which we must now turn.

## 5 Resale price maintenance

### (a) THE NUMBER OF SELLING POINTS

We can probably lay down with some degree of confidence the proposition that the less capable the general public is of recognising distinctive qualities in rival brands of merchandise, and in developing for them the intensity of 'consumer insistence' which each manufacturer desires, the more necessary it becomes for each manufacturer to persuade the greatest possible proportion of retailers in every area to stock them. Unless that is done, the customer is likely to be content with a substitute 'which is just as good' rather than bother to walk out of one shop and go in search of another. The smaller the intrinsic difference which the mass of customers is capable of recognising in actual consumption or use of the article, the greater is the trouble to which the manufacturer is put in maintaining sales. He becomes committed to sustained and expensive campaigns of press advertising, designed to represent any failure to discriminate blindfold between his brand of whiskey or chocolates or cigarettes and all others as a social crime of no mean order, and to encourage the undiscriminating at least to *pretend* to the palate of a connoisseur. But relatively few people are capable of maintaining these pretences very seriously in their private, as distinct from their public, behaviour. In the privacy of their dealings with local shopkeepers they will relax the strain. The manufacturer is, therefore, prone to try to persuade every trader to support him in his campaign at least to the extent of stocking his article and supplying it when asked for.

The usual method of doing this is for the manufacturer to announce to every dealer his desire to make the trade in his product both profitable and easy. National advertising will create the public interest in the brand: it remains, it is presumed, for the manufacturer to fix an attractive trade discount for the retailer, and to undertake to make it effective. Although for the most part manufacturers are convinced that the volume of their sales will be greater, the lower the final price at which the public can buy their articles, they generally proceed to involve themselves in a movement to maintain resale prices, enforcing a minimum rather than a maximum final price to the public. Thus, despite the differences that undoubtedly exist in the buying habits of the public, in the kinds of service they expect of retailers, with corresponding price variations in different places and at different times, and despite the wide variations in the margins of gross profit which dealers of varying competence will find most profitable to themselves in different locations, manufacturers of branded goods have generally arrived at a marketing policy which endeavours to impose a rigid uniformity of final selling price over a vast area.

### (b) ECONOMISTS AND RESALE PRICE MAINTENANCE

Students of the abstract science of political economy may surely be excused if they find so prevalent a practice completely at variance, *prima facie*, with the expectations which their science arouses in their minds. Can it really be in the interests of manufacturers to insist that no matter what reductions in costs of distribution an efficient retailer may introduce, he shall not be allowed to benefit either himself or the manufacturer or the consumers by lowering his prices in order to increase his sales? It was an eminent permanent secretary of the Board of Trade who, sixty years ago, giving evidence before a Royal Commission, described in the following terms an unusual attempt which had been made many years earlier to introduce this practice into the retail trade in books: 'I remember the thing very well, for I was just beginning to read Political Economy, and I wondered whether there could be anything true in the science of Political Economy, when such an absurd practice as that contended for by the publishers could prevail in what ought to be the most intelligent trade in the country.' (T. H. Farrer in evidence before the Royal Commission on Copyright, on Friday, 9 March 1877.) Lord Farrer (1819–99) nevertheless lived to see the practice, which had been abandoned by general consent in 1852, revived in 1890 by one of the most enlightened and respected of publishing firms, the proprietary article selected for the revival being strangely enough the most famous economic treatise ever published since the days of Adam Smith; for Professor Alfred Marshall himself apparently personally approved the selection of his *Principles of Economics* as the first book to be sold on conditions which refused all trade discount to any retailer who sold copies below the stated net price. Today the 'net book agreement' is almost universal in the book business of this country.

When students of economics find an important and widely prevalent business practice at variance with their expectations they may react in a number of ways. They may shut their eyes to the practice: and one may certainly wish that a greater measure of attention had been bestowed by economists upon the growth of resale price maintenance during the last forty years. They may, again, decide at once that the practice is absurd and doomed to speedy failure, a conclusion which implies in this case the assumption that many of the most able leaders of business policy are too ignorant to realise wherein lies their own interest. Most economists today would, I hope, decline to base any conclusion upon so improbable an assumption. They prefer, I believe, in so far as they devote time to the matter at all, to assume a likelihood that the practice, with all its inherent defects and possible long-period instability, serves to further the interests of at least a number of the leading business men who maintain it, with the result that others who imagine a coincidence of interest are led to imitate their betters, although in their own circumstances a very different policy might well be more appropriate. There has, in fact, in recent years been a welcome tendency among economists studying business practice to analyse the working of resale price maintenance in different sets of circumstances, with the object of establishing the conditions that make for permanence or for collapse, for profit or for loss, for satisfaction to some and disappointment to others who practise it. I shall myself venture to suggest some relevant considerations.

### (c) IS IT ESSENTIAL?

It may be observed first of all that a manufacturer may be able to induce traders to stock his brand of merchandise without concerning himself with the question of retail margins. An increase in effective advertising is to some extent an alternative. A trader who is repeatedly asked for an article which he does not stock may end by taking it up, although the manufacturer declines to regard the problem of fixing the resale price as a matter on which he is either competent to express or desirous of expressing an opinion. The recent Board of Trade committee hazarded the view that half the goods sold by an ordinary grocer, for instance, are not branded at all, and that of the branded goods about one-third are not subject to any price restriction. Branding does not *necessarily* imply resale price maintenance.

### (d) TRADE REGULATIONS CONCERNED TO FIX AGREED DISCOUNTS

A second observation of relevance is that manufacturers who practise resale price maintenance for the most part recognise the futility of competition among themselves in the amount of trade discount which they offer to retailers as an inducement to stock and push their brands. It is not merely that more liberal discounts involve higher final prices and presumably a reduction in total sales, but that a discordant element of instability and suspicion is thereby introduced into trade relations. Various trade associations, therefore, regulate the terms which their members may offer. Manufacturers may thus be left free to fix their final price as high or as low as they like, but they may not vary the percentage of trade discount. Thereby it is hoped that the retailer will have no other incentive to discriminate between rival brands than that aroused by a proper desire to give satisfaction to his customers: if he wishes to increase his profit on each sale, he must take the risk involved in trying to persuade his customer to choose the dearer article. Yet even though manufacturers standardise both their discounts and their final prices, and even also the qualities of their goods, while maintaining separate brands, they will not succeed in eliminating the incentive under which retailers operate to develop 'leading lines' and encourage customers to accept particular brands; for the greater the number of distinct brands, the greater the stock that must be carried by each retailer in order to meet a given volume of demand. There will be an economy in concentrating sales as far as possible on one or two brands of which stocks are carried, while maintaining a skeleton display of the others to keep up appearances. Particularly will this be true if manufacturers offer graded quantity discounts.

Quantity discounts would seem, therefore, to be a means whereby a manufacturer might encourage traders to influence their customers to buy his brand, but it is most unlikely that the same trade associations would fail to regulate quantity discounts as well as ordinary trade discounts, if their members considered such practices undesirable. There are, moreover, other reasons which may induce manufacturers to decline to give large inducements to retailers to buy in bulk. One is the pressure from organised wholesalers. A second is the determination of many manufacturers to avoid becoming dependent upon a few chains of retail stores for their access to an important section of the buying public. A third reason, of particular reference to the trade in rapidly perishable articles, is the necessity for discouraging small retailers with a limited market from over-stocking, and thereby injuring the manufacturer either by selling stale goods to the customer or by continually returning them for replacement.

### (e) IS THE POLICY SELF-FRUSTRATING?

The references which I have already made, firstly, to the significance of differences in rates of stock-turn, in relation to retailers' costs and to the selling margins which they will accordingly find most profitable and, secondly, to the varying emphasis which buyers may place upon the relative advantages of convenience of service and lower prices, will probably suffice to explain the *prima facie* doubts entertained by economists on the wisdom of imposing rigid uniformity of retail prices over large areas. If the trade-marks do not distinguish characteristics to which the buying public attaches much significance, there will be a tendency for at least part of the demand to be transferred to substitutes which continue to offer a choice between convenience and cheapness. It must be added that the attempt to make a branded article particularly attractive to all retailers who may operate in an area by enforcing a minimum gross profit will tend to defeat itself wherever the effect is to raise the aggregate profit of the retailer above the normal return to be secured on transferable capital and enterprise in that region. The gross margin necessary to maintain a retailer in sparsely populated districts, where only a small volume of trade can be secured, will be higher than that which retailers can secure in market streets much frequented by shoppers. When a manufacturer insists upon all retailers maintaining the higher margin, he raises the aggregate profits of retailers in the busier market areas above the normal and thereby encourages other retailers to enter the trade in these districts. The total trade to be secured at the higher retail price is limited in each region, and the rate of stock-turn secured by each retailer falls as the trade is shared among more and more shops, until his aggregate profit is once more no greater than normal. But a new element of instability has thereby been introduced into the system. Each retailer in these areas, unlike those who are in isolated villages, knows that if any one of them cuts his price to the competitive level his business will expand at the expense of the others and his aggregate profit will rise accordingly. The higher prices ruling in sparsely populated districts owe their origin to the inevitably higher costs which are a symptom of greater natural scarcity: they cannot be reduced, if costs are to be covered, because lower prices cannot in such regions evoke a sufficient expansion of sales. But this is not so in the areas of concentrated demand. Particularly in times of depression, when receipts fall more rapidly than rentals and other costs, there will be a strong inducement to cut prices, as a direct consequence of this effect which price-fixing has of increasing the number of retailers when the gross profit is fixed above the competitive level for the district. Resale price maintenance is itself responsible for the price-cutting which is so prevalent in such districts.

Manufacturers are, of course, well aware of this consequence, and many of them are alive also to the increase in aggregate sales which frequently results from the lower prices obtaining during a so-called 'price-war'. During the recent depression they did not all make serious attempts to stop price-cutting, and those who abstained saw their business expand in consequence. The retailers who were 'loyal' to their undertaking to maintain prices suffered for their loyalty, and goodwill was thereby impaired. The manufacturers may by increasing their direct advertising to consumers have prevented many of the dealers from ceasing to stock their brands, but they could not thereby prevent their disillusionment.

A direct consequence of the maintenance of resale prices is that some degree of substance has been added to the age-long complaint of retailers that there are 'too many shops'. The rigid maintenance of resale prices reduces the turnover accruing to each shopkeeper and justifies his contention that if there were fewer shops, retailers' profits would rise without raising final prices. Certain consumers, it should, however, be added, would then lose a measure of convenience of service and in that sense prices would be higher; while if price maintenance were abandoned the retailers who survived would continue to distribute a possibly greater volume of goods at lower average prices. Moreover, the abandonment of price maintenance would not by permitting lower prices in the market-place necessarily mean the closing-down of higher-priced shops in the scattered suburbs. That the convenience of a local service is appreciated by large sections of the public, who are prepared to pay the extra costs involved, is shown by the flourishing condition of shops in such localities, selling non-branded merchandise at prices and costs above those ruling in central markets.

It is possible that the increase in the number of shops in areas offering relatively high rates of stock-turn, as a consequence of enforcing a fixed gross margin of profit upon all dealers throughout a large zone, will actually lead to an increase in the total sales of the manufacturer. The fact that supplies are more conveniently accessible to the public may offset the higher price. But the increase in sales is certainly unlikely to be as large as proportionate to the increase in number of selling points, and as their rate of stock-turn falls the expectations which the original retailers are likely to have entertained of the benefits from the maintenance of trade margins are almost bound to be disappointed. The manufacturers themselves may also experience a decline in net profit, as the result of a further difficulty which arises, when costs of delivery of the article are high, out of the fact that the fixed retail price normally includes delivery costs from the factory to any retailer. Total delivery charges on all estimated sales will be allowed for by an averaged allowance in the price, with the result that the manufacturer may find his sales declining in the markets most adjacent to his factory and expanding in the most distant regions, so that the allowance for delivery costs will prove inadequate. In that way his competitive position may be weakened. The larger the price zone, and the more bulky the article, the greater this tendency will be. Transport costs alone have therefore largely prevented the application of resale price maintenance to furniture; and in the motor-car business it is customary to advertise the price *ex* works, the local dealer possibly being left free to add such transport costs as he considers feasible and wise.

### (f) THE 'LOSS-LEADER'

Let us now turn to examine what is frequently adduced as the most conclusive justification of resale price maintenance; that is, the policy adopted by some price-cutting retailers of using a widely advertised branded good as a 'loss-leader', to attract custom to their shop in the hope (no doubt in part realised) that buyers will make other purchases there also. It will be realised, of course, that for this policy to be most effective the 'loss-leader' must already be fairly strictly price-maintained by the manufacturer, or the reduction in price will not be sufficiently spectacular; and this practice may therefore with some justice be regarded as a further consequence of price-maintenance itself. The contention of the manufacturer in its most convincing form may be put as follows: that although his sales may indeed be increased temporarily, trade is in part diverted from other retailers in the district, who become the recipients of complaints of overcharging from their customers which they, not unnaturally, find difficulty in answering; with the consequence that they accuse the manufacturer of breaking faith and are prone to withdraw his brand in disgust from their stock.

Of the possibility of this happening there cannot of course be any considerable doubt. It is most likely to occur where the appeal of the brand is not in fact particularly strong, for otherwise the retailers who do not lower their price would hesitate to risk offending their customers by refusing to stock it and would be unable, usually, to divert trade to substitutes. In any case, the whole of the trade will not be diverted to the price-cutter, for as we have argued, the public is frequently prepared to pay more for convenience and courtesy of service. Low prices at the market-place and high prices at the periphery may well represent long-period equilibrium. The unsettling effect of the 'loss-leader' is probably most serious in the case of widely-advertised packet goods, such as cigarettes or tea or soap, which sell at a low unit price and particular brands of which are bought largely from habit, rather than on account of a general capacity on the part of the public to distinguish significant intrinsic differences between them and their perhaps equally widely advertised substitutes. Not a large proportion of buyers will in such cases take the trouble to transfer to the price-cutter. The general body of retailers may not retaliate with a similar price cut, for if the unit price is low the smallest reduction which is practicable on single packets will cut severely into the gross profit allowed (often as low as 7½ per cent to 15 per cent on such articles). The manufacturer may conceivably find that the trade which is left with the general retailers is being switched over by them to rival brands, as in their spleen they cease to stock his line to an extent which is not compensated by the increased sales of the price-cutter. If the loss-leader campaign is terminated, the manufacturer's sales in the whole district may conceivably be lower subsequently than before. It will, however, be clear that in the case of articles of higher unit value the buying public will take greater pains to patronise the price-cutter and the manufacturer is more likely to find his total sales rising as price-cutting develops.

It cannot be disputed that as retailing methods are gradually improved, the more progressive retailing organisations will find it profitable to expand their scale of operations by passing on to the public a share in the economies which they introduce, in the form of lower prices and better service. Manufacturers who, for whatever motive, refuse to allow these pioneers to distribute their product, whether in order to avoid domination by large chain organisations, or because they wrongly believe that small retailers in remote locations will not secure an adequate turnover unless all other retailers elsewhere are compelled to levy similar charges per unit sold, run a grave risk that their share of the market will gradually decline as the more efficient retailing system supersedes that to which they entrust their own distribution. In fact, of course, there is a growing tendency for manufacturers to attempt to secure the best of both worlds, reserving the goodwill of the general body of retailers by preserving in their hands the trade in the nationally advertised brands and price-lines, while extending their trade through the large chain-store organisations under contracts which adequately safeguard their long-period interest. These special contracts may provide either for supplying the product under the traders' or some other name instead of their own brand-mark, or alternatively for creating a special wrap and price-line which enables the new retail organisation to maintain its customary mark-up policy, but which is not nationally advertised and is not generally compared by the buying public with the more standard output.

### (g) SOME SPECIAL CASES

Peculiar technical conditions have compelled certain classes of manufacturers to make special arrangements for the distribution of their branded merchandise. A first category is that of highly perishable products. Reference has already been made to the discouragement of over-stocking by the device of refusing to offer special quantity discounts for bulk orders, proportionate to the saving in costs accruing to the manufacturer. In addition, to extend still further their control over the physical condition in which their product reaches the retailer, the manufacturers of, for example, chocolates and biscuits may themselves undertake the greater part of the wholesale function. The safeguarding of reputation and the reduction in the costs of replacing defective stock are considered to outweigh the loss from integrating the manufacturing and wholesale function under one control. The most perishable product of all in this category of branded goods is undoubtedly the newspaper. By six o'clock in the evening the lunch edition of an evening newspaper is little more than an encumbrance to be left in the first convenient corner. The distribution problem is, therefore, greatly complicated in the case of periodicals by the necessity, on the one hand, to ensure that stocks are carried at every location at which sales are likely to be made, while, on the other hand, reducing to a minimum the loss from the allowances that must be made on surplus stocks returned unsold. The compromise of the 'distance limit' between newsagents represents the attempt of a highly organised trade to solve that problem. It is clear, nevertheless, that any distance limit for an article of this kind, bought largely upon impulse on seeing a newsvendor, inevitably results in a reduction of sales, and it is to be observed that the individual evening newspaper offices at any rate supplement the distribution service themselves through their own street vendors. It must, however, be borne in mind that increased circulation is in these days almost an end in itself, to be secured by a newspaper at virtually any cost.

The device of the 'distance limit' has nevertheless been imitated for other articles, partly as a means of checking the tendency to price-cutting in areas in which price maintenance has led to higher prices and abnormal retailers' profits. It has more justification when it has arisen out of the special problem of distributing highly technical products, uch as electrical equipment and motor-cars, which require dealers with special skill, both for demonstration and selling, and also for providing after-sales service in each locality. The problem presents special difficulties which cannot be fully elaborated here. The trade in each area may not, especially in the early years, be sufficient to induce suitable persons to undertake expensive specialised training unless an exclusive dealership is offered by way of encouragement; on the other hand, it is doubtful whether the manufacturer can wisely insist that the dealer shall confine himself also exclusively to the handling of his brand, for buyers of such products are naturally hesitant to decide definitely upon a particular make without first having an opportunity for comparing it with others. The buyer will doubt whether the advice he receives from an exclusive agent is entirely disinterested; he will prefer to wait until the opportunity occurs of visiting a larger centre where an adequate choice is available for inspection. The manufacturer, therefore, hampered in part by the dealer's possible ignorance of technique and in part by his possible clash of interest when advising a client, must resort to expensive direct mail advertising, and to direct house-to-house canvassing by specially trained representatives, in order to set in detail before all potential buyers a more comprehensive explanation of the merits of his product than can be conveyed through press advertisements or through the mouth of the local dealer.

As a device for the prevention of price-cutting, the 'distance limit' is a more doubtful instrument. That it puts a limit to the local competition between rival dealers in the same product is certain; it is unfortunately almost equally certain that it applies a limit also to the development of the trade, especially in articles of low unit price in search for which the buyer is unlikely to take a long journey. No matter how carefully 'market areas' are defined, for the purpose of locating a single dealer in each, it remains true that for the great majority of branded goods an increase of sales will result, the maintained price remaining the same, from any increase in the number of market areas and of dealers. The dilemma confronting the manufacturer is, as we have seen, that the difficulties of maintaining fixed prices increase with every increase in the number of shops, on account of the loss of turnover experienced by the original dealers.

It would not be proper to conclude this account of resale price maintenance without some reference in these circumstances to the expense and trouble to which manufacturers are put in their endeavour to make their minimum retail prices effective. Most people are aware of the expensive systems of coding packages and articles with secret marks which will reveal, on re-purchase by a private detective from a price-cutter, the channels by which he has succeeded in securing his supplies, in order that those channels may be closed. It will not be necessary to elaborate here the methods of detection by which the 'loyalty' of suspected dealers is tested, or to outline the systems of organised boycott by which collaborating manufacturers all agree to penalise the offenders. Such systems are enormously expensive to the manufacturers and associations which maintain them, and yet the ingenuity of those who devise them continues to be generally excelled by that of the price-cutters who still contrive to evade them. Those who delight in discovering anticipations of present troubles in the annals of the past will find an amusing account in the *Westminster Review* for April 1852 of the elaborate, expensive, and yet unsuccessful attempts of an Association of London Booksellers and Publishers over a hundred years ago to trace and close the channels by which price-cutting booksellers secured their supplies.

Manufacturers of branded goods have usually realised that their insistence upon fixed resale prices throws additional risk upon shopkeepers by limiting their discretion. Particularly in times of falling prices, failure to reduce market prices promptly may leave the trader with unsaleable stock upon his shelves. It is therefore customary when prices are reduced to pass credit notes to retailers in respect of unsold stocks, but this in itself clearly does not compensate for loss through the locking-up of working capital. Significance therefore attaches to the suggestion that the trade in price-maintained proprietary articles would be more equitably conducted upon a consignment basis.

### (h) THE FUTURE OF THE PRACTICE?

The conclusion of this paper has been already too long delayed, and yet some sort of answer will nevertheless be expected to the question what the future is likely to hold in store for those who are concerned in practice with resale price maintenance. The view already advanced here is, firstly, that by a nice balance of conflicting considerations the practice may be held to serve the interests of particular manufacturers, especially in the case of certain widely-advertised branded products selling at low unit prices to consumers, the great mass of whom at any rate are quite unable to find any significant feature other than name to distinguish one brand from another. Secondly, it is suggested that manufacturers of many other types of branded goods have followed that lead without appreciating that the fine balance of considerations that justified it in the one case is quite inapplicable to their own peculiar problems. The whole question of advertising policy is today in a very fluid condition; the business world is far from stability of opinion in regard to either the optimum scale of appropriation or its distribution over the various publicity media which are available. Is it therefore not timely to query further, for each type of proprietary article, the necessity for stating retail prices in national advertisements as a condition for successful publicity? If that were deemed not to be essential for the development of 'consumer preference', one at least of the principal reasons for retail price-fixing would have disappeared. If in the case of particular products it is decided that national publicity must be given to price, would it not suffice for at least some of these commodities to name a figure at which supplies are obtainable direct from the manufacturer, making it clear that some retailers will be in a position to offer the identical product at lower prices, but that the manufacturer's guarantee goes with the goods in every case, irrespective of the channel of distribution? There are cogent reasons for the belief that public confidence in a proprietary article depends far more upon the effectiveness of the steps taken by the brander to implement his guarantee than upon elaborate attempts to prevent progressive traders from expanding their sales and their service by sharing with the public the benefits from their improvements in the system of distribution.

CHAPTER II

# The economic approach to the peaceful use of nuclear power*

## I An amateur's apologia

It will be abundantly evident to the readers of this paper that the account which it presents of contemporary progress and prospects in the development of the peaceful use of atomic energy as a source of power is written by a layman. I may cite the opinion of an eminent world authority on this highly specialised and technical field of scientific advance that the choice of a non-specialist author for a contribution on occasions such as this is rather to be commended than to be deplored. Under the terms of the Fawley Foundation established in the University of Southampton in 1953 by Esso Petroleum Company Ltd, an annual public lecture is delivered under the general title of 'Science and Industry', treating important aspects of the application of scientific thought to industrial and social needs. I had the honour of delivering the third Fawley Lecture. The fourth, on the subject 'The strategy of research', was given in October 1957 by Sir George P. Thomson, FRS, under the chairmanship of Sir Henry Tizard, and I quote in this context the following sentences from Sir George's concluding remarks:

> It is of the first importance that a class of men should be encouraged whose business it will be to explain scientists to one another. We are used to the writer of popular science writing for a non-scientific audience. He has a most valuable function, it is difficult, carries too little prestige and not much money. But besides encouraging him, we want two other kinds of populariser: the man who will explain advances in one science to workers in

* Paper read at the Meeting on the Peaceful Uses of Atomic Energy, UNESCO, Paris, 15–19 September 1958.

> another, which is perhaps particularly important for advances in technique, and the man who will explain one branch of science to those working in another branch of the same science. We already have review articles. Unfortunately, they tend to become more and more detailed, useful only to the specialist in the field described, though very useful to him. . . . It comes from having the articles written by specialists who know too much, or perhaps feel that if they omit anybody's works they will be suspected of not having read it. Such articles are best written by a man who has learned the subject up for the purpose. He is not too near it and can retain a sense of proportion. . . . There is room for many such articles, but it is difficult to find people to write them. It is greatly to be hoped that such men will be forthcoming and that they will be adequately rewarded. I should like to see them as Fellows of the Royal Society.

At any rate the present author has made some effort to 'learn the subject up'.

## 2 Atomic and solar energy

Viewed from the angle of the evolution of scientific discovery in the development of new sources and forms of energy available for doing useful work, atomic fission makes a special appeal to the imagination.

A vast resource of energy is for the first time tapped for employment in doing mechanical work. The world enters a new phase in the age-long process which the late Sir Frederick Soddy epitomised in the phrase 'the unbroken flow of energy from the inanimate world into life'.[1]

> With few and economically unimportant exceptions [he wrote over thirty years ago] the whole of the energy that makes a world a going concern comes from the sun. The internal energy of the living organism is neither created by the organism nor provided by Providence or usury. It gets there through the bodies of plants, and of animals that in turn feed upon plants, from the sun in the form of radiation. . . . Everything living draws the wherewithal to live from the vegetable kingdom through the instrumentality of the dye chlorophyll acting as a transformer of solar energy.

Soddy distinguished the internal energy of life, which maintains metabolism, from the external energy which an animal or plant can use in doing work on its environment.

> Just as a clock must be wound up and provided with a store of available energy before it will go, so a man has to be wound up before he can wind a clock, and the economics of life deals primarily with the ways in which Nature winds up man. The natural tendency of energy to degrade itself at one stage into worthless heat must be circumvented, so that there is something useful at the end to show for it, something, that is, that, at will, can be turned into work again, and used in life.

The internal energy of life all still comes through the plant. But the vast increase in the supply of vegetable plants which sustain the greatly increased human and animal populations of our times has been indirectly effected by the introduction of purely inanimate prime-movers which today aid and displace human and animal labour on so great a scale, both in agricultural production and in the transport of produce.

So far as concerns the external energy of life, the doing of useful work, scientific development has bypassed life itself by using purely inanimate energy as it is found in nature, without passing it through living bodies. The development of better machines has been found more productive than the breeding and maintenance of more muscular brute labour. Throughout the world, the function of the worker is changing rapidly in our day. By and large, he now contributes from his own body only an insignificant part of the work done. As a producer he tends increasingly to provide diligence rather than strength, attention rather than physical energy. Muscular effort is reserved more and more for exercise and recreation. Today, human labour supplies perhaps no more in aggregate than 1 per cent of the energy used by man in the world.[2]

The summary account which Soddy gives of the origins of available energy, as they were understood thirty years ago, helps to put atomic energy into the general picture. When solar energy falls, as it mainly does, on opaque objects, it instantly becomes heat, which is swiftly transformed by conduction into the immediately worthless form of heat at the temperature of its surroundings. A minute fraction of the solar energy, however, is naturally transformed into a useful form by evaporating the waters of the ocean, to ascend as vapour and recondense as rain which forms the rivers and provides the power for waterwheels and turbines as it returns to the ocean. Similarly, naturally and without the intervention of life, some solar energy creates the winds, which have had so large an economic significance to mankind in navigation and for driving windmills. When however it falls on vegetation it is converted into chemical energy rather than heat, because of the presence of chlorophyll, presumably acting as a catalyst, and produces the many different carbohydrates which have provided our food and so much of our fuel and raw materials.

Our coal resources are an accumulation of the fossilised vegetation of the carboniferous era. Soddy was reluctant to be certain about the origin of the world's deposits of mineral oils. If, as was more generally the belief, their origin was traceable to the action of heat and pressure on the decomposed remains of fishes and other marine organisms, then the ultimate source of oil energy was sunlight, once again. On the other hand, their origin might be due to the formation of inorganic metallic carbides, in the conditions of high temperature and high pressure almost certainly existing deep in the interior of the earth, from which petroleum might eventually be produced by the subsequent infiltration of water. If it be true that the heat of the earth is being continuously maintained by radio-activity, then it could be inferred that oil derives its energy from the atom, and its use 'represents an early step in the emancipation of life from entire dependence upon solar supplies'. This explanation would apply to the hot springs long utilised by man in New Zealand, Iceland, Tuscany and elsewhere. And, when Soddy wrote, 'as regards the energy of the sun itself, there seems little reason to doubt that it also is due to atomic energy'.

Briefly, then, the picture we have is that of mankind probably having depended ultimately, throughout the ages, on atomic energy. In the main, man has acquired the energy which he has needed, both for his internal metabolism and for his external effort, from the current flow in the form of solar energy. He has derived it subconsciously, as it were, through the media of the vegetable and animal kingdoms. At an early stage he learned also to make conscious use of other solar energy, provided naturally through the wind and the rain. Later he delved into the capital stock of past solar energy accumulated in the coal deposits of the world, and with them created a new age of power-driven machinery. More recently he tapped other reserves of either solar or direct atomic energy stored up in the world's petroleum supplies. Finally, he has in our time extended his command over the sources of energy by beginning himself to release the supplies still locked up in the atomic world.[3]

How vast are the usable resources of atomic energy is still a matter of conjecture. It is however quite clear that, so far ahead as we can see, the animal kingdom, including man himself, must continue to depend on solar energy transmitted through the chemistry of plants for the internal energy of life itself. To that extent the middleman cannot be eliminated. Profitable discussion must be confined to the question of the timing and extent of the probable contribution which direct atomic energy can be made to yield, through the agency of inanimate prime-movers, for the doing of useful work.

## 3 Scientific discovery and technological development

From the economic standpoint the main question is the probable cost of nuclear power relative to human and animal energy and to power obtained from other sources and fuels. Set against the effective demand for energy, as it exists today and as it is likely to arise at different locations throughout the world, the question can be resolved into two parts. First, where is nuclear energy likely to become available at sufficiently low cost usefully to *augment* existing supplies, within the range of effective demand? Second, in which areas, if any, is the cost of nuclear energy likely to be sufficiently low to *replace* alternative sources of fuels at present being used?

In the second case, it will be important to bear in mind that to the extent that the sources of energy displaced by nuclear power are capable of serving or being transferred to other areas, there may be a gain from the standpoint merely of increasing supplies of energy available in those areas from conventional sources, to be derived from the substitution of nuclear energy elsewhere. For example, if some oil is released in areas which substitute nuclear energy, it may pay to use more oil elsewhere. In the first case, direct gain in other areas will be a matter for the future. The immediate gain elsewhere will be indirect, to the extent that increased productivity in one area benefits other regions in an exchange economy. The increased output of goods and services resulting from an increase in energy consumption in areas which add nuclear power to existing supplies from conventional sources will, in an exchange economy, raise the level of prosperity in at least some other parts of the world which trade with them.

Consideration of the question of the relative cost of nuclear energy requires some preliminary study of the relevant science and technology, and of technological history. Atomic energy for peaceful purposes has emerged as a by-product of the development of atomic weapons since the early 1940s. Much of the scientific knowledge and technical experience acquired during the manufacture of the first atomic bombs has been utilised subsequently in the development of equipment for peaceful uses of atomic energy. The first commercial supplies of electricity produced since the war from energy released by atomic fission are moreover in part a joint product of continuing scientific and technological collaboration and of the use of equipment concurrently engaged in manufacturing warlike weapons. So long as this continues, the total costs incurred in installing, operating and maintaining the equipment necessary for both purposes, as distinct from that required for only one of them, is capable of being charged in some measure against each of them. There seems to be no reason to doubt that this joint production has up to now resulted in electricity being produced from atomic energy at a lower cost, charged to the accounts of the electricity supply authorities, than would have been incurred if the same nuclear supplies had been wholly financed by the electricity authorities. That is not of course to say that the same additional supplies of electric current could not have been produced more cheaply from conventional fuels and other sources.

Let us look first at the elementary scientific facts. The nucleus of the atom consists of neutrons and protons held together by immensely strong internal forces, normally incapable of being disturbed by any force smaller than that provided by bombarding it with another sub-atomic particle. When the nucleus of the atom of one of the components of the heavy metal uranium, as it exists in nature, is hit by neutrons, it splits into two (atomic 'fission'), releasing an enormous amount of energy, most of which causes the two fragments to move apart at high speed among the uranium atoms. The metal is so dense that their movement is quickly slowed down, transforming their energy of motion into heat. It is in part this heat which is used in nuclear electricity stations to provide steam for the turbo-generators.

In atomic fission, however, neutrons are released as well as energy, and some of these neutrons split neighbouring nuclei, spreading the fission reaction through a mass of uranium. To split the nuclei most effectively, the bombardment must be by low-energy neutrons, whereas those released by fission are of very high energy. They have to be slowed down between their release and their impact with neighbouring fuel, by letting them collide sufficiently with the atoms of a suitable 'moderating' material, such as graphite, or hydrogen or heavy hydrogen, until their thermal energy has been adequately reduced. This is achieved by arranging the lumps or rods of uranium fuel in a block of moderator, with appropriate spacing.

Natural uranium is made up of two sorts (isotopes) of atoms, uranium-235 which can be split by neutrons of low energy, and uranium-238 which virtually cannot. Only one atom of uranium-235 exists in 140 atoms of natural uranium; but it has been found that if some of the liberated neutrons enter atoms of the non-fissile uranium-238, they become atoms of plutonium, which is fissile. It is thus possible to utilise a larger proportion of the energy in natural uranium. There is also a third isotope of uranium, uranium-233, which does not exist naturally, but is produced by bombarding thorium with neutrons. This is also fissile.

Thus there are three known nuclear fuels, uranium-235 which occurs in nature, and plutonium and uranium-233 which can be produced by neutron bombardment; the requisite supply of neutrons being furnished by the action of the nuclear reactors themselves.

In a nuclear reactor using natural uranium as fuel, each separate uranium rod is enclosed in a can of light magnesium alloy which prevents the escape of the fissile products, and these fuel elements are introduced into vertical channels inside a vertical cylinder built up of blocks of graphite, the moderating element. The reactor is controlled by inserting into the core more or less of a material which easily absorbs neutrons, such as boron, which can be moved in and out of the core in special channels, in the form of rods of boron steel. The heat generated by fission may be transferred by pumping up pressurised carbon dioxide through the fuel channels, the hot gas being then piped to outside boilers in which steam is raised. The whole reactor is contained in a strong steel drum surrounded by a thick shield of reinforced concrete. In essence, the first nuclear power station to supply electricity on a commercial scale, which went into operation at Calder Hall in 1956, was of this type – natural uranium, magnesium alloy clad, graphite moderated, carbon dioxide gas cooled.

Since the Calder Hall reactor was designed, many technical advances have been made, both with slow or thermal reactors, and with fast reactors. If we are to get a grasp of contemporary achievement and current trends of development, it is now necessary to sort out the variations of types of nuclear stations which are already operating, or under construction, or the subject of experiment, or still at the conjectural stage.

All nuclear power stations consist of four parts:

1 The reactor in which neutrons are released in atomic fission of the fuel.
2 The coolant which extracts the heat produced by the reacting fuel.
3 The cladding material which provides the container or 'can' in which 1 and 2 are confined.
4 The heat exchanger in which the heat extracted by the coolant is passed to a secondary circuit, a suitably designed boiler, in which steam is raised to drive the turbo-generator of electricity.

The efficiency of nuclear power stations depends on the temperature at which the heat is extracted from the reactor. This in turn depends on the properties of the particular fuel when reactive, the type of coolant used to extract the heat, and the efficiency of the cladding material.

Although reactors burning natural uranium in Britain produce from one pound weight of fuel as much heat as four or five tons of coal, their technical efficiency is still remarkably low. The fuel contains only 0·7 per cent of fissile uranium-235 and less than half of this is actually burnt up, for the process of bombardment by neutrons distorts the metal fuel and some of the fission products which accumulate themselves absorb a significant proportion of the neutrons. Work is in progress to reduce these losses in later designs of reactor, which may also burn the plutonium formed in the uranium-238, but these improvements are not expected to raise the utilisation in stations already programmed to more than 1 per cent of the natural uranium.

In the present ten-year nuclear power programme in Britain, the three atomic stations following Calder Hall in the first stage will each produce about three times the gross output of Calder Hall. They are gas-cooled. The second stage will involve reactors of still higher rating, for which gas coolant will not be as effective for transferring heat from the reactive uranium to the steam generator as would liquid cooling. With liquid cooling a greater electrical output could be obtained, at a cost, from a given amount of uranium. Two such types of reactor are under consideration, and each introduces new problems. Both require enriched fuel. One uses graphite as moderator and liquid sodium metal as coolant. Sodium permits high temperatures to be attained at comparatively low pressure, which avoids complications concerning the pressure resistance of the containing drum, but design problems arise because the sodium coolant must not be allowed to make contact with either the moderating graphite or the water in the heat exchanger. The other type uses pressurised water as both moderator and coolant. One problem here is that the hydrogen in the water itself absorbs a higher proportion of the neutrons, and this must be compensated by enriching the fuel. Another complication is that, since high pressures are necessary if the temperature of the heat is to be usefully high, design of the containing drum presents problems of its own. The provisional conclusion about these liquid-cooled reactors therefore is that, though cheaper to build, the necessity to use expensive enriched uranium raises fuel costs, and it remains problematical whether they will generate electricity at a lower cost than gas-cooled reactors. However, the present programme in Britain envisages twelve nuclear power stations completed in about eight years' time with a nuclear capacity of 5 to 6 million kilowatts, using about 100 tons of uranium, and replacing the equivalent of about 18 million tons of coal, per annum.

In Britain the authorities concerned are sufficiently impressed by the rate of technical advance to place on record their expectation that by 1975 all new electricity stations could be nuclear fired, and that there would by then be a generated output of 10 to 15 million kilowatts from nuclear fuel equivalent to 40 million tons of coal per annum. The saving in coal equivalent may indeed prove to be substantially greater.

The very low extraction of energy from the reactive fuel has concentrated much research and development on securing greater fuel economy. The experts concerned believe that it will in due course prove practicable to use up to 30 per cent of the fuel in the reactor by the development of 'breeder' reactors, in which, if neutron losses are reduced, more new fuel atoms are created than are burnt up. These breeder reactors may be of either the thermal (or slow) type, or fast reactors; in both the reacting core is surrounded by suitable fuel into which the neutrons escape from the core to produce further atoms of fissile material. If the fuel is natural uranium, plutonium is created; if thorium is used, uranium-233 is the fissile product. Thermal breeder reactors are 'homogeneous', i.e. the fuel element is not kept separate from the moderator but is distributed through it. In one system, in which the moderator is ordinary or heavy water, the fuel is a uranium compound (it may be ceramic) dispersed in the moderator and kept circulating, becoming reactive only when passing through a central reactor vessel. In another, using a graphite moderator, the fuel is enriched uranium dissolved in a molten metal such as bismuth. In these ways the losses from distortion of the fuel under reaction are overcome, and as it is also possible to remove continuously the other fissile products which absorb neutrons, the supply of neutrons available for breeding new fissile materials is increased. The fast reactor dispenses with the moderating material, but as fast neutrons are less effective in producing fissions than are moderated neutrons, a nearly pure fissile fuel is necessary. The experimental plant at Dounreay, to generate about 60,000 kilowatts, is of this type; the fuel, highly enriched uranium (later plutonium), clad in niobium, and surrounded by natural uranium, with a liquid sodium-potassium alloy as coolant to extract the heat. There is still much conjecture about the most effective type of breeder reactor that is likely to emerge, and about the best system of using the fissile material which is bred. The speed of breeding to be achieved is obviously important: expert opinion at present inclines to the view that fast reactors breeding plutonium from the non-fissile uranium-238 in natural uranium will probably give the quickest build-up. If a 30 per cent utilisation of uranium is ultimately achieved, one ton of uranium will do the work of 1 million tons of coal. In the meantime some satisfaction can be derived from the prospect that during the next decade the world's output of uranium oxide can rise to 30,000 tons or more, which in itself will more than match the supply of capital available for investment in nuclear power programmes. Breeders are important from the standpoint of the relative cost of the fissile material they can create, rather than to overcome an absolute shortage of natural uranium which would hold up development which would otherwise be both practicable and expedient.

## 4 Regional specialisation in experimentation and development

Although this brief account of technological development has necessarily centred on experience in Britain, it nevertheless provides a sufficient elementary basis for some understanding of contemporary progress in the other leading world centres of experimentation and construction. The diversity of types of nuclear power plants emerging in the various centres reveals a measure of specialisation. This specialisation undoubtedly reflects the influence of a number of factors. In some countries, nuclear power is a joint product, if indeed not merely a by-product, with nuclear weapons. In some, the types under development reflect special advantages due to the availability of particular fuels or other materials. Again, the influence can be traced of the fact that particular countries enjoy the advantage of special access to other conventional sources of energy, such as hydro-electric plant. Finally, the different rates at which the development of nuclear power plants has been pressed forward in various regions reflect the relative urgency of quickly filling the gap between the growing effective demand for power in those countries, and the contribution which can be expected from other conventional sources. In consequence, the rest of the world is offered a diversity of choice. Wherever the need arises to supplement conventional power supplies by acquiring nuclear installations, the chance is increased that particular types will become available which will prove specially suitable for adoption in regions in which economic circumstances are comparable with those in which these types have been developed.

Thus, for example, in Britain the first installations at Calder Hall were constructed primarily to produce plutonium, with electrical power as a by-product. The fuel is natural uranium, clad in magnesium alloy, the moderator is graphite and the coolant is carbon dioxide gas. The same constituents were retained in the subsequent nuclear power plants, of 'improved Calder Hall' type, designed, however, primarily to produce electricity, with plutonium as by-product. When they were planned, supplies of natural uranium and graphite were still limiting factors controlling the rate of development, and the programme envisaged a relatively slow start, during which period a small selection of consortia of private manufacturing corporations participated and acquired know-how and experience. It was thought that the additional fissile material produced in these first reactors would provide extra fuel to enable an accelerated build-up of nuclear power capacity to be achieved in the second stage, without recourse being necessary to securing expensive enriched fuel by importation from dollar sources. Events soon showed that the delay need not continue so long. New supplies of natural uranium came into the picture, particularly from Canadian deposits, and facilities were developed to produce graphite on a much enlarged scale. It emerged also that the power rating of the next reactors could be increased substantially. At the same time the need to increase quickly the contribution of nuclear plants to the total electricity supply became more pressing. It became clear that coal was not likely to provide the share that had been anticipated, and the Suez threat to imported oil supplies strengthened doubts as to the prudence of making the future expansion of electrical generating capacity so dependent on a steady and increasing use of oil fuel. In these circumstances, the nuclear power programme was trebled in 1957. The decision to make an early start in Britain was taken on grounds of special urgency to meet known demand for power; in the knowledge that efficiencies would be lower, and costs higher than those which would be obtainable a few years later, but in the confident belief that these improved types would still be needed when available. A start had to be made, if the knowledge and experience were to be acquired to make possible the improvements in efficiency which have followed so quickly. It was considered that the relative high cost of nuclear power during the early stage of development was a reasonable initial price to pay.

In France, a similar combination of circumstances has also favoured the construction of nuclear stations using natural uranium fuel, graphite moderators and gas coolants, but the opportunity to develop important new hydro-electric power plants has afforded a breathing space for a more deliberate approach.

Canada, Norway, Sweden and Russia have had a special interest in developing nuclear stations using heavy water as moderator, with natural uranium as fuel and either heavy water or gas as coolant. They enjoy special advantages in the production of heavy water, which has attractions as a moderating material in that it is far less absorptive of neutrons, which may offset the more difficult technical problems to be solved, as compared with graphite moderators.

In the United States, preoccupation with strategical considerations no doubt explains the special concentration on developing reactors using enriched fissile fuel, moderated and cooled by ordinary water, either pressurised or boiling. Ordinary water captures so many neutrons that costly enriched fuel is necessary to compensate for the high proportion lost; and the capital costs of the first installations are proving higher than was anticipated. Russia is also developing reactors with enriched fuel, moderated by water or graphite, and water-cooled. Both the United States of America and Russia are also experimenting with other variations of reactors using enriched fuel. For example, the United States is working on plants with an organic liquid as moderator and coolant, and with graphite as moderator and sodium as coolant. Homogeneous reactors in which the enriched fuel is dispersed in heavy water, or in liquid metal, are under experiment, in both the United States and Russia.

Fast breeder reactors, using enriched fuel with sodium as coolant, are not only represented by the large British experimental plant at Dounreay but are also under construction in Russia and the United States.

## 5 The cost of nuclear power

The picture which emerges from this survey of progress reported to date reveals a great variety of experimental and development work in different countries. Many different types of nuclear reactors are under construction or reaching the prototype stage of actual operation. In some cases experience has already been obtained of the costs of operation of large-scale installations. Improved plants designed to secure much greater efficiency are well advanced, and the authorities concerned have released confident estimates of the operational results which they expect to attain, both from nuclear stations to come early into commercial operation on dates already announced, and also from later installations of still greater efficiency which are planned in the foreseeable future. Thus in Great Britain, as we have seen, a phased programme of commercial nuclear power stations which will make a significant contribution to the total electricity generating capacity of the country during the next eight years is well under way.

It must however be emphasised that data relating to actual performance on a commercial scale are still very meagre, and cost figures portraying the relative efficiency of the various widely different types of installation at present under construction are highly conjectural. In Great Britain, the first country to operate a large-scale installation, the only figures of realised achievement relate to the Calder Hall plants which have been operating since 1956, in which the generation of electrical power is no more than a by-product from installations whose primary purpose is to produce plutonium. In this case published reports give the cost of producing electricity as 0·8 or 0·9 pence per kilowatt hour; or 0·7/0·8 pence net after allowing for the value of the plutonium produced. In the United States, the production of electricity by prototype reactors has hitherto been quite incidental to their main purpose, and only since December 1957 has a nuclear power station been in operation solely for commercial purposes. This reactor, at Shippingport on the Ohio River near Pittsburgh, is of the enriched fuel, pressurised water type, and its full capacity is given as 60,000 kilowatts. It is experimental, to furnish experience and information, and the Atomic Energy Commission is reported to have found £35 millions of a total capital cost of £43 millions. The published estimate of the cost of the electricity produced is as high as 6·5 cents per kilowatt hour, compared with a range of less than half a cent to nearly one cent, according to location, for coal-fired stations. Since May 1958 the Shippingport reactor is being operated under contract by the Duquesne Light Company to augment the electricity supplies to consumers in the Pittsburgh area.

The next best cost estimates relate to the future. Progressive improvements in efficiency are expected to accrue from the first batch of commercial stations now under construction in Great Britain. Thus, as regards capital costs, at the third station in the programme (at Hunterston) it is expected that the heat rating of the plant will yield 2·5 megawatts of heat energy per ton of uranium compared with 1·3 at Calder Hall: and the fourth at Hinkley Point is designed to reduce overall costs per kilowatt hour by a further 10 per cent as compared with Hunterston. As regards the cost of metallic uranium fuel elements, the plans of the United Kingdom Atomic Energy Authority for producing these elements from uranium ore should (on the authority of Sir John Cockcroft) make fuel available for early stations in Great Britain and for exported British type plant installed in other countries at a maximum price of £20,000 per metric ton, and the minimum price at which irradiated fuel elements would be bought back for their plutonium and other content should not be less than £5000 per metric ton. Professor J. M. Kay of the Imperial College of Science and Technology has recently published an estimate of operating costs which should now be achievable by a nuclear plant constructed in Great Britain on the most up-to-date model. It relates to a large reactor designed to produce 250 megawatts of electricity from a heat output of about 900 megawatts. The capital cost of the installation at present prices would be £27·5 millions, equivalent to £110 per kilowatt. This figure shows a considerable reduction on those for plants already under construction, but it is still twice as high as that for a comparable coal-burning station. The capital cost of the fuel charge (350 tons) would be £5·5 millions. On running costs, he assumes a fuel life in the reactor of 3000 megawatt days per ton, and a net fuel replacement cost of £15,000 per ton. Capital costs being so high, the assurance of a high load factor is important. If the plant is assured an operating load factor of 80 per cent, the total cost of the electricity generated (including interest and depreciation on the plant, interest on the fuel, fuel replacement, and operating and maintenance charges) works out at 0·6*d* per kilowatt hour (with interest at 6 per cent) or 0·67*d* (at 8 per cent interest). Under demand conditions as favourable as that, the unit cost estimates are not markedly out of line, in the opinion of Professor Kay, with those for an equivalent coal-burning station at a coal price of £5 per ton. On the other hand, for a load factor of only 20 per cent, the cost per kilowatt hour of the nuclear plant would be trebled, a performance which would compare very adversely with that of conventional stations for which the capital costs are so much lower.

This estimate is for a new plant started now and finished in five or seven years, with the advantage of the higher heat ratings and economies of size now known to be achievable. Sir John Cockcroft has recently forecast that the figure of £110 per kilowatt given for the capital cost of the plant should be further reduced to about £80 for new installations within ten years' time. These estimates indicate significant progress towards greater efficiency, in as much as the capital cost of the nuclear stations comprising the present 10-year programme to be completed in Great Britain by 1966/7 is reported to be £775 millions greater than it would have been for a wholly conventional-type programme of like capacity.

The upshot is that even in regions where the demand for power is as intensely developed and highly concentrated as it is in parts of Great Britain, nuclear power plants only begin to approach comparability with conventional stations, from the standpoint of cost of electricity produced per kilowatt hour, where they can be run continuously at their optimum load factor. The variations of load obtaining in Great Britain, between the highest winter peak and the summer weekend valley, mean that so favourable a load factor is available for only one quarter of the total installed capacity. Because it can run continuously, that quarter produces about one half of the total electricity generated. Improved technical efficiencies are yielding steadily reduced capital costs for new conventional stations as well as for nuclear plants.

It appears therefore that the scope for nuclear capacity will continue to be severely restricted in Great Britain, if comparative economic efficiency is the determining factor, unless relative capital costs are found to be capable of much greater reduction than is at present anticipated. New conventional-type stations will continue to be more advantageous wherever there is easy access to abundant coal; nuclear stations will make their greatest impact in regions of heavy continuous demand for power which are more remote from coal supplies. The precise balance may of course be influenced by the price policy of the coal authority, to the extent that negotiation with the electricity authority resulted in a pattern of delivered prices for coal which does not add to pithead prices the full transport cost to each generating station.

Other policy decisions may also influence the proportion of nuclear to conventional capacity. For example, the pattern of demand might in due time be changed by a differential electricity tariff for peak and valley periods of demand which provided a sufficient incentive to power users to secure a more even spread of load. Again, arrangements for long distance distribution of electricity at high voltage may have important effects. The situation in Great Britain is once again a case in point. The two areas of southern and north-west England are seriously deficient in local coal for electricity generation. Where practicable, the cheapest method of transporting energy to such regions, where there is a large demand for electric power, is to ship coal by sea for use in local generating stations. Where rail transport of coal would be involved, high voltage supply systems from electricity generating stations located near the coal are less expensive than moving the coal. Because coal supplies are expected to be insufficient to meet the growing demand for power, recourse may be had to fuel oil, either from local refineries or from direct import, to fire the boilers of generating stations in the areas which are deficient in coal. There are however political risks associated with making electric power supplies too dependent in present circumstances on imported oil. It is therefore in these regions that nuclear power stations are being introduced. Against their high initial capital cost may be set their lower fuel costs, relative to those of conventional stations. It is however necessary to locate them on somewhat remote sites, and high voltage distribution lines will be required to transmit the power to the demand centres. It is planned to incorporate them into a 'super-grid' system of very high voltage, which has a much greater carrying capacity and will facilitate the most economic use of the power from the nuclear stations. Nevertheless, in many areas of Great Britain there will remain, as far ahead as can be foreseen, a clear cost advantage in continuing to meet the growing demand by constructing new large generating stations of conventional type.

The situation in Great Britain is paralleled in many of the economically developed communities elsewhere. There are many regions comparable to southern England, which have become highly industrialised on account of a variety of locational advantages which outweigh the relatively high cost of power. They may for example serve a large but localised market for particular products, which on a balance of considerations is best catered for by local factories. Other regions may be plentifully supplied with essential materials which lose a large proportion of their crude weight or bulk at certain stages in the manufacturing process, and are therefore better processed near the source of supply than transported to other regions where power is cheaper. Suitable labour may be more plentiful there, industrial sites more easily provided, and so on. Nevertheless, the high cost of power, whether due to the transport costs on fuel brought in for local electric generating stations or to the high transmission cost of electricity produced in other areas where fuel is more abundant, must remain a factor which limits the rate of industrial development of these areas. If their demand for power has the appropriate characteristics – an adequate volume to justify a large installation and a sufficiently steady load factor to permit continuous operation under optimum conditions – a local nuclear plant may provide electricity for further expansion more cheaply than from any other source of energy. Such conditions frequently obtain in countries which embrace other regions in which power is unusually cheap, due to plentiful coal or lignite or to waterfalls which are harnessed for hydro-electric stations, and which are particularly favourable for the development of industrial processes which depend on abundant cheap power. The power authorities in these countries are therefore keenly interested in the possibility of importing complete nuclear power installations from specialist firms, such as those in Great Britain, which are already in a position to supply plant of the improved Calder Hall type on a commercial basis, with efficiencies calculated to show lower costs for particular areas of demand than can be offered by supply from conventional sources in remote situations within the country concerned. The terms of agreement concluded or under negotiation for Italy, Japan and elsewhere cover not only the supply of the complete installations and the provision of operational 'know-how' by the contractors, but also, under agreement with the United Kingdom Atomic Energy Authority, the requisite supply of prepared uranium fuel elements and, on a continuing basis, the return of irradiated fuel elements to Great Britain for the extraction of plutonium and for refortification or replacement, on terms stipulated in the contract. The United Kingdom Government has announced its desire to conclude agreements with the European Atomic Energy Community and member governments, which will provide the framework within which individual power undertakings may acquire fully developed power reactors on ordinary commercial terms.

An important parallel development is that incorporated in the provisions of the Memorandum of Understanding, published in June 1958, between the United States' Government and Euratom. This provides the framework for the joint construction in Euratom countries of prototype reactors, of pressurised or boiling water type using enriched uranium, which are still in the development stage in the United States, and which will be partly financed by America. The arrangement is designed to provide the countries concerned with an opportunity to press forward with nuclear power development to meet their ever-growing shortage of power, and at the same time to provide America with experience of large-scale reactors in Europe which the lower cost of conventional power stations in the United States would make it less economical to install in America.

A recent policy decision in the United Kingdom focuses attention on the problem of security arising from the export of nuclear power plants to countries which have not hitherto entered the field of experimental work and development in atomic fission. Nuclear plants supplying electric power can at the same time produce fissile material, such as the plutonium isotope-239, from which bombs and other nuclear weapons may be made. British contracts for the export of nuclear power installations provide either that the irradiated or partially burnt-up fuel elements shall be returned to Great Britain for processing, or, as in the recent arrangement with Japan, that the importing country may keep the fissile material under an agreement that it shall be used only for peaceful purposes. In the new arrangement between the United States and Euratom it will be left to Euratom, subject to the sanction of the US Congress, to ensure by approved methods of inspection that none of the fissionable material provided is used for warlike purposes. The recent announcement in the United Kingdom that some of Britain's commercial nuclear stations are to be adapted during the course of construction to permit the production of fissile material illustrates the importance of the problem.

A conflict arises between the aim of operating the nuclear stations in such a way as to produce electricity at the lowest cost per kilowatt hour, and that of so running them as to yield the required output of fissile plutonium-239. To produce electricity most economically it would appear to be desirable to extract the maximum energy output from the fuel elements by keeping them in the reactor until all the fissionable content is irradiated. The useful life in the reactor is at present believed to be 3000 megawatt days per ton of uranium, and it is hoped that improvements in design will raise this figure to 5000 megawatt days. All of the plutonium produced during the reaction process begins in the form of the fissile isotope-239. Some of this is burnt up with the uranium in the reactor, and what remains in the spent fuel when the elements are not withdrawn until irradiation is complete has by then become plutonium-240, a non-fissile isotope, small in quantity and poor in quality. It is apparently still uncertain (indeed there has not yet been sufficient time to be certain) whether it can be used after extraction as a commercial nuclear fuel and at what processing cost. Sufficient is known already, however, for the recovery value of plutonium extracted from fully irradiated fuel elements to have fallen substantially. In recent estimates it has been reduced from 0·35*d* to a mere 0·07*d* per unit of electricity produced, but notwithstanding this the electricity authority would have continued to keep the elements burning up in the reactor until the fissile plutonium was all irradiated, rather than withdraw them much more frequently so that the plutonium-239 could be extracted from the partially spent fuel by an expensive chemical process. The new situation is that further development on the military side of various new types of nuclear weapons may call in the future for additional supplies of fissile plutonium. It has accordingly been officially announced in June 1958 that the United Kingdom Government has arranged with the Central Electricity Generating

Board for modification of the equipment in some of the power plants under construction, at an additional cost, to permit more frequent charging and withdrawal of the fuel elements, should it be wished to extract the plutonium produced while still fissile. This may mean that the plants programmed to commence operations after 1962 may have considerably higher running costs than was previously envisaged. Expensive fuel elements would be withdrawn perhaps five times as frequently to be reworked into new rods and fortified with additional fissile uranium by an expensive process. Additional processing capacity may be required to treat the greater volume of partially spent fuel. In these circumstances it is quite possible that it will be the latest British-type reactors supplied to other countries which will operate under optimum conditions as electricity producers, and yield the most significant operational results, rather than those installed in Great Britain; but everything turns on the relation between the credit received for fissile plutonium extracted and the increased fuel costs involved in withdrawing elements only partially burnt up. Fortunately the modification in operational practice does not appear likely to involve so large an increase in the demand for natural uranium, to produce the additional supply of fuel elements to keep the plants running, as would outstrip the estimated output from the mineral deposits known to be available.

## 6 Some tentative conclusions

It may be useful to end this paper with a few broad conclusions that suggest themselves.

1 The authors of the 1956 Report of the Electricity Committee of OEEC, entitled *Europe's Growing Needs of Energy. How can they be met?*, thought it wise to strike a note of caution. The following abstracts from paragraphs 37 to 41 of that Report deserve quotation:

> 37 Unfortunately the popular enthusiasm aroused by this new form of energy and the headline publicity given to developments of relatively small importance in this new field have created a false impression of the contribution that nuclear energy is likely to make to Western Europe's energy needs during the next twenty years and of the extent to which we must continue to rely on the existing sources of supply.

> 38 In the absence of definite long-term plans from the other member countries, we have taken as a basis the estimate made by the United Kingdom that nuclear power stations in the United Kingdom will produce in 1975 the equivalent of 40 million tons of coal. After consulting various authorities and taking into account official reports from the United States, we regard as a reasonable forecast an equal production from other nuclear power stations in Western Europe in 1975. The rate of progress will depend on the co-operation between the countries concerned.
>
> 39 If our forecast is correct, nuclear energy is unlikely to provide more than 8 per cent of the total energy demand in Western Europe in 1975. No doubt after 1975 the output from nuclear reactors should increase rapidly, but our forecast indicates that it is a mistake to assume that atomic energy on a large scale is just round the corner....
>
> 41 Nothing we have said in this section must be taken to imply any mistrust on our part of the essential contribution that nuclear energy will make in later years.

There seem to be no sound reasons for regarding this forecast as over-pessimistic.

2 The high initial capital cost of nuclear power stations, even of the most advanced and improved design, needs emphasis. As against the average figures assumed in the OEEC Committee's report of $145 per installed kilowatt for thermal stations and $315 for hydro stations must be put Professor Kay's estimate of about $300 per kilowatt for a nuclear station with an electrical output of 250 megawatts, not counting the capital cost of the initial fuel charge. The comparative running cost of a hydro plant is of course very low.

3 The most efficient nuclear power stations promise to show comparable efficiencies with conventional stations only when they can be introduced to take over a substantial basic and continuous demand at a high constant load factor.

4 Opportunities for securing a high basic load factor by extending the area serviced by a nuclear station, so as to obtain any evening out of fluctuations which diversification of demand might offer, are limited, as is already the case for stations of conventional type, by the high costs of long-distance transmission of electrical energy.

5 The scope for nuclear stations would therefore appear to be greatest in areas of substantial and non-fluctuating demand for power which are remote from the sea-board and from internal supplies of cheap conventional fuels.

6 In Western Europe, over nine-tenths of the electric power at present produced is based on lignite, coal and oil fuel. If the growing demand is to be met, a steadily rising proportion of the coal and oil consumed will have to be imported. The development of nuclear power in Western Europe will therefore reduce the pressure of aggregate world demand for transportable conventional fuels, and in that way confer indirect benefit on more or less developed countries elsewhere which are dependent for their power supplies on imported fuel.

7 Other industrialised countries such as Japan which are dependent for a substantial proportion of their power on fuel imported from a considerable distance will have the same incentive as countries in Western Europe to introduce nuclear power plants to meet concentrated demands offering a high load factor.

8 In less developed areas, the direct help to be obtained from nuclear plants in meeting their growing demands for power is likely in the foreseeable future to be very small. Instances to the contrary will be justifiable on economic grounds in quite exceptionable conditions. An example would be the exploitation of rich deposits of valuable minerals, located in districts remote from conventional fuel supplies or hydro-electric stations, and particularly in cases where chemical processing involving heavy consumption of power is required on the spot. Continuous night and day operation year in year out might then offer the appropriate conditions for a nuclear station; but present indications are that the deposits would need to be very rich and valuable for the enterprise to be successful.

9 There remains the possible recourse to nuclear power to accelerate industrialisation of densely populated agricultural communities on comparatively low levels of subsistence. It seems most unlikely that in the early stages of industrialisation the emerging demand for power would have the load factor which alone would give nuclear stations a cost advantage over conventional types. The conditions are more appropriate, generally speaking, for relatively small oil-driven generating plants. The same considerations would seem also to apply to the development of power aids to irrigation projects, agricultural improvements and domestic activity.

## Notes

1 Frederick Soddy, *Wealth, Virtual Wealth, and Debt*, Allen & Unwin, 1926.

2 OEEC Report, *Europe's Growing Needs of Energy. How can they be met?*, 1956 (ENC(56)63).

3 Cf. Soddy, *op. cit.*: 'From the energetic standpoint progress may be regarded as a successive mastery and control over sources of energy ever nearer the original source.'

## Bibliography

OEEC, 1956 Report: *Europe's Growing Needs of Energy* (ENC(56)63).
*The Electricity Industry*, a *Financial Times* Survey, London, 3 February 1958.
*The Times* Calder Hall Supplement, London, 17 October 1956.
'Energy and Man', *Esso Magazine*, London, September 1957.